WHOSE DEMOCRACY?

WHOSE DEMOCRACY?

Nationalism, Religion, and the Doctrine of Collective Rights in Post-1989 Eastern Europe

Sabrina P. Ramet

ROWMAN & LITTLEFIELD PUBLISHERS, INC.
Lanham • Boulder • New York • Oxford

ROWMAN & LITTLEFIELD PUBLISHERS, INC.

Published in the United States of America
by Rowman & Littlefield Publishers, Inc.
4720 Boston Way, Lanham, Maryland 20706

12 Hid's Copse Road
Cummor Hill, Oxford OX29JJ, England

The EuroSlavic font used to print this work is available from Linguist's
Software, Inc., PO Box 580, Edmonds, WA 98020-0580 USA tel (206)
775-1130.

British Library Cataloguing in Publication Information Available

Library of Congress Cataloging-in-Publication Data

Ramet, Sabrina P., 1949–
    Whose democracy? : nationalism, religion, and the doctrine of
collective rights in post-1989 eastern Europe / Sabrina P. Ramet.
        p.   cm.
    Includes bibliographical references and index.
    ISBN 0–8476–8323–0 (alk. paper). — ISBN 0-8476-8324-9 (pbk. :
alk. paper)
        1. Europe, Eastern—Politics and government—1989–
2. Nationalism—Europe, Eastern.   3. Europe, Eastern—Ethnic
relations.   I. Title.
DJK51.R35   1997
320.947—dc21   97–7819
                                                                                       CIP

ISBN 0–8476–8323–0 (cloth : alk. paper)
ISBN 0–8476–8324–9 (pbk. : alk. paper)

Printed in the United States of America

To Ida M. Ramet, my mother
and
to Irmgard Beller, my friend

Contents

Tables

Preface

A specter is haunting Eastern Europe—to steal a line from Marx—the specter of collective rights. But where Marx drew encouragement from the specter that he identified, I fear that, when it comes to the "doctrine of collective rights," the sooner Eastern Europe is "exorcised," the better. At issue is not whether peoples are entitled to dignity and respect; on the contrary, that ought to be assumed under any and all circumstances. At issue is rather the contention, advanced by the new "ethnarchs," that peoples have a right to suppress the cultures and religions of minorities that happen to live within their borders, to dictate moral agendas, and to expel or massacre those who do not fit into their fantasies of homogenized utopias.

This book is explicitly moral in purpose and presumes the existence of objective, absolute, and universal moral laws. This assumption is Kantian and Lockean in derivation, and not Platonist, as those with short memories might suppose. In undertaking to write in a moral-philosophical mode about contemporary events in Central and Eastern Europe, I am clearly challenging (1) those who believe that scholarly writing should be "value free" (an absurdity, if I have ever heard one); (2) those who believe that morality has only relative validity and application and that there are no acts that may be construed as clearly and unambiguously evil, not even genocide (although one rarely hears argument for moral relativism presented in an entirely straightforward way); (3) those who believe that political history should be divorced from philosophical concerns and influences; and, although I am anticipating my argument, (4) those who believe that rights exist prior to, or independent of, duties, rather than as a by-product of duty.

Philosophy was my first love. As an undergraduate at Stanford University majoring in philosophy, I discovered the joy of contemplating the theater of ideas and of following the implications of certain ideas to their logical conclusions. Logical consistency has always impressed me as an essential ingredient in the beauty of an argument. But rigorous adherence to logical consistency may sometimes lead one in a direction in which one had not originally expected to travel; then the choice is either to follow one's path to new conclusions or to retrace one's steps and reexamine one's original premises. In attempting to be faithful to this principle, I have found myself arriving at a conclusion that one cannot ground autonomism in anterior moral precepts—a conclusion that surprised me, since there was a time when I considered autonomism to be an extremely positive phenomenon, regardless of system. But if I have followed the threads of my own logic correctly, then whatever the positive effects of autonomism may be, the principle itself cannot be grounded in a moral justification.

I am indebted to Robert Stacey for suggesting certain sources on the medieval world, cited in the introduction; to Peter Mentzel for drawing my attention to the writings of Chandran Kukathas; to Frank Cibulka for feedback on earlier drafts of the introduction, chapter 5, and the conclusion; and to Michael Shafir for feedback on earlier drafts of the introduction, chapters 1 and 2, and the conclusion. I am also grateful to George Schöpflin for his feedback on earlier drafts of the introduction and conclusion, to Sami Repishti and Nemanja Marčetić for their feedback on an earlier draft of chapter 6; to Katarzyna Dziwirek for assisting me with the diacritical marks in chapter 4; and to Dasha Koenig for assisting me with the diacritical marks in chapter 5. I also wish to express my gratitude to the anonymous reader contracted by Rowman & Littlefield for most helpful advice and suggestions (including for having suggested the title); to Joan McCarter for preparing the tables used in this volume and for printing out the final manuscript submitted to the press; and to my editor, Susan McEachern, for her interest in this project, her encouragement at every stage, and her helpful suggestions along the way. Finally, I would like to thank my spouse, Chris Hassenstab, whose interest in this project has been unflagging, who has listened to successive drafts as I have read them to her, sharing her reactions with me, and who remains an inspiration to me in my work.

A few of the chapters collected here have previously appeared as journal articles. I gratefully acknowledge permission from the journals to use the following material in this volume: An earlier version of chapter 1, "Back to the Future in Eastern Europe," was originally published under the same title as an article in *Acta Slavica Iaponica,* volume 13 (1995). Chapter 2, "Eastern Europe's Painful Transition," was published in an earlier version in the March 1996 issue of *Current History.* An earlier version of chapter 5 was originally published under the title "The Reemergence of Slovakia" in *Nationalities Papers,* volume 22, no. 1 (Spring 1994). An earlier version of chapter 6, "The Albanians of Kosovo," was originally published under the same title as an article in the *Brown Journal of World Affairs,* volume 3, no. 1 (Winter/Spring 1996).

Introduction

The Holy Trinity: Rights, Legitimacy, Political Succession

The history of Eastern Europe is often told as if it were reducible to a long struggle for the realization of the right of national self-determination and associated "national rights." What in Revolutionary France was called "the Rights of Man" comes in Eastern Europe—or so it sometimes seems—to be called "the Rights of Nations." It is striking that in no other part of the world is there so much fussing over nation-related terminology—whether a particular group is a nation or a nationality or a national group or an ethnic group or a minority or, even if it constitutes less than 50 percent of the local population, somehow "not a minority"—a question that sometimes assumes huge importance in the minds of locals.[1] One imagines that the locals somehow believe that a "state-forming nation" of 20 percent, for example, is somehow "larger" than a "minority" of 20 percent. Larger or not, a state-forming nation claims the right to play a determinative role (though not necessarily *the* determinative role) in constructing the political order of the state, whereas a minority is held to enjoy the right, at most, to lobby for group-specific concessions.

But telling the East European story in terms of national self-determination, in terms of a search for the freedom of *nations,* lures one into the trap of representing East European history as if its dynamics were somehow different from the dynamics of politics elsewhere, as if it were not merely a matter of differences in factors at hand but rather a matter of entirely different laws of politics holding sway in the region long known as "the lands between."

Yet the appeal to rights does not hang in the void. On the contrary, the notion of rights is one component of a kind of "holy trinity" of political order, consisting of legitimacy, succession, and rights. The three are interrelated, and changes in any of the three variables have consequences for the other two.

The concept of *legitimacy* refers to the acceptance of a state by the people under its jurisdiction or, in more formal terms, to "the moral value which

1

citizens attach to their state."[2] The moral value gives the state's actions "a quality of appearing to be 'right' or 'just' or, if you will, 'legitimate.'"[3] This has the consequence that a state viewed as moral cannot be illegitimate, while a state viewed by its citizens as immoral cannot be legitimate. Morality is organically bound up with the idea of legitimacy. Many people think that economic performance can be determinative of the legitimacy of a particular system, but this is quite false. On the contrary, a legitimate system can easily weather economic reverses, while an illegitimate system can sometimes be pushed over the edge by economic difficulties precisely because it is already viewed as morally decrepit by its citizens. Needless to say, the dynamics of change of administration (which do not call into question the legitimacy of the system) are entirely different from the dynamics relating to system change.

The concept of *political succession,* as Guglielmo Ferrero has pointed out, lies at the very core of the notion of legitimacy.[4] Indeed, the central issue at stake for the question of political legitimacy is the nature of political succession: what principle, in essence, does a system employ to change its rulers—dynastic succession, divine sanction (determined by an accepted method), direct vote by the citizens, or election by the magnates of society? The acceptance of the given methodology of political succession has much to do with the legitimacy of the overall system.

And finally, the concept of *rights* is connected with both of the preceding concepts, both because legitimacy, as a moral concept, provides the groundwork for notions of rights and duties and because both legitimacy and political succession entail notions of what is "right" in a given society. For example, the notion of the divine right of kings, a principle of political succession, entailed as well a notion of the rights of both monarch and subject, as well as of their respective duties.

It is important to keep in mind that different concepts of legitimacy entail different concepts of political succession, as well as of rights. For example, the legimating concept of liberal democracy entails notions of political succession through popular election and, in some incarnations, of the primacy of individual rights over societal rights.[5] Communism, by contrast, promulgated notions of political succession by elite selection (albeit sometimes ratified by popular "election" from single-candidate slates) and of the primacy of societal rights over individual rights. And as we shall see in more depth in chapter 5 and the conclusion, authoritarian nationalists base their appeal on the primacy of the unqualified rights of the state-forming nation (collective rights, as I refer to this claim) over both the claims of other groups and the claims on behalf of individual rights. Political succession is less articulated as a principle, though there is an assumption that nonmembers of the state-forming nation are to be excluded from positions of power.

State-Forming Nations

What is a "state-forming nation"? In a word, a declared (or in Benedict Anderson's terminology, "imagined")[6] community that claims the right to speak on behalf of all the citizens inhabiting a certain territory and that claims to enjoy the exclusive right to determine what constitutes the language, culture, and customs of both the community itself and its territory, or that, if it shares that status with one or more other groups, claims the right to exercise a veto over any changes to the political order. Understood in this way, it appears that a state-forming nation is not so different, in certain ways, from a Church. Certainly in Poland the Catholic Church has claimed the right to speak on behalf of all the citizens inhabiting the country as well as the exclusive right to determine what constitutes the morals, acceptable culture, and legitimate customs of the people inhabiting Poland.

It might be thought that the Church, as a body dating itself back two thousand years, must necessarily operate rather differently from nationalist movements that trace their lineage back to the Enlightenment and the French Revolution. But the Church has changed with the times. Without denying elements of constancy in the Church's self-concept, one may observe that where it once spoke the language of truth and mission, the Church now champions the "right" of Catholic children to Catholic religious instruction in state schools. Such language would have been entirely alien to the medieval Church. Indeed, it is interesting to note that while medieval Europe developed highly articulated legal codes regulating the rights, privileges, and duties of individuals, guilds, and sundry professions,[7] even providing a legal basis in twelfth- and thirteenth-century England (building on the precedent of Roman law) for certain groups to obtain "corporate status,"[8] a notion of collective rights in anything like the modern sense could not be developed until the modern concept of the collectivity had emerged. The closest equivalent known to the Middle Ages was the concept of the "common good" or "common interest," found, for example, in the writings of John of Salisbury (d. 1180).[9] But even this referred, not to the common interest of subgroups within a society, but to the common interest of the society as a whole. It is within the framework of the same understanding that St. Thomas Aquinas writes, in his Summa Theologica, that "law, to be effective in promoting right living, must have . . . compelling force. . . . The power of compulsion belongs either to the community as a whole, or to its official representative whose duty it is to inflict penalties."[10] Aquinas's concept was, as this passage makes clear, legalistic and formal.

Among the diverse factors that shaped the post-1989 Eastern European context, I would like to highlight two. The first is the impact of the West (chiefly Britain and France) in defining the territorial conflicts in the region. As I shall show in chapter 2, the territorial disputes in the region are, without exception, the result of Western diplomatic involvement and not the spontaneous outcome of purely indigenous problems. The West has, however, tried to cover its tracks by concocting and promulgating the myth of "ancient ethnic rivalries" with which Eastern Europe is supposedly riddled. On the contrary, Western designs for the region have contributed to stimulating resentments among peoples, and these resentments, in turn, reinforce the allure of appeals to collective identities.

The second factor I should highlight is the legacy of communism. From the very beginning, the communists in all the countries of the region tried, with varying degrees of success, to suppress and extirpate all independent associations and social infrastructure, allowing only the Churches to continue their activity. The result, as Ognyan Minchev has pointed out, was the near-total atomization of society, as people could turn only to family and friendship circles for support but lacked any institutional resources (except, to some extent, the Church) with which to resist the state. The upshot is that with the collapse of communism, nationalist movements and Churches faced less competition for people's time than they would have if not for the communist era.[11] This generalization is especially true for societies such as Romania, Bulgaria, Serbia, Albania, and Slovakia, less true for societies such as Slovenia, the Czech Republic, and Poland. Hungary and Croatia occupy intermediate positions in this gradation.

The Moral Derivation of Rights

Rights do not spring forth out of nowhere. Quite to the contrary, they make their appearance as the epiphenomenon of corresponding duties. I have a right to life because others have a duty to respect my life. I have a right to privacy because others have a duty to respect my privacy. If there were no duties, there would be no rights.

But duties do not arise autonomously either. Nor is it satisfactory, as conventionalists try to argue, to trace all duties, and hence all rights, merely to conventions adopted one way in one society and another way in another society. Quite apart from the fact that this mode of thinking denies natural rights altogether, asserting instead that there are only positive rights, conventionalism rather transparently slides into moral relativism, by holding that there are no rights or duties that have absolute validity, indeed no moral order except as determined by convention.

If it means anything at all to speak of a natural right to life, liberty, and the pursuit of happiness enjoyed by all living, sentient beings—or, if one prefers to opt for mere humanism, by all humans—then those rights can be included only in a universal and objective moral foundation. That foundation is commonly called Natural Law or Universal Reason. The latter term is, to my mind, the more useful—even if the less common—because it alerts us at once to the attendant claim that the most essential moral precepts are discernible by unaided reason and that all humans, except for sociopaths and other mentally deranged persons, share the ability to comprehend rationally the difference between good and evil.[12] As Bernard Yack put it, summarizing John Rawls, "all mature individuals share . . . the nature of 'free moral persons.'"[13] But on the point of morality, Kant draws an interesting distinction. A person may discern what action may be morally best and may even execute that action, but unless that action is undertaken "for the sake of the good," it cannot be considered a "good" action, merely an action with pleasing results. In setting this high standard, Kant seems to be taking aim at persons who do good works either to earn a reputation as good persons or to earn a spot in heaven. Either way, so Kant tells us, the persons in question show themselves to be self-serving hedonists who are ultimately not concerned with the good at all.

In recent decades it has been common to banish moral philosophy from political discourse, as if the former could find no legitimate home in the conceptual fortresses constructed by political model builders and analysts. In his 1988 work, *Morality within the Limits of Reason,* Russell Hardin bemoans this tendency. In Hardin's words:

> Moral theory has become primarily the province of those who inhabit philosophy departments while political theory has become that of those who inhabit political science departments. This separation makes nonsense of many of the concerns of Athenian philosophy, of the Scottish Enlightenment, and of much that went between them. Any effort to grasp moral theory in full must lead to concern with the nature of politics and of institutions for regulating human affairs. The term "moral philosophy" once meant everything from what is now narrowly construed as ethics to political economy.[14]

For Hardin, the divorce of moral philosophy from political analysis leads to problems. Among those problems are (1) that, cut free from a moral anchor, one has no clear standards on the basis of which to appraise policy actions or recommend corrective policies (a deficiency most clearly evident in Western policy responses to the genocide in Bosnia 1992–95);[15] (2) that one may construe the state as merely an apparatus for assuring security, without reference to moral law and moral life, in what one could call the *mechanistic fallacy;* and (3) that one might divorce rights from their moral foundation in Universal Reason, losing, in the process, the standard for distinguishing authentic rights from bogus rights or purely contingent rights.

Moral universalism (as the theory of Universal Reason may also be called), which holds that certain basic and discernible moral tenets existing independent of, and without regard to, any divine being have universal validity, underpins this book. It is not, however, the only moral theory. Alternatives include contractarianism, conventionalism, consequentialism, and theocracy; the first three of these are discussed in chapter 3, while aspects of the fourth (theocracy) are discussed in chapter 4. In the context of the discussion in those chapters, it will become apparent that the entire nature of rights is transformed depending on the moral theory to which one subscribes.

In the pages that follow, I shall argue that individual rights and societal rights (to be explained below) can be grounded in Universal Reason and can thus be shown to be fully legitimate. I shall, on the other hand, argue that the same cannot be claimed on behalf of so-called collective rights and that the legitimate rights that subgroups of society enjoy are in fact extensions of individual rights and/or societal rights, rather than special rights of a separate category.

Defining the Doctrine

It is perhaps time to define what I mean by the expression "doctrine of collective rights." I shall understand, by this expression, the claim that one's own group has certain rights that are superior to those of others, perhaps in some sense transcendent, and that one's own group is entitled to set the rules for members of other groups to follow within a certain territory, or to assert territorial autonomy within specified boundaries. I do not mean, by referring to this doctrine, the rights of suppressed minorities, except insofar as they are translated into "national rights" or "ethnic rights." I do not mean the cultural rights that every individual has, both as an individual and as a voluntary member of any given association. Nor do I mean mere nationalism, although nationalism generally carries with it the baggage of so-called collective rights. But the two are, all the same, distinct. It is, on the one hand, the claim to superiority and to an entitlement to rule or, on the other hand, the demand that the group be granted autonomy and provided with state-funded cultural institutions that lies at the core of this "doctrine."

It should be clear enough that the doctrine of collective rights is often limited to claims within a specified territory. For example, the Greater Serbian doctrine of collective rights has extended in recent years, *at the very most,* to the Serbian core, Kosovo, Bosnia, and parts of Croatia and Macedonia. On the other hand, the aspirations of religious organizations are not, on the whole, so clearly demarcated; the Roman Catholic Church has never, for example, been secretive about its aspiration to global expansion.

The doctrine of collective rights is not the same as the legitimacy of collective interests. One can defend the legitimacy of the aspirations of the ethnic Hungarians of Romania to obtain education in their own language or, alternatively, the legitimacy of the Romanian state's requirement that all its citizens obtain fluency in Romanian, without conceding either Hungarians' right to "control" Transylvania (e.g., through some form of autonomy) or the Romanian state's right to set limits to the culture and language use of local Hungarians. Indeed, it is often incomplete democratization—that is, inadequate respect for the rights of individuals—that kindles demands for territorial autonomy in the first place. The question emerges: can a society be satisfied with the honoring of firm and explicit guarantees of *individual* rights, or does the appeal to *collective* rights expand the realm of freedom and right? It is my argument that, if anything, the appeal to collective rights threatens to limit and subvert individual rights and that, on the contrary, a strict observance of individual rights *and societal rights* (as explained below) is sufficient to meet all those needs of the inhabitants of any society that champions of collective rights seek to defend by more circuitous routes.

Individual rights standing alone may not be enough to ensure a balanced system. The difficulty with basing a system exclusively on respect for individual rights (an enterprise perhaps most clearly assayed in the case of the United States) is twofold. First, there is the danger that higher principle may be abandoned on the supposition that citizens taken individually should be assumed to be "the best judges of their own interests"[16] on any and all matters, including those of a technical or complicated nature. And second, there is the distortion that ensues when systems deny or ignore the notion that the entire body politic may have legitimate interests that may, indeed, transcend the interests of individuals qua individuals. These distortions have been magnificently outlined and analyzed by Frank Coleman in his brilliant book, *Hobbes and America*.[17] But respect for the interests of the entire body politic, as a collective entity, is what I call *societal rights*. It is, however, fundamentally at variance with any appeal to the supposed rights of one sector of the body politic against other sectors. The word "against" is of the essence here, and insufficient stress on this word would result in a complete obfuscation and misconstrual of my meaning.

From a notion of individual rights one may derive: the right to obtain education in one's own language, where there are enough students with that native language to warrant classes; the right to develop and pursue one's own culture, together with fellow members of that culture (including converts); the right to establish cultural and educational institutions funded from private funds or from funds generated by the members of that community; and the right to practice one's own religion, whether or not it is the dominant religion of one's group, or to abstain from religious practices.

From the notion of societal rights, one may derive notions of society's rights: to public security, to a functioning public education system, to low-cost medical care, to the state-provided maintenance of public transport and sewage systems, to the state's ensuring a favorable flow of trade with external partners, and to the commitment of the state to defend a system of justice based on Natural Law or Universal Reason.[18] These are not merely the rights of one particular segment of a society (e.g., the Hungarians of southern Slovakia) nor merely of individuals qua individuals; they are the rights of the entire body of citizens taken as a whole. Some people may be inclined to dispute my suggestion that the state needs to defend Natural Law or Universal Reason, but this was indeed the assumption made by John Locke, and it constituted the foundation of his defense of the legitimacy of rebellion against unreasonable authority; what made authority "unreasonable" was precisely its departure from Universal Reason. If authority is not bound to adhere to Universal Reason, then there can be no appeal that it has grown "unreasonable," since the standard of measure has been discarded.

By contrast, an appeal to "collective rights" serves to justify rather distinct demands. The following demands are dependent on the promulgation of a doctrine of collective rights: notions that violence against group "outsiders" is morally justified (as in the case of "ethnic cleansing"); claims of a right to take houses from "another nation" to redress losses by one's "own nation" (as in the eviction of ethnic Hungarians from their homes in Vojvodina, in order to offer them to Serbian refugees from the war against Croatia and Bosnia);[19] demands for territorial and local autonomy (demanded by Albanians in Macedonia, by Serbs in Hungary, by Hungarians in Slovakia and Transylvania); demands for state funding of group cultural institutions, radio stations, newspapers, and ethnic or religious events (demanded by Serbs in Croatia in 1989–91, by Albanians in Macedonia since 1991, etc.); assertions of a right, on the part of numerical minorities, to secede, even against the wishes of the numerical majority (as claimed by the Bosnian Serbs in 1992); and equations of the nation with the state. Hence, when Yugoslav president Dobrica Ćosić told the Bosnian Serb Assembly (in Pale) in 1993 that "wherever Serbian houses are, wherever Serbian land is, and wherever the Serbian language is spoken, the Serbian state will exist," he was equating the Serbian nation with the Serbian state and thereby invoking the doctrine of collective interests.[20] Or, again, when Bosnian Serb leader Radovan Karadžić told a Russian interviewer in 1995, "This is the only correct path for the Serbs—to create a single state" and claimed that Serbs enjoyed some transcendent "right to unite," he too was invoking the doctrine of collective rights.[21]

It might be thought that policies such as affirmative action depend on notions of "collective rights," but in fact quite the contrary is the case. Affirmative action or, for that matter, any program designed to correct or remedy injustices and inequalities suffered by individuals because of their race, ethnicity, religion, or gender takes as its starting point the right of individuals to equal treatment. It has nothing to do with the so-called historical rights of one Nation or another Nation. Affirmative action can thus be more authentically justified by appeals to individual, or even to societal, rights. On the other hand, it turns out that the doctrine of *collective* rights is inimical to notions of affirmative action. In its hegemonist variant, the doctrine advances the argument that members of the state-forming Nation are entitled to the protection of their culture, language, and history, while members of "non-state-forming nations" are not. In its autonomist variant, the doctrine advances the argument that equality within society as a whole should be shelved in favor of a sytem of differential rights in which each subgroup enjoys differential rights and status according to which province one finds oneself inhabiting or visiting. In either variant, the doctrine of collective rights undermines the moral and political presuppositions of affirmative action.

Furthermore, the concept of individual rights—which is anchored in Natural Law[22]—provides sufficient basis on which to assert the legitimacy of cultural differences and even to mobilize people for action on the basis of shared policy interests and goals, without regard to group membership. The doctrine of collective rights goes much beyond this, however. The doctrine translates cultural *differences* into cultural *divisions,* so that we find Radovan Karadžić telling a Bulgarian interviewer that it is "impossible" for Serbs, Muslims, and Croats of Bosnia, who had lived together in the same state for hundreds of years, to live together in the same state.[23] The doctrine, further, makes religion and/or nation the basis for political action and mobilizes people on the basis of membership in the (religious or ethnic) cultural collectivity. In the religious sphere, the doctrine of collective rights underlies demands to introduce creationism in state schools (as in the United States), to hang crucifixes in the classrooms of state schools (a phenomenon in post-1989 Poland and Germany), to pray (Christian) prayers in the classrooms of state schools, and to dictate the moral agenda in gray areas such as abortion, as well as the policy of conducting Catholic prayers in the confessionally mixed state schools of Croatia. In the nationalities sphere, the doctrine of collective rights underlies efforts to legislate the language to be used in local communities and churches (as in Bratislava's efforts to Slovakize ethnic Hungarian communities in southern Slovakia) and to limit property transfers according to ethnic criteria (as in Belgrade's proscription of the sale of land in Kosovo to Albanians).

Underlying the assertion of the doctrine of collective rights is the demand for conformity—the demand that all persons within a certain territory speak the same language, believe the same things, worship the same God, observe the same customs, and, ideally, identify with the same collective construct ("We are all Serbs here" or "We are all Muslims here"). For the doctrine to obtain moral grounding, one would have to be able to demonstrate that the state has a duty either to suppress the languages and cultures of disfavored groups in the name of the supposed rights of the favored group (the hegemonist variant of this doctrine) or, on the other hand, to create special autonomous zones for all groups and to finance the cultural artifacts and institutions of all self-declared peoples living on the territory under its jurisdiction (the autonomist variant of this doctrine). One would have to be able to demonstrate, further, that members of the subgroup have a duty to conform in language, religion, social beliefs, customs, and culture to the standards declared to be appropriate by those wielding power. In other words, if the appeal to collective rights has moral validity, at least in its hegemonist variant and, in some cases at least, arguably also in its autonomist variant, then we must embrace intolerance and limit the rights of individuals where they threaten group unity and homogeneity. But the appeal to intolerance and homogeneity is itself incompatible with respect for individual rights, which is grounded on the principle of tolerance.[24] Therefore, the doctrine of collective rights cannot be said to be grounded in Universal Reason.[25] On the contrary, it is grounded in a rejection of Universal Reason, not only because it cannot accept the tolerance required by Universal Reason but also because it must reject Universal Reason's tenet that all persons be viewed as equal moral actors. This is not the view of the nationalist, who thinks inherent rights vary depending on the territory in which one finds oneself (and sometimes on whether the given group is declared to be a "historical nation" or an "ahistorical nation," to use Marx's own terminology), and the moral field is narrowed in such a way that nationalists (or their religious equivalents) deny the universal character of morality. As Andrei Simić has explained:

> Within a moral field, members [of the self-designated group or subgroup] are expected to act towards each other with reference to a common set of shared ideas by which behavior is structured and evaluated. In contrast, behavior outside the moral field can be said to be amoral in that it is primarily idiosyncratic and as such may be purely instrumental or exploitative without being subject to sanctions. Thus, for the individual, those belonging to other moral fields can be said to form part of his or her amoral sphere.[26]

As I explained in a 1996 epexegesis on this text, the consequence of this mode of thinking is, for the nationalist, that "actions which might be deemed morally reprehensible when committed against a fellow member of the moral field (such as murder, torture, rape, confiscation of goods) may be seen as commendable when committed against persons not included in the group's moral field."[27] And yet, from what has been said earlier, it should be clear that the more narrowly any doctrine defines its moral field, the more distant it is from Universal Reason and the deeper its problems of moral illegitimacy.

The doctrine of collective rights has yet another debility, that is, the implication that larger groups have "larger" or more extensive rights than smaller groups—a position incompatible with Universal Reason, and hence with classical liberalism. In fact, the doctrine of collective rights strikes right at the heart of the assertion of common "societal" rights and interests and sows the seeds of faction. This is what James Madison had to say about the doctrine of collective rights:

> By a faction I understand a number of citizens, whether amounting to a majority or a minority of the whole, who are united and actuated by some common impulse of passion, or of interest, adverse to the rights of other citizens, or to the permanent and aggregate interests of the community.
>
> There are two methods of curing the mischiefs of faction: the one, by removing its causes; the other, by controlling its effects.[28]

Rejecting the option of eradicating the causes of faction, a remedy that could only be premised upon the complete extirpation of liberty, Madison urged the adoption of a system that would short-circuit the tyranny of either majority or minority. As he noted elsewhere:

> It is of great importance in a republic not only to guard the society against the oppression of its rulers, but to guard one part of the society against the injustice of the other part. Different interests necessarily exist in different classes of citizens. If a majority be united by a common interest, the rights of the minority will be insecure. There are but two methods of providing against this evil: the one by creating a will in the community independent of the majority—that is, of the society itself; the other, by comprehending in the society so many separate descriptions of citizens as will render an unjust combination of a majority of the whole very improbable, if not impracticable.[29]

Madison realized that to the extent citizens come to define themselves exclusively in terms of one difference, political polarization will result, provoking an intensification of conflict. This insight has been confirmed by more recent political science literature. Take, for example, Donald Horowitz, author of *Ethnic Groups in Conflict*. Horowitz's argument in the book is quite simply that "the organization of political parties along ethnic lines tends to foster rather than moderate competition between ethnic groups."[30] The same argument may be extended to notions of securing harmony by establishing autonomous zones. As early as 1929, Oscar Jászi, taking the Austro-Hungarian monarchy as his case study, showed the folly of endeavoring to ensure harmony and stability by recourse to autonomous zones and autonomous powers.[31] While a system of autonomous zones may produce certain positive side-effects, it is also apt to stimulate and intensify both polarization and conflict, by providing an institutional framework within which differing interests may contend on the basis of greater resources. There are, however, conditions that justify autonomism, both in moral terms and as a practical consideration; these conditions will be taken up in chapter 6.

Thus, I have argued that the doctrine of collective rights can be justified neither on moral nor on practical grounds. Not only can the doctrine of collective rights not be justified, but even the broader notion of linking rights with species membership is open to serious question. As Diana Meyers has observed:

> Salubrious as the conjunction of basic rights with universality in the domain of the human has been from a practical standpoint, the implication that individuals possess certain rights because they are members of a select species sanctifies a conceptual muddle. Individuals qualify for rights as individuals, not as members of [a] species. It may be the case that all or nearly all of the members of a species have a certain right. But if so, they have this right because of properties that characterize all or most members of the species.[32]

But if we accept Meyers's argument that "human rights" are the rights of *living beings* and not the rights of *members of the human species,* then we may find ourselves convinced of her corollary that the whole notion of specifically *human* rights is a form of "speciesism" and that all living beings have rights.[33] She offers the following suggestive argument:

> That membership in a species is not by itself relevant to possession of rights becomes clear once attention is diverted from members of the human species and focused on some other species, like gophers and robins, to which we are less emotionally attached. Let us grant for the sake of argument that most gophers have a right to a burrow because digging a burrow is the normal gopher's natural way of providing itself with shelter. Along the same lines, suppose that robins have a right to a nest. Is membership in these species the basis for this attribution of rights? The fatuity of attributing a right to a burrow to a mutant gopher who instinctively climbs a tree and constructs a nest of twigs and leaves reveals that species membership is not the critical factor. If anything, this sport should have a right to a nest despite the fact that it is a gopher. Evidently, the properties that usually characterize gophers, not gopherhood, would constitute the basis of our attribution of rights to gophers.[34]

Meyers's argument serves us in two ways. First, it suggests that the entire notion of rights of groups is founded on mythology and, further, that Locke's linkage of Universal Reason with specifically individual rights was well founded.[35] Second, it invites us to speculate as to whether a demand, for example, that Slovaks have a right to speak Slovak anywhere in Slovakia should not, perhaps, be rephrased as a right to speak any language they choose anywhere in Slovakia. Or, to put it another way, which Slovak is freer: the Slovak who is guaranteed the right to speak Slovak (but not any other language) anywhere in Slovakia or the Slovak who is guaranteed the right to speak Slovak or Hungarian or Spanish or Swahili or Esperanto or any other language without fear of punishment?

Nationalism versus Civic-Mindedness

This book represents an effort to come to grips with the phenomenon of collective rights and is premised on the supposition that there is a fundamental distinction between civic-mindedness and care for one's fellow citizens (both of which may be subsumed under the concept of societal rights, as elaborated in the conclusion) and nationalism (which involves the exaltation of one particular community or culture within and over a given society). The notion that a nation or a religious community has certain rights quite apart from and beyond the rights abiding in its members as individuals is a doctrine with far-reaching consequences. Invented in the eighteenth century, this notion is premised on the unspoken assumption that full guarantees of the civic rights of individuals will not suffice to provide protection for culture and community, suggesting in turn that the supposed special rights of a subgroup of society may, at times, bypass, if not actually come into conflict with, the rights of its members qua individuals.

But it is only in times of system collapse, political chaos, and sociopolitical transition that such grand questions are even raised. And it is most especially in times of transition and political chaos that societies are vulnerable to appeals to collective rights in the first place.

I do not aspire in this book to provide a general survey of Eastern Europe since 1989. A glance at the table of contents should suffice to indicate how remote such an ambition is from my mind. My purpose, rather, is to explore the manifestation of repressive action on behalf of supposed collective rights in the region since 1989, and for that reason I have elected to focus on three case studies that best illustrate the role played by the doctrine of collective rights in peacetime. On the other hand, I have decided to omit the most dramatic case of struggle over collective rights in the region, the Yugoslav wars of 1991–95, in part because I have written extensively on the subject before,[36] and in part because I believe that given the overexposure of that case, the subject of collective rights may actually emerge more clearly by looking at cases that have been less frequently examined. Bosnia receives only brief discussion, therefore, and that limited to post-Dayton Bosnia, in which, in theory at least, peace has been restored.

The first two chapters in this book describe regionwide trends since 1989. Chapter 1 investigates parallels between challenges facing the region in the years since 1989 and those confronting the region in the years after 1918. Parallels are found in challenges of relegitimation, violence, border changes, heightened nationalism, and the like. Chapter 2 summarizes the chief tasks that the countries in the region have had to face since 1989, specifically in the areas of economic rehabilitation and privatization; political institution building; and coping with chauvinistic nationalism, religious zealotry, and rising crime.

Chapter 3 is, at least in part, a moral-philosophical essay, in which the moral theory underpinning this book is further developed. The remainder of that chapter is devoted to an examination of five case studies in miniature: the Hungarians of Transylvania, the Turks of Bulgaria, the Serbs of Croatia, the Albanians of Macedonia, and post-Dayton Bosnia. The cases of the Turks and the Serbs most clearly show the importance of ethnopolitical and religious factors in minority disputes, although both factors are present in the other three cases as well. Autonomy has been attempted in all these cases but one, the Albanians of Macedonia—and the Albanians have not failed to demand it. Yet autonomy does not solve all problems. It solves some, creates others, and transforms still others.

Chapters 4–6 explore particular case studies relevant to the doctrine of collective rights. Chapter 4 explores the claims registered by the Roman Catholic Church in Poland on behalf of its flock, which, according to some of its prelates, is endangered by the alleged secularization of post-1989 Poland. Chapter 5 takes up the theme of Slovak nationalism and its effects in stunting the development of democratic institutions and laws and in provoking fear and defensive behavior among the minority Hungarians of southern Slovakia. And chapter 6 probes the case of Kosovo, a region in southwest Serbia (which until 1989 enjoyed the status of an autonomous province), in which ethnic Albanians, who still constitute at least 80 percent of the local population, have been relegated to second-class status on the strength of Serbian claims that the region is "sacred soil" and that the emotions attached to Serbian history there in the fourteenth century have greater weight in determining the political arrangements in the region than demographic or democratic arguments; in essence, an appeal to the collective rights of the Serbs has been pressed in an area where, in 1987, they composed less than 10 percent of the local population.[37]

Finally, in the conclusion, I examine the major categories of rights (of kings, of society, of the collective, of the individual), discussing their alternative sources of legitimation, and explore in greater depth the dynamics of nationalism understood as politicized culture.

The view that one adopts about nationalism depends on one's definition of it. One can define nationalism in such a way that perhaps no one would object to it. For example, if by nationalism one means merely cultural awareness or civic-mindedness, then it is apparent that a society is enriched and protected by the presence of these phenomena in large amounts. If, on the other hand, one means destructiveness and chauvinism, then it is hard to be positive about the phenomenon. On an understanding of nationalism as destructive chauvinism, John Keane has recently written:

> Nationalism is a scavenger. It feeds upon the pre-existing sense of nationhood within a given territory, transforming that shared national identity into a bizarre parody of its former self. Nationalism is a pathological form of national identity which tends (as Milorad Pavić points out in *Dictionary of the Khazars*) to destroy its heterogeneity by squeezing the nation into the Nation. Nationalism has a fanatical core. In contrast to national identity [or civic-mindedness], whose boundaries are not fixed and whose tolerance of difference and openness to other forms of life is qualitatively greater, nationalism requires its adherents to believe in the belief itself, to believe that they are not alone, that they are members of a community of believers known as the Nation, through which they can achieve immortality. . . . Nationalism has nothing of the humility of national identity. It feels no shame about the past or the present, for it supposes that only foreigners and "enemies of the nation" are guilty. It revels in macho glory and fills the national memory with stories of noble ancestors, heroism and bravery in defeat. It feels itself invincible, waves the flag and, if necessary, bloodies its hands on its enemies.[38]

My approach in this book is Kantian and Lockean, which is to say it is fully within the classical liberal tradition. I do not claim that only liberal democracy can constitute a legitimate system, but I do claim that the moral underpinning of liberal thought can provide a framework for assessing the legitimacy or illegitimacy of any and all systems, whether they be monarchies or theocracies or fascist dictatorships or communist systems or variations on the theme of nationalism. As a neo-Kantian, I take Universal Reason as my starting point, construing all political questions as, at least potentially, moral questions. As a neo-Kantian, I consider Universal Reason to be independent of a divine order. Or, to put it another way, the existence of God is immaterial to the establishment of a binding and universal moral code; whether God exists or not, there are some actions that are inherently good (e.g., kindness) and some actions that are inherently evil (e.g., the torture of infants). To refer the question to consequences, as if reason is not sufficient to inform one as to the moral character of at least some actions, is to abandon moral universalism for moral relativism. As a neo-Kantian, I do not argue or assume that Universal Reason can assure consensus on all moral questions. Some questions, such as abortion, seem likely to remain moral gray areas. But other questions, such as mass murder and mass rape, can more readily be judged. And as a neo-Kantian, I take it as a given that human rights, tolerance, and human freedom are among the most cherished values that must be protected in any social and political system.

I depart from Kantianism in two areas. The first is with respect to Kant's teaching on revolution. For Kant, as for Hobbes, rebellion against established authority can never be justified.[39] On this count, I find myself in agreement, not with Kant, but with Locke, who argued that when a government violates the precepts of Universal Reason, its subjects no longer owe that government their obedience but, on the contrary, enjoy the right (and, I would argue, duty) to overthrow it.

The second area in which I depart from Kantianism has to do with the concept of the state itself, where I find myself much closer to Hegel (a much maligned democrat).[40] It was, after all, Hegel who, in The Philosophy of Right, called attention to the need for political organizations responsive to the citizenry: "It is of utmost importance," wrote Hegel, "that the masses should be organized, because only so do they become mighty and powerful. Otherwise they are nothing but a heap, an aggregate of atomic units. Only when the particular associations are organized members of the state are they possessed of legitimate power."[41] For Hegel, who I believe was inspired in part by medieval writings concerning Natural Law, the state has a moral essence and is duty-bound to protect morality and to behave morally. This concept moves considerably beyond Locke's position. I understand Locke to have a rather passive concept of the state in relation to Universal Reason, while Hegel construes the relationship in more active terms.

It is thus on the groundwork of a more or less Kantian metaphysics that I propose to highlight the way in which appeals to the doctrine of collective rights complicate efforts to construct a liberal democracy and, more grandly, to make a small contribution toward clarifying the relationship between doctrines of rights, legitimation, and system content, taking certain societies of Eastern Europe as my cases.

1

Back to the Future in Eastern Europe

———————————————

Twice in this century Eastern Europe has been liberated from foreign rule and new indigenous elites have taken power, promising democracy and a more equitable division of the wealth. In 1918, the end of World War I saw the tumbling of the Habsburg and Hohenzollern dynasties, the final disintegration of the long-crumbling Ottoman Empire, and the withdrawal of Russia from Finland and the Baltic States and, for a brief period, also from Belorussia (as it was commonly called then) and Ukraine. In 1989, the sudden collapse of the communist political order in Eastern Europe, accompanied by the rapid shrinkage of Soviet power, swept virtually all the region's communist elites out of power—everywhere except in Serbia and Montenegro, although some still consider Romania a hybrid case. In 1918, the new postwar configuration of states was justified in terms of the doctrine of collective rights (under the rubric of national self-determination); in 1989, the collapse of the communist order reopened questions of national boundaries in accord with a reawakened doctrine of collective rights.

The purpose of this chapter is to assess points of comparison between the two historical situations, to consider the similarity in the challenges and complications confronted and in the responses devised, and to examine some mitigating factors that, in spite of all the commonalities, might enable at least some of the states in the area to chart a different course.

The argument unfolds over the five succeeding sections. In the first three sections, I explore seven aspects in which there are some significant parallels between the two historical periods, then I list briefly some additional factors in which there may also be a comparison. In these sections, I develop the argument that there are some respects in which Eastern Europe's leaders are returning to tasks undertaken in the interwar period, noting the ways in which the outlook and assumptions of present-day elites reproduce, albeit with variations, those of the interwar elites. The next section is devoted to exploring certain significant differences between Eastern Europe in the interwar period and Eastern Europe today and makes an effort to assess what these differences will mean in political terms. The chapter closes by identifying certain crucial policy tasks that analysts should watch closely to gauge the overall political tendencies.

In part, the question of the potential for the political recapitulation of the past is conjoined to an ineluctable choice of one view of history over others. There are, as far as I am aware, at most four alternative views of history, two of ancient vintage and two more modern. The ancient approaches, developed and articulated in Greece some twenty-four hundred years ago, are the cyclical view of history (associated with Parmenides and Plato) and the linear-dialectical view of history (associated with Heraclitus and, more recently, with Hegel). The birth of the liberal tradition with Machiavelli, Hobbes, and Locke gave rise to two further possibilities: the linear-nondialectical (liberal optimistic) view, which I would associate with nineteenth-century social Darwinism (especially Herbert Spencer); and the chaotic-antiteleological (liberal pessimistic) view, which underlies much popular and journalistic writing about world politics.

In developing my argument, I suggest that the cyclical view of history may be more useful than any of the linear approaches—whether dialectical or nondialectical—though this should not be given a crass interpretation nor lead the observer to expect exact replications of historical developments. The point is that certain themes reappear; certain problems recur or, perhaps remaining permanently unresolved, are confronted in ways that evolve cyclically; certain historical patterns return, like ships coming into port.

Parallels between Then and Now

In looking for parallels between the post-1918 and post-1989 situations in Eastern Europe, there are a number of aspects in which comparisons may be drawn. I propose, in the following pages, to take up these aspects: the general historical context; the rupture of transport systems and trade regimes as a result of border changes; the reopening of border questions and the stimulation of local conflicts; difficulties of adjustment in the legal, cultural, and economic spheres; the delegitimation of the old order and the need for entirely new principles of legitimation; the challenges of democratization in lands hitherto ruled by authoritarian systems; and the kindling (or rekindling) of ethnic animosities. Certain other factors will be noted very briefly after that: comparisons with regard to economic duress, land reform, controversies about the place of religion in society, and challenges associated with the need to construct a new infrastructure, especially in education and in the media.

Historical Context

Both periods involved regionwide political and economic transition, in which the prevailing sociopolitical order collapsed very abruptly. *Transition* may be understood as the processes that span the period of instability between the breakdown of a once stable political pattern and the attainment of a new equilibrium, a new stability; this understanding is founded on the principles of systems theory. The goal of any transition is stability. The goal of the post-1989 transition, as seen by at least some of the elites in most countries in the region, is *stable democracy.* By this, the East European elites understand parliamentary democracy on the West European model, albeit with some American admixture. The focus on democracy is evident: from the work habits of the region's constitutional commissions that, in framing their own constitutions, have first studied and reviewed the constitutions of many other states, mostly of Western Europe and the United States; from the invitations to American and British constitutional and legal scholars to present seminars to legislators in these countries (mostly in the years 1990–91); and from the important role that lawyers and judges of the American Bar Association have played in assisting the elites in drawing up legislation in many policy spheres.[1]

Both transitions (post-1918 and post-1989) are characterized by what we might call "the acceleration of history." The triumph of the Western Allies in World War I, together with the revolutionary upheavals in Russia and throughout the region, led to the sudden collapse of the Romanov dynasty in 1917, of the Hohenzollern and Habsburg dynasties in 1918, and of the Ottoman Empire, also in 1918. The entire region was affected by these changes. In 1989–90, the communist order collapsed throughout the region; only in Serbia and Montenegro were the incumbent communist elites able to prolong their hold on power, and there only by abandoning the communist program and embracing a new nationalist-chauvinist program. The Habsburgs and the Ottomans had attempted major systemic reforms during the last decade of their sway, and the Habsburg monarch offered the federalization of the realm in 1918 in a last-ditch effort to save the empire and his throne. In the 1980s, the communists undertook various reform schemes, and the words "reform" and "democratization" were constantly on the lips of communists everywhere in the region except in Albania.

The end of World War I put six new states on the map: Poland, Czechoslovakia, Yugoslavia, and, insofar as its sovereignty had been limited within the

Habsburg Dual Monarchy, Hungary, as well as city-states in Fiume and Danzig. The number increases to ten if one also counts the Baltic states and Finland. Between 1989 and February 1994, the division of preexisting states gave rise to seven new states: the Czech Republic, Slovakia, Slovenia, Croatia, Bosnia-Herzegovina, Macedonia, and the Federal Republic of Yugoslavia (consisting of Serbia and Montenegro). Again, adding the resurrected Baltic states brings the total to ten.

In both cases, political transition brought into politics many persons who either were not professional politicians or who were actively fighting the pre-existing system, or both. In both cases the new elites have included literary intellectuals (Masaryk, Havel), musicians (Paderewski, Landsbergis), professors (Tsankov, Antall), revolutionaries (Piłsudski, if I may characterize his rather complex career in this way, and Wałęsa), and chauvinistic nationalists (Horthy, Milošević). Some of these had been engaged in behind-the-scenes politicking for years, even though their professional careers were prima facie nonpolitical (here: Marasyk, Havel, Paderewski, Tsankov).

And in both cases, the incoming elites, with few exceptions, have promised democracy and a more equitable division of resources.

Rupture of Transport and Trade Systems

The wholesale border changes in 1918 and again in 1989 inevitably complicated transport systems and trade regimes.

This problem confronted almost all the East European states in 1918. Czechoslovakia was a case in point:

> The railroad and road networks of Bohemia and Moravia-Silesia had been designed to connect them with Vienna, while those of Slovakia and Ruthenia had focused on Budapest; consequently, the transport connections between these formerly Austrian and formerly Hungarian parts of Czechoslovakia were poor. Initially, indeed, the only main railroad line between them was the one passing through the disputed Tesin area, and by the end of the interwar period there were only four additional secondary connections.[2]

Yugoslavia, stitched together from Serbia, Montenegro, and parts of the dissolved Habsburg Empire, faced even more severe problems. Again, railroads in formerly Habsburg areas (e.g., Slovenia, Croatia, and Bosnia) had been laid out with an eye to integrating these regions into Austria-Hungary, and hence connections to regions east and southeast were poor. This situation was further complicated by differences in railway gauge and by the generally lower level of development of non-Habsburg regions. Thus, while the new Kingdom of

Serbs, Croats, and Slovenes inherited 59 kilometers of railway lines per 1,000 square kilometers in Croatia and Slavonia and 65 kilometers per 1,000 square kilometers in Slovenia and Medjimurje, the corresponding figures for Bosnia Herzegovina, northern Serbia, and southern Serbia were 33, 34, and 20 kilometers of railway lines per 1,000 square kilometers respectively.[3]

Other new states had similar problems. There were, thus, almost no rail connections between the three sections of Poland (the sectors occupied by Germany, Austria, and Russia) or between Transylvania and the Regat (the Old Kingdom).[4]

The breakup of the old empires also meant the end of de facto customs unions. The new state of Czechoslovakia soon renounced its trade treaty with Hungary, and the two states erected tariff walls.[5] Until 1918, Slovakia had been entirely integrated into the larger Hungarian market, but in the 1920s, Slovak trade was gradually reoriented to the Czech lands, and Czech capital bought out Hungarian interests in Slovakia. The Budapest industrial region suffered, of course, from being cut off from a number of its former sources of raw materials (especially in Slovakia and Transylvania) and from its former domestic markets. In Poland, the new frontiers produced an element of chaos in local industry and agriculture for similar reasons, and also because of Russia's disappearance from world trade.

The post-1989 transition does not involve (at this writing) the merger of any hitherto separately administered regions but is characterized throughout by tendencies toward fragmentation and secession. But in this sphere, much of the transport infrastructure in Bosnia-Herzegovina was destroyed as a result of the Serbian Insurrectionary War of 1991–95.

The trade sector, however, provides a much closer parallel. The breakup of COMECON, the economic and political decline of Russia, and the disappearance of the Soviet-era trade regime based on the "transferable ruble" are macro-level factors that have been the driving force for major reorientations of trade in the region. In addition, there are factors specific to certain countries. The breakup of Czechoslovakia and Yugoslavia had a major impact on trading patterns. Trade between the Czech Republic and Slovakia, for example, fell 60 percent in January 1993 compared with the average monthly level for 1992.[6] Both republics, like other states in the region, scrambled to boost trade with the West, and by May 1993, 55 percent of Slovakia's exports, for instance, went to Western Europe.[7] The former Yugoslav republics have also had to adjust to changing markets. In their case, the outbreak of war between Serbian insurgents in Croatia and Bosnia and forces loyal to the elected governments in those republics compelled these states, together with Serbia (which was supplying Croatian Serb and Bosnian Serb forces), to make even more drastic adjustments. The imposition of the United Nations economic embargo on the Federal Republic of Yugoslavia (hereafter, Serbia and Montenegro) in May 1992 (toughened in April 1993) forced Serbia to rely on trade with sympathetic states willing to defy the embargo—in particular Greece, Romania, Russia, China, and Libya.[8]

In both transition periods, the disruption of transport and trade systems was sudden, compelling the states concerned to make major economic adjustments under duress, while still in the process of establishing, or transforming, their political systems.

Creation or Reopening of Border Questions

What is especially striking about the two transitions is that both began with widespread social chaos, revolutionary upheavals, and local conflicts. World War I officially ended at the end of 1918, but the borders of several states in the region were settled only in 1921, after Czechoslovak troops had seized Polish-inhabited Tešín, Austrian-inhabited Sudetenland, and Hungarian-inhabited areas that became part of southern Slovakia; after the Serbian/Yugoslav army seized the Hungarian-inhabited Vojvodina by force; after Romanian troops had penetrated deep into central Hungary, securing Romanian conquest of Transylvania; and after Poland went to war with Russia in an ultimately successful endeavor to annex a large swath of Ukrainian and Belorussian territory. The only plebiscites conducted in Eastern Europe were held in what became Austrian Burgenland and in Silesia (divided between Germany and Poland).

The entire region was riddled with border disputes. Germany and Poland quarreled over the "Polish corridor," inhabited mostly by Germans, while German-Lithuanian relations were strained over Lithuania's occupation of the Baltic port of Memel. Lithuania resented Poland's occupation of the Wilno district, and the Poles in turn resented Czechoslovakia's seizure of Tešín. Hungary had border disputes with Czechoslovakia, Romania, and Yugoslavia, which in turn formed the anti-Hungarian "Little Entente." Bulgaria resented the loss of the Southern Dobruja to Romania; of Macedonia to the Kingdom of Serbs, Croats, and Slovenes (later renamed Yugoslavia); and of its Aegean outlet to Greece. Albanian irredentism riveted on sections of Yugoslavia and Greece, while Greece, in turn, craved southern Albania, which it referred to as "Northern Epirus." There was not a country in the entire region free of border conflicts. The situation was so extreme, and the borders drawn with such utter contempt for the actual wishes of the local inhabitants, that by 1932 even Britain and France, the countries most responsible for the Versailles system, were showing some sympathy for the idea of revising the peace treaties in favor of the Hungarians and the Bulgarians.

In addition, there were revolutionary upheavals in Germany in 1919, 1921, and 1923; instances of violent resistance to incorporation into the new South Slav Kingdom in Kosovo and Montenegro; and, in Albania, a series of revolts against King Zog, beginning in 1931.[9]

Happily, the post-1989 scenario is not as extreme. Even so, a number of border conflicts have flared up, some of them with pernicious effect. The most obvious border conflicts have been those between Serbia and Croatia and among Serbs, Croats, and Muslims in Bosnia. But there are other border conflicts in the region, with varying potency to influence domestic and foreign policy agendas. Here I might mention Russian separatism in Moldova, which has already entangled Romania to the extent that Romania supplies some of Moldova's import needs. Other border conflicts have included the Serb-Albanian dispute over Kosovo, Hungarian sensitivities about the treatment of Hungarians in Slovakia and Vojvodina, Greek frictions with Albania over what Athens still refers to as Northern Epirus,[10] and Greek refusal to recognize the Republic of Macedonia. Interestingly enough, two border disputes that were occasionally cited during the communist era—between Romania and Hungary over Transylvania, and between Bulgaria and Yugoslavia over Macedonia—seem to have largely faded from view. This development is due, at least in part, to caution in Budapest and Sofia lest reckless rhetoric inflame political passions and stoke interethnic conflict.

Difficulties of Adjustment in the Legal, Cultural, and Economic Spheres

After 1918, Poland, Czechoslovakia, Romania, and Yugoslavia were all faced with the task of integrating into a common system territories with disparate legal, cultural, and economic traditions and pattern. This process of integration took years and in some respects was not even complete when the region plunged again into war.

The three sections of Poland operated initially under different systems of taxation and education. Only Germany had introduced universal education, but the Germans had not permitted *any* Polish-language schools, not even at the primary level. In Austrian Galicia, by contrast, the educational system had been under Polish control and there were two universities (Kraków and Lwów); but the system itself was primitive, and illiteracy was widespread in ex-Austrian Galicia. In Warsaw, the Poles inherited a university that had been offering classes in Russian only.

During late 1918 and 1919, as many as six currencies were in circulation in Poland: German marks, Austrian crowns, Russian rubles, Polish marks, "occupation marks" issued by the German High Command in the east, and varieties of Russian currency. Until 1920, a tariff barrier remained between former Prussian Poland and the rest of Poland, and one even needed a passport to travel from Warsaw to Poznań. There was no unified transport system either: more than fifty Austrian- and German-built railway lines extended to the limit of their former holdings; where the Russians had ruled, there were only ten rail lines.[11] The differences in the rail system extended to differences in signaling, in braking systems, in safety devices, and in gauge.

Four legal systems functioned in the emergent Poland (in the Russian sector, the region of the Congress Kingdom retained a modified version of the Napoleonic code, while elsewhere the same legal system had obtained as in the rest of the Russian Empire). The long separation had affected the political culture and even the perceived identity of the Poles, so that in Galicia a kind of dual identity had taken hold, and locals thought of themselves simultaneously as Poles and Austrians.[12]

In Czechoslovakia, the Czech provinces inherited the Austrian legal code, while Slovakia and Ruthenia initially operated under the less liberal Hungarian code. There were also economic differences between the Czech and Slovak regions. Farm holdings in the Czech regions, for example, were significantly larger than those in Slovakia, contributing to a higher standard of living for rural Czechs. Indeed, the Czech peasantry produced for the market and thus welcomed increases in agricultural prices, while the Slovak smallholders had to purchase a substantial portion of their diet and therefore were averse to such price increases.[13] There were also important differences in religious temper between the two regions. It bears recollecting that Father Andrej Hlinka (1864–1938) founded his clerical Slovak People's Party in 1912 in order to combat and resist the influence of Czech "free thinking" among Slovak intellectuals and the spread of socialist ideas from Czech workers to Slovak workers; Slovak autonomism thus was born of differences in religious and cultural outlooks.

The situation in the new Kingdom of Serbs, Croats, and Slovenes was even more complex. At first, six distinct legal-administrative systems prevailed, fueling uncertainty and administrative chaos. Even though the government soon established a special ministry to standardize the laws, progress was slow.[14] Even the Serbian Orthodox Church found itself saddled with significant administrative differences from one region to another. Orthodox bishops in Karlovac and Bosnia-Herzegovina were especially dogged in resisting changes that they feared would reduce their local autonomy, and it was not until 1929 that the Serbian Orthodox Church achieved organizational and administrative unity.[15]

Similar problems also plagued Romania in the years shortly after 1918, as authorities confronted the need to synchronize the diverse legal and administrative systems in the Regat, Transylvania, Bukovina, and Bessarabia.[16]

I have already suggested that the post-1989 transition is characterized by a more general tendency toward fragmentation. In only two places so far has this issue presented itself in the form of integration: in Germany (with the integration of East Germany into the Federal Republic of Germany) and—albeit so far only in the form of desire—in the Serbian sector of Bosnia, which, as Bosnian Serb leader Radovan Karadžić admitted in 1993, he and his collaborators hoped to see absorbed into a "Greater Serbia."[17] But other states in the region may yet face parallel tasks, such as Albania (if Kosovo is eventually conjoined to it), Croatia (if it were to annex what it calls "Herzeg-Bosna") and Romania (if and when Moldova is ever finally reunited with Romania proper).

In the short run, the German experience betrays some parallels to the earlier cases. These parallels include local resistance to specific changes in legislation (especially among women opposed to the delegalization of abortion,[18] and also in regard to regional consciousness, with a sudden realization on the part of East Germans that they do not share the same cultural and political outlooks as West Germans)[19] and differential levels of unemployment, which feed interregional resentments.

But if there are some differences between the post-1918 and post-1989 transitions in terms of the *roots* of the problem, elites in both transitions have nonetheless faced the *same result:* chaos in bureaucracy and administration. All the elites in the region have been confronted with the urgent need to adopt entirely new legislation affecting all spheres of public life, to mold and change the institutional structures of the system, to eliminate the overlap of functions that was a hallmark of the communist system, and to train new personnel or carryovers to function according to new procedures within the framework of new legislation. When I visited Ljubljana in March 1992 for two weeks of interviews with government ministers and party leaders, I was struck by the degree to which most of them felt overwhelmed by the enormity of the tasks that confronted them; I was also impressed by the large number of bills passed into law each month. I encountered much the same situation on visiting Skopje in March 1995.

Legitimation of the New Order

In interwar Eastern Europe, after the overthrow of the dynasties, there were several competing sources of legitimation, among which the most important were (a) the appeal to peasant democracy (associated with Stamboliski in Bulgaria, Radić in Croatia, and Tărănism in Romania);[20] (b) the appeal to nationalism, always associated with the glorification of past history and, when appropriate, also with irredentism; (c) the appeal to religion (this was most overtly manifested in the loud appeals to religion made by the Slovak People's Party of Hlinka and Tiso and by Codreanu's League of the Archangel Michael, but it is also relevant for other politicians, including Masaryk, who believed that one of the primary tasks in politics was "how to resurrect the values of Christianity,"[21] and Hungary's Bishop Ottokar Prohaszka, generally regarded as the spiritual leader of the Horthyite counterrevolution, who traced Hungary's territorial losses in the Treaty of Trianon to Jewish influence and championed "positive Christianity," order, traditional values, and opposition to Jewish influence;[22] (d) the appeal to charismatic authority (the most obvious example being Poland's Marshal Piłsudski, who once described himself in a speech before the State Tribunal as "the greatest man in Poland,"[23] although after Piłsudski's death in 1935, Poland's ruling elite, the Sanacja, tried quite deliberately to build a new hero cult around Piłsudski's chosen successor, General Edward Rydz-Śmigly);[24] (e) the appeal to radical egalitarianism (briefly promoted in Hungary by coercive means, by Béla Kun, before his overthrow by Admiral Horthy in the summer of 1919); and (f) parliamentary politics.

I pointedly refer to parliamentary politics rather than to liberal-democratic values, because, in spite of the familiarity of some of the elites with liberal ideas, they lacked sufficient force to serve as an exclusive vehicle for legitimation. Parliamentary politics is, of course, the formal institutional expression of what might be liberal democracy. But in its East European interwar incarnation, parliamentary politics was too often understood in terms of everyone getting his or her share—hence, Stamboliski's well-known contempt for the old-style political parties. Liberal democracy thus lacked independent force for legitimation in interwar Eastern Europe, and even parliamentary politics was often viewed as a rather shabby, even sordid, display. Hence, something else was needed. And given the shared history of lengthy struggles against foreign rule, combined with border problems rife in the area, nationalism was the most obvious and most commonly employed legitimating force, typically harnessed with other available legitimating resources.

In fact, despite the professed desire to create functioning democratic systems, the interwar elites frequently rejected the individualism that is entailed in liberal concepts of democracy.[25] The ideas of Heinrich von Treitschke were the common currency of the age, and most East European ruling elites in the interwar period would have agreed with the following remarks by Treitschke:

> How far is the individual responsible for the morality of the State to which he belongs? Here the Natural Law, which defines the State as nothing but a collection of small individualities, goes seriously astray. We have already recognized that *la volonté générale* is not the same thing as *la volonté de tous*. The pure individualism of the Natural Law teaching came to the preposterous conclusion that the citizen has the right to desert the State if it declares a war which he holds to be unjust. But since his first duty is obedience, such unfettered power cannot

be granted to his individual conscience. For me, the upholding of the mother country is a moral duty. The machinery of the political world would cease to revolve if every man made bold to say "the State should not; therefore I will not."[26]

But if the claims of the state come first, the claims of nationality, for Treitschke, are not far behind. As Treitschke put it:

> Even at present a man feels himself primarily a German or a Frenchman, and only in the second place as a man in the wider sense. This is stamped upon every page of history. It is then both historically and physiologically untrue that human beings enter upon existence first as men, and afterwards as compatriots.[27]

Thus, for Treitschke, one is a citizen first, a national second, and a human being only third and derivately. This same ordering inspired the social and political systems of interwar Eastern Europe. Little wonder that the East European elites of the interwar era did not give birth to liberal-democratic systems.

The interwar elites dealt with the question of legitimacy by construing it in terms of the state's boundaries, rather than in terms of its form of government. It is for this reason that the "Czechoslovak nation" and the "tri-named people" (Serbs, Croats, and Slovenes) were invented and that the Polish government made energetic efforts to Polonize the Ukrainian and Belorussian peasants in Poland's eastern territories.[28]

The collapse of communism in 1989–90 reopened the question of legitimacy in Eastern Europe, and of the five most common appeals for relegitimation, three recapitulate interwar options. The three "old" options are nationalism, religion, and charismatic authority; the "new" options are appeals to liberal democracy valued either as a safeguard against oppression or as a route to economic prosperity. The appeal to nationalism has been central to most secessionist states in the area, especially Slovakia, Croatia, and Serbia, but much less so in Slovenia and Macedonia; and where nationalism has been raised to a dominant position, chauvinism has followed in its wake.[29] In Romania, as in other states in the region, appeals to nationalism may disguise deep-seated hostility to democratic reform.[30]

Religious legitimation has figured as a secondary, even ancillary, resource in Poland, Croatia, and, perhaps surprisingly, Serbia as well, where Milošević received the Orthodox patriarch at one time and arranged to have the Orthodox Church praised as a bulwark of Serbian national culture.[31]

The two new appeals have a common feature: they both appeal to the welfare of the community as a collectivity. One appeals to the *political* welfare of the community, the other to its *economic* welfare. And unlike appeals to nationalism, religion, and charismatic authority, they admit of some "objective" neutral criteria of success.

Comparing the two transitions in light of the question of legitimation, one may say that the interwar endeavor to build democracies was subverted in advance by the strong appeal to nationalism, while the post-1989 endeavor shows greater diversity from state to state, suggesting one reason the prospects for democracy in the region vary at this juncture from state to state.[32]

The Challenge of Democratization

It is commonly noted that Eastern Europe's experimentation with democracy in the interwar era was short-lived. In Hungary, liberal democracy did not even have a chance to entrench itself. Count Mihály Károlyi, an aristocrat with liberal-democratic views, took office as prime minister on 2 November 1918 and attempted to carry out a liberal program, but pressures from the victorious Allies contributed to the fall of the Károlyi government in March 1919. He was succeeded first by a communist dictatorship of the proletariat (under Béla Kun), lasting 133 days, and subsequently by the antidemocratic, reactionary government of Miklós Horthy.[33] A new franchise law of 1922 reduced the Hungarian electorate by about 25 percent; intricate restrictions included minimum education requirements, effectively disenfranchising almost the entire agrarian sector, and opposition parties were, in any event, barred from organizing in the village.

In Poland, Marshal Piłsudski seized power in May 1926 and thereafter established a "soft" dictatorship by combining manipulation, preemptive arrests, and curtailment of the right to form associations. The elections of 1930 were held after the summary arrest of several thousand opposition leaders, and the government's electoral commissioners invalidated 214 election lists before allowing the voting to take place.[34] On 1 March 1932, the autonomy of the universities was curtailed, and the Ministry of Education was given the power to remove professors who were (politically) "unfit."[35] A 23 August 1932 decree revoked the irremovability of judges, and in October of that year the right to form associations was subjected to new limitations. In 1935, one of the first acts of Piłsudski's successors was to restrict the franchise—a move justified as eliminating professional politicians and making the Sejm "less partisan and more patriotic."[36]

Elsewhere royal dictatorship was imposed—in Yugoslavia in 1929, in Romania in 1938, and in Bulgaria in 1935 (where it was toughened in 1938).[37] Only in Czechoslovakia did democracy fare somewhat better. But even there, the founders of the state pointedly excluded German, Hungarian, and Ruthenian deputies from the provisional National Assembly's deliberations about the state constitution; only when the constitution had been adopted were the representatives of the national minorities permitted to participate in the proceedings.[38] What the Slovaks and Ruthenes wanted above all was political autonomy (which in fact had been promised to them), and neither Masaryk nor Beneš was willing to discuss this. The Sudeten Austrians and the Hungarians wanted plebiscites to be conducted in their areas to allow them to determine whether they wished to be conjoined with the new state of Czechoslovakia. "A vicious circle was soon established [in Czechoslovakia]. [The] national minorities were denied regional autonomy because their loyalty was in doubt, and they remained disloyal because they were given no self-government."[39]

Why did democracy fail to take root in interwar Eastern Europe? I believe that at least five reasons may be cited. The first, already discussed above, is the fact that the borders of these states were drawn by force without regard to the wishes of the populations concerned. The only problem-free borders in the entire region were the Hungarian border with Austria and Romania's borders with Czechoslovakia and Yugoslavia. It is not without significance that the first of these was one of only two borders in the region that had been fixed by the outcome of a plebiscite and that the parties involved in the latter two cases were cosignatories of the so-called Little Entente. In this respect, the contemporary situation is somewhat more promising; the borders of Poland and the Czech Republic, at least, are problem free, and Hungary has, after a series of highly problematic statements by Prime Ministers Jozsef Antall and Peter Boross,[40] ostensibly renounced any irredentist notions under Prime Minister Gyula Horn. During 1995 and early 1996, Jozsef Torgyan, an antidemocratic, homophobic demagogue with overt irredentist views, seemed to be building a sizable following among the Hungarian citizenry. But after March 1996, his popularity and credibility plummeted precipitously.[41] Be that as it may, in post-1989 Eastern Europe, problematic borders are largely restricted to the Balkans.

A second factor was the sheer proliferation of political parties. In Czechoslovakia in 1920, 23 parties contested the elections, and 17 of them elected deputies to the parliament; in elections for the Constituent Assembly in Yugoslavia, held that same year, 22 political parties or groups fielded candidates, and 16 of them elected deputies. In Poland, 92 political parties registered to contest the 1925 elections, and 32 of these obtained representation in the Sejm. And in Romania, 102 political parties vied for seats in the elections of December 1933. Moreover, the number of political parties actually increased over time in Yugoslavia and Romania.[42] The proliferation of parties in parliament made necessary elaborate coalitions that could only prove highly unstable. Cabinets fell with regularity throughout the region, including

Czechoslovakia. Moreover, in these conditions, responsible government was more difficult to attain, and ambitious politicians found it expedient to resort to extremist and even alarmist rhetoric in the effort to build their electoral bases.

In this respect, Eastern Europe since 1989 has gotten off to an inauspicious start. As early as the beginning of 1990, 17 political parties were operating in East Germany, 80 in Poland, 35 in Czechoslovakia (with 22 of them actually fielding candidates in the June 1990 elections), 22 in Hungary, 78 in Romania, 35 in Bulgaria, and at least 86 in Yugoslavia.[43] As in interwar Eastern Europe, some of these parties have focused on narrow issues: the Rock 'n' Roll Party in Serbia; the Liberal Sexual Party in Hungary; the Hungarian Health Party; and the Friends of Beer Party and the Union of Rabbit Raisers, both in Czechoslovakia. And as in the interwar period, the plurality of parties has contributed to parliamentary weakness in Poland (at least until the elections of September 1993), Romania, and Bulgaria.[44] In Croatia and Serbia, on the other hand, the same result (parliamentary weakness) has resulted from other factors.

A third factor underlying the failure of democracy in the interwar period was the rise of fascist parties throughout the region, gaining special importance in Croatia, Serbia, Romania, and Hungary.[45] Indeed, in Romania the growing strength of the fascistic Iron Guard contributed directly to King Carol's decision in February 1938 to outlaw all political parties, enlarge his own powers, and appoint a nonparty government under the nominal prime ministership of Orthodox patriarch Miron Cristea.[46]

In contemporary post-1989 Eastern Europe there are both atavistic neofascist and neo-Nazi parties operating throughout the region,[47] as well as "new-style" nationalist formations such as the România Mare party in Romania and István Csurka's Hungarian Truth Party,[48] not to mention the authoritarian regimes of Slobodan Milošević in Serbia and Franjo Tudjman in Croatia.[49] Vladimír Mečiar's governing style in Slovakia also shows some marked tendencies toward chauvinistic nationalism, and he has been accused of making anti-Semitic comments in public speeches.[50] The neofascist and neo-Nazi parties do not have any chance of coming to power anywhere in the region, at least not in the foreseeable future, but they still have the capacity to make a great deal of trouble, harassing people who are "different" in any way, polarizing societies, and distorting political agendas. But in both the short and the long run, it is the new-style nationalists who are apt to constitute the greater threat to tolerance and democracy in the region.

The fourth factor that I would like to highlight as corrosive of democracy in the interwar period was the lack of a "civic culture" in the East European societies. This lack was itself a reflection of the absence of an educational philosophy that stressed the importance of tolerance, of compromise, of coexistence, of the capacity for empathy. On the contrary, the educational system of interwar Eastern Europe placed special emphasis on the times of "glory" when the armies of one's own country savaged and occupied other peoples' territories, and East European youth in the region as a whole were taught to regard their own nations as racially, morally, intellectually, and psychologically superior to their neighbors.[51] Hugh Seton-Watson highlighted the importance of this factor in 1942. As he wrote at the time:

> The most essential condition . . . for the establishment of democratic Government in Eastern Europe is an improvement and intensification of general Education. This means not only the education of the youth, but the raising of the tone of the press, literature, and all forms of expression of public opinion.[52]

The failure to educate the populations for democracy was reflected in the rapid growth of authoritarian parties in several of these states and in the ease with which democracy was subverted.

Yet, the elites of the interwar era were not oblivious to the importance of this factor. Kazimierz Bartel, Piłsudski's first prime minister, said as much in May 1926:

> The Government understands that it is not enough today to maintain legal order provisionally. It is further necessary to raise public life to a level of morality which will be the measure of the internal regeneration and recovery of the Republic. This moral regeneration, this development of the Republic, through respect for law and social justice, and by the elimination of all party and individual egoism, the Government considers, not only its future function, but also its present task.[53]

The communists, of course, promised to educate people in such a way as to foster coexistence and harmony among peoples and "democratic behavior"; but in fact the communist regimes completely failed in this ambition to fashion a "new socialist person." And in some societies, the communist system actually worked in the opposite direction, to foster social atomism and withdrawal.[54] The overall effect of communist rule in Eastern Europe was to replicate a pattern that Alexis de Tocqueville identified in all despotic systems (I would say *some*), in which people become

> far too much disposed to think exclusively of their own interests, to become self-seekers practicing a narrow individualism and caring nothing for the public good. Far from trying to counteract such tendencies despotism encourages them, depriving the governed of any sense of solidarity and interdependence; of good

neighborly feelings and a desire to further the welfare of the community at large. It immures them, so to speak, each in his private life and, taking advantage of the tendency they already have to keep apart, it estranges them still more.[55]

As Ken Jowitt has suggested, the Leninist legacy in Eastern Europe is to have fostered just such a frame of mind (though, I would add, with less success in Poland than elsewhere, and with more success in Romania than anywhere else), so that contemporary political culture in Eastern Europe, despite all the professions of desire to build democracy, may be on the whole more conducive to authoritarian capitalism than to liberal democracy.[56] I would add only that the Czech Republic and Slovenia, and to some extent Poland and Hungary, constitute important exceptions to this general trend, although Hungary has an additional challenge of having been rather "Budapest-centric" in economic investments through much of its history. It is interesting to note in connection with Poland that in an August 1992 poll, 46 percent of Poles said that democracy was only "useful" if it produced economic prosperity, while only 13 percent felt that democracy actually contributed to economic development.[57]

The fifth and final factor that contributed to the failure of democracy in interwar Eastern Europe is that, to a considerable extent, the elites of Eastern Europe either did not know what they were doing (this certainly applies to many of the politicians in Poland, Romania, and Yugoslavia, and to some Czech politicians) or were more interested in feathering their own nests than in creating workable democracies (this applies to most of the politicians in interwar Romania, as well as to most Bulgarian politicians after the fall of Stamboliski).

Ethnic Animosities

I have already discussed the border problems endemic in the region in both interwar and post-1989 Eastern Europe. In both periods, serious ethnic animosities have existed within the states themselves. In the interwar era, this was especially true of Yugoslavia and Czechoslovakia, both of which were dismantled at the end of the earlier period, Czechoslovakia in 1938–39, Yugoslavia in 1941. But other states in the region also confronted serious internal problems of this kind—among them, and most obviously, Poland, but also Romania, with its Magyar, German, Ukrainian, and Russian minorities.

The policies pursued in this area in Poland, Romania, Yugoslavia, and Czechoslovakia showed some surprising consistencies. In each of these cases, the government resisted demands for autonomous status and pursued policies of linguistic assimilation and religious favoritism. In the Yugoslav case linguistic assimilation policy went so far as attempting to deny that the Slovenian language was anything more than Serbian that had been bastardized as a result of Austrian manipulation.[58]

All four states adopted land reform packages that discriminated against ethnic minorities. Thus, in Czechoslovakia, the land reform bill was designed essentially to confiscate the estates of Austrian or German and Hungarian landlords and turn them over to Czech and Slovak tenants, and in Ruthenia land reform was carried out in such a way as to benefit Czech colonists from the western part of the country rather than local Ruthene peasants.[59] In Yugoslavia, a similar reform was applied in Bosnia, principally with an eye to breaking up the large estates of Muslim landowners, while the Yugoslav government also authorized the seizure of Hungarian estates in Bačka (Vojvodina) and the Banat, and the possessions of the Croatian nobility. In addition, under the pretext of agrarian reform, Belgrade authorities seized 154,287 acres of land from Albanians in Kosovo, turning about a third of it over to Serbian "colonists" and retaining the remainder for government and military uses, and drew up plans for the settlement of fifty thousand Serbian families in Macedonia.[60] Similarly, in Poland, land reform included an element of ethnic Polish "colonization" in erstwhile Ukrainian and Belorussian areas,[61] while in Romania, the "wholesale removal of Magyars from Romanian government posts" was accompanied by "the expropriation of rural property belonging to 'foreign' [i.e., Hungarian and Saxon] landholders in Transylvania, Crisana, Maramureş, and the Banat."[62]

In education, too, ethnic discrimination was official policy in Yugoslavia, Poland, and Romania. After forcibly suppressing a renewed effort by the Albanians of Kosovo to join Albania, Belgrade authorities closed down all Albanian-language schools in the region.[63] As Ivo Banac records:

> The authorities first tried to assimilate Albanian children and youth by allowing them only Serbian language education, using Bosnian Muslim teachers of proved pro-Serbian orientation for the purpose. But when it appeared that the Serbian schools, far from Serbianizing [the] Albanians, were providing them with the intellectual skills that could be used against the regime, Belgrade started discouraging public education for Albanians, permitting them only catechetical instruction, conducted by Muslim imams and Catholic priests. The authorities were convinced that these predominantly Muslim schools . . . would keep the Albanians . . . ignorant.[64]

In Vojvodina, the Yugoslav government closed all Hungarian-language schools, both primary and secondary, although two were eventually reopened. Later, the government used the assassination of King Alexander as a pretext to expel a large number of Hungarians from Vojvodina.[65]

In Poland, authorities largely liquidated the existing system of Belorussian primary schools by 1924–25 and curtailed the number of Ukrainian-language elementary schools by 80 percent between 1921–22 and 1934–35. In fact, both the pre-Piłsudski and Piłsudskiite governments obstructed Ukrainian and German efforts to obtain schooling for their children in their own languages.[66]

Linguistic assimilation was pursued through vigorous policies of linguistic discrimination. Czech efforts to "Czechize" the Slovak language have already been noted, as well as parallel efforts in Yugoslavia to promote the Serbian variant of Serbo-Croatian as the country's sole language. A similar course was pursued in Poland, where the 1931 census showed that only 68.9 percent of the population claimed Polish as their native language.[67] In spite of that, a law passed in March 1933 made Polish the official language in all local government bodies and curtailed the rights of self-governing villages. Needless to say, non-Poles resented the policies, and among the Ukrainian minority, extremist organizations sprang up and burned crops as a means of resistance. As early as 1930, the Polish government replied to resisters by dispatching "pacification squads" that burned down entire Ukrainian villages, slaughtered innocent peasants, and tortured both adult and child Ukrainians taken into custody.[68] Ironically, all of these excesses occurred after the Polish parliament had passed a law in 1922 recognizing the right of the Ukrainian-inhabited regions of Poland to local autonomy. In spite of that formal recognition, the Ukrainians of Poland did not fare any better in their efforts to obtain autonomous status than the Slovaks in Czechoslovakia or, until 1939, the Croats in Yugoslavia.

In many ways, the ethnic question remains the most troublesome in post-1989 Eastern Europe; it has considerable potential for destabilizing given political systems, polarizing societies, and, as events have shown, fueling internecine war. Autonomism has recurred in the post-1989 period with special force. Some Serbs of Croatia, for example, demanded wide-ranging autonomy as the price of remaining within Croatia during 1989–90, although others began talking in terms of annexation to Serbia once it became clear that Yugoslavia was breaking up.[69] Tudjman's refusal to extend an offer of political autonomy alienated a sector of the Croatian Serb population, and intercommunal violence soon escalated into full-scale war, thus playing into Serbian president Milošević's hands. In Serbia, similarly, authorities suppressed the autonomy of the provinces of Kosovo and Vojvodina between 1989 and 1990 and have consistently rebuffed requests from the Muslims of the Sandžak for autonomous status.

In Slovakia and Romania, petitions by local ethnic Hungarians for autonomous status have been rejected,[70] while in the neighboring Czech Republic, there has been strong sentiment among the public against *any* negotiations with the expelled Sudetenlanders regarding any form of restitution.[71]

Demands by Istrians for autonomy within Croatia and by ethnic Serbs in Hungary for their own autonomous zone seem even less likely to be met, but also less likely to lead to local turmoil.[72]

Other Issues

Space limitations do not permit a detailed exploration of other spheres of policy. In brief, it is striking that in both transition periods the elites had to deal with the question of land redistribution (agrarian reform in the 1920s, decollectivization in the 1990s); with economic stresses and dislocations rooted in regionwide, even continent-wide, processes; with controversies between clericalist forces eager to place religion at the center of public life, to incorporate religion into the school curriculum, and to draft certain laws on the basis of dogmas of the dominant religion, and those opposed to such measures; and with the sundry complications associated with establishing or restructuring educational and media systems.

Conclusion

Given the parallels between Eastern Europe then and Eastern Europe now, it is not surprising that some energies that were let loose in that earlier era are once again making their presence felt—whether nationalist chauvinism, or intolerant religious zeal, or even varieties of fascism. But, tallying up the balance, what factors might one cite that might dispose one to expect a less erratic developmental course in what remains of the 1990s and beyond than the region took in the 1920s and 1930s?

A number of factors come to mind that, taken collectively, lead to the conclusion that however similar the challenges, it is not the same Eastern Europe confronting them.

The first—and it is in many ways a crucial variable—has to do with literacy and education levels. Illiteracy was a major problem in the earlier period. By 1918, illiteracy was minimal in Western Europe—for example, 0.2 percent in Denmark, 0.4 percent in Germany, 6.8 percent in Sweden. But it stood at 33 percent in Hungary that year[73] and was still in excess of 30 percent in Poland in 1931, after twelve years of compulsory education.[74] In Romania, illiteracy in 1930 ranged from 27.5 percent in the Banat to 33.6 percent in Transylvania, 34.2 percent in Bukovina, 44.1 percent in the Old Kingdom, and 61.4 percent in Bessarabia.[75] But universal compulsory education was introduced throughout the region after World War I, and in the years 1918–41, the East European states made huge strides in reducing illiteracy, even if certain regions (Bosnia-Herzegovina and Bessarabia in particular) lagged dramatically behind; the illiteracy rate in Bosnia was in excess of 80 percent even as late as 1941.[76]

In contemporary Eastern Europe, illiteracy has been reduced to less than 10 percent. This reduction fundamentally changes the nature of the body politic and its receptivity to political messages. However, as the history of Serbia since 1986 has shown, this change is not always in the direction expected by humanists. The printed word, with its implied authoritative factuality, alongside television—now commonplace in the countryside as well as in the city is able to disseminate political messages quickly and with greater efficacy. This means, ironically, that the public may be *more easily manipulated* in the 1990s than it could be in the 1920s and 1930s.

A second difference between Eastern Europe then and Eastern Europe now has to do with social structure. In 1918, the peasantry accounted for 80 percent of the population in Bulgaria, 78 percent in Romania, 75 percent in Yugoslavia, 63 percent in Poland, 55 percent in Hungary, and 34 percent in Czechoslovakia.[77] Even in Czechoslovakia, where the proportion was exceptionally low, most Czechs and Slovaks were at most one or two generations removed from the countryside, and this fact reduced the psychological distance from the village. Moreover, in Serbia, Bulgaria, and Slovakia, there was no native aristocracy and no old commercial class; so the peoples of these three countries were overwhelmingly peasants.[78]

Urbanization has changed all of this, and peasant culture has been considerably marginalized or transformed in the years since 1945. These changes make it less likely that clerical parties like that of Hlinka and Tiso could dominate the political landscape of any of these countries,[79] although authoritarian populist movements, with their appeals to "the simple people,"[80] are still within the realm of the possible, as the governing styles of Milošević and Tudjman have amply shown. This difference, like the first one mentioned, reflects universal processes.

A third important difference between the two periods is, by contrast, specific to the East European context and has to do with the stability of the northern tier. In the post-1918 era, Germany and Hungary were driven by irredentist yearnings, while Poland and Czechoslovakia were internally weakened by serious ethnic discontent. In the 1990s, however, Germany, Poland, the Czech Republic, and Hungary have all become status quo powers, and the latter three have few internal ethnic problems.[81] While this has not prevented the appearance of chauvinistic groupings in these countries, it does make it less likely that they could be sucked into a maelstrom of Balkan-style strife.[82]

There are other differences between these two periods, including differences in relationships with Germany and Russia; the greater skills possessed by contemporary elites; NATO's presence; and (on the negative side) uncertainties about Greece's ambitions in Albania and Macedonia. Moreover, it should not be forgotten that the European economic depression of 1929 played a crucial role in undermining stability in the region and in fueling fascism. Any drastic economic reversal in the years to come could possibly have a similar effect.[83]

So where does that leave us? I have argued that the dilemmas, developments, and tendencies in the post-1989 period show a striking parallel to those in the post-1918 period, but I have also highlighted some important differences. I would argue, then, that Eastern Europe is at the same point in the cycle in the 1990s that it was in the 1920s, but that the cycle itself has shifted so that it is not exactly the same cycle. To use an image from music, it is as if we were listening to Vaughan Williams's "Variations on a Theme by Thomas Tallis": each variation bears a relationship to the others but yet is somewhat different—and will not necessarily entail everything found in the previous variation.

Historical development is the outcome of the combination of predictable cycles, unpredictable contingencies, and programmatic policies adopted by decision makers. If, for example, we could predict whether there would be a major economic crash at the end of the 1990s, as there was in 1929, we would be in a better position to make some predictions about the prospects for the radical right. Moreover, if we knew now what policies would be pursued over time in key policy spheres and which adaptations would be stressed, again the prospects for prediction would be enhanced. In this regard, political science is not much different from medical science: a physician, to make the point explicit, cannot know whether the medication she prescribes will cure the patient unless she can be sure that the patient will actually take the medicine and follow her instructions.

And yet there are some lessons to be drawn from this comparison. In the first place, the failure of the interwar effort to stabilize democratic systems can be traced to the ways certain challenges and tasks were confronted; this in turn will suggest other routes to be preferred in confronting parallel tasks today. Second, the pernicious effect of chauvinistic nationalism cannot be doubted after the experience of the 1930s and 1940s, and this should induce both political observers and decision makers to take this phenomenon more seriously than was the case in the 1930s. Third, this analysis suggests certain key policy spheres to be watched as measures of the ultimate tendencies of the system. These would include, first, the educational system and the content of instruction about politics and history; the resolve and success of policymakers in working toward a distribution of wealth that is accepted by the population in question as fair and equitable; policies affecting Church-state separation; policies regarding the media, and the uses that the media make of their possibilities; and the ability of policymakers to move beyond border squabbles and beyond petty attempts to suppress the national cultures of minority peoples. And fourth, the mere reappearance of something like the earlier pattern alerts one to the folly of self-congratulatory complacency of the "end of history" variety; on the contrary, the same or similar battles must be fought and refought ad infinitum.

2

Eastern Europe's Painful Transition

Six years after the collapse of the communist one-party system, the societies of Eastern Europe confront a new array of problems for which they are not prepared. Many East Europeans are disappointed with what political change has brought them. Throughout the region, polarization is the keynote, as nationalist and reformed communist parties gain in strength. Their electoral successes reflect widespread discontent with the status quo and a deep desire for a new direction.

Amid the myriad challenges that the societies of Central and Eastern Europe have faced in the political transition since 1989, the doctrine of collective rights has loomed large, manifesting itself in both the religious sphere and the ethnic-national sphere. None of the societies of the region has been entirely immune to this doctrine, although the Czech Republic, Hungary, and Slovenia have been much less affected than other countries by the energies associated with this doctrine. In Croatia and Bosnia, between two hundred thousand and five hundred thousand persons were impaled on the horns of this doctrine between June 1991 and December 1995, while the Bosnian war obliterated much of the Bosnian economy.

There have been other challenges, too, above all in the economy, but also with regard to political institution–building, management of the mass media, and the regionwide desire to affiliate with Western economic and military blocs.

This chapter will take a look at the chief tasks facing the societies in the region, setting them in context and assessing their relationship to one another. It thereby sets the stage for the more in-depth analysis in subsequent chapters of the dynamics of ethnarchy and of the demands registered on behalf of collective rights in Poland, Slovakia, and Kosovo.

Economies in Transition

Of all the tasks with which the postcommunist elites have had to wrestle, perhaps the most urgent is that of economic rehabilitation. The communist systems collapsed amid growing institutional and economic disarray, and the years 1990–93 saw variable rates of shrinkage in all of the economies of the region.[1] Poland, the Czech Republic, Hungary, and Slovenia were the first to begin the process of economic recovery, and by 1994 most of the states in the region could boast of positive rates of growth of both gross domestic product (GDP) and industrial production (see table 2.1).

The big success story in the region is the Czech Republic, which, thanks to the austerity program of Václav Klaus, could boast the completion of its conversion to a free market economy by 1995, with a low unemployment rate of 3.5 percent (0 percent in Prague). The Czech inflation rate of 8.4 percent in 1996 is, moreover, the fourth lowest in the region. The Czech Republic recorded a 5.2 percent growth in GDP in 1995 and projected GDP growth of 5.2 percent in 1996, as indicated in table 2.2.[2]

Hungary, whose recovery had looked quite sturdy in 1992–93, began to go into a slump in mid-1994 as export earnings dipped and foreign investment

Table 2.1
Economic Indicators, 1994–95 (in percentages)

	GDP Growth 1994 (%)	GDP Growth 1995 (%)	Unemployment 1995 (%)	Inflation 1995 (%)	Industrial Growth 1995 (%)
Poland	5.2	7.0	14.9	21.6	9.4
Czech	2.6	4.8	2.9	10.0	9.2
Slovak	4.9	7.4	13.1	8.4	8.3
Hungary	2.9	1.5	10.9	28.0	4.8
Slovenia	4.9	3.5	14.5	14.0	2.0
Croatia	0.8	-1.5	17.5	3.7	0.3
Macedonia	-3.9	3.0	37.7	6.0	-18.6*
Yugoslavia	6.5	4.0	27.0	120.0	3.8
Romania	4.0	6.9	8.9	21.0	9.4
Bulgaria	1.8	2.6	11.1	32.9	5.4
Albania	8.0	5.0	25.0	10.0	6.7

Sources: Neue Zürcher Zeitung, 13–14 July 1996, 9; and *New Europe* (Athens), 12–18 November 1995, 22; 3–9 December 1995, 35; 10–16 December 1995, 23; 24–30 December 1995, 22; 21–27 January 1996, 16, 35; 28 January–3 February 1996, 17; 11–17 February 1996, 32–36; 10–16 March 1996, 21; and 17–23 March 1996, 19.

*First three months of 1995 only

slowed.[3] Between 1994 and 1995, only two of the states in the region (leaving aside the Yugoslav successor states) experienced significant slowdowns in GDP growth rates: Hungary and Albania.[4] A contributing factor to the Hungarian economic slowdown may well have been the government's tendency to concentrate investments in the capital city, Budapest. In October 1995, however, after months of recording central budget deficits, authorities chalked up a budget surplus, signaling the beginning of an economic rebound.[5] Industrial production between January and May 1995 was 9.5 percent higher than for the same period the preceding year, projecting a 1995 growth rate of 6.5 percent in industrial production and 6 percent in GDP overall.[6] Officials in Budapest began to talk of an economic "comeback." But these preliminary projections were not borne out, and at year's end Hungary showed a 1.5 percent growth in GDP and a 4.8 percent rate of growth in industrial production (as shown in table 2.1). Moreover, as 1996 drew to a close, the GDP was expected to have shown only a 0.5 percent growth rate in that year (lower than the 1.5 percent preliminary report shown in table 2.2) and to expand by a modest 2 percent in 1997. Hungarian economists advised that real wage growth is the key to a sturdy economic revival in their country.[7]

Poland's recovery has been slower than the Czech Republic's, but sturdier than Hungary's. As of November 1994, the underground economy still accounted for as much as 40 percent of Poland's economic output, as compared with 30 percent in Hungary and 20 percent in the Czech Republic.[8] Warsaw has

Table 2.2
Economic Indicators, 1996 (in percentages)

	GDP Growth*	Unemployment	Inflation (June)	Industrial Growth[†]
Poland	5.5	14.3	19.5	9.2
Czech	5.2	2.7	8.4	9.6
Slovak	6.0	12.0	6.2	4.5
Hungary	1.5	10.6	23.6	1.6
Slovenia	3.0	13.7	10.5	-1.1
Croatia	3.5	18.1	4.1	0.8
Macedonia	3.0	38	6	n/a
Yugoslavia	3.0	30	120	n/a
Romania	4.0	7.1	33.8	7.1
Bulgaria	0.0	10.0	70.4	-1.2

Sources: Neue Zürcher Zeitung, 13–14 July 1996, 9, and 26 July 1996, 10.

*Preliminary figures

[†]Based on the first five months of 1996

moved somewhat more slowly than Prague with privatization, but thanks to a robust growth of the private sector, private enterprise accounted for about 56 percent of the GDP by the end of 1995.[9] Poland's economic recovery owes something to the willingness of Western banks to write off repeatedly large portions of the Polish debt.[10] Poland's economic recovery was well on the way by 1995, when the Polish economy recorded a better-than-expected growth in the GDP of 7.0 percent, compared with a projected growth rate of 6.1 percent. As of 1996, investment growth remained strong, inflationary pressure was subsiding, and both imports and exports were growing at a rate exceeding GDP growth. Economists forecast a slower but still healthy growth in Polish GDP in 1996.[11]

While the lethargic pace of Poland's privatization has only whetted the appetite of foreign investors, delays in the capitalization of the Slovenian market have frustrated foreign investors and slowed economic recovery.[12] In fact, privatization in Slovenia began in earnest only in 1994, and as of October 1995, only 342 of the 1,500 enterprises up for conversion had been transferred to private ownership.[13] All the countries in the region had to deal with the loss of assured supplies of raw materials. For most countries in the region, it was the loss of the Russian market that presented the most immediate difficulty in this regard. For Slovenia, as for Croatia, the loss of the unified Yugoslav market created the greatest pressure to seek new sources and outlets for goods and raw materials. Still, Jože Mencinger argues that Slovenia was, all in all "the least affected by the disruption in coordination and by the transfer from a seller's market toward a buyer's market which characterized the transition to a market system [also] in other socialist countries."[14] Slovenia's modest 3.0 percent rate of GDP expansion in 1996 was, moreover, suggestive of an economic recovery. With strong performance in the manufacturing of electrical machines and appliances, basic chemicals, nonferrous metals, wood products, rubber, machinery, and transport equipment, the Slovenian economy has benefited from a strategy of export-led growth, combined with a successful anti-inflation strategy and sound public finances.[15]

Romania, by contrast, was much harder hit by the evanescence of COMECON. Within a matter of months, Romania lost half of its foreign markets; moreover, the mechanisms of a centrally planned economy simply disintegrated before new institutions and laws could be created to take their place. As a result, by 1992 Romanian industry was operating at half of its real capacity.[16] Indeed, aside from Serbia (under the burden of the UN embargo) and Bosnia (scourged by war), Romania was the only country in the region whose GDP declined faster in 1992 than in 1991. It was only in the latter half of 1994—thanks to a new economic strategy and assistance from the International Monetary Fund (IMF) and the World Bank[17]—that Romania began to pull out of its nosedive. In that year, Romania recorded its first growth in GDP since 1988, albeit at the cost of seeing its external public debt rise to $4.4 billion as of December 1994.[18] But by 1995, Romanian GDP growth stood at 6.9 percent, with a marked rise in the manufacturing sector; this rate slowed in 1996 but was still a healthy 4.0 percent. On the negative side, Romania racked up a trade deficit of $1.7 billion in 1995, with year-on-year inflation recorded at 27.8 percent that same year.[19] But in spite of energetic rates of growth, the Romanian economy remained vulnerable, because of delays in enacting responsible structural reforms, as well as because of continued high levels of state subsidization of inefficient state industries.[20]

Privatization in Romania, as in Slovenia, Slovakia, and Bulgaria,[21] was delayed as a result of internal differences, and as of November 1994, only 700 out of a total of 6,700 state enterprises had been transferred to private hands.[22] After several postponements, the Romanian government announced that shares accounting for 60 percent of the stock in some 3,905 state firms would be distributed by the end of the year. But the government made only incomplete information available to its citizens, resulting in further delay. The deadline for completion of this phase of privatization was extended to 31 March 1996.[23] By July, the government had distributed privatization coupons to its citizens, who in turn invested them in the company or plan of their choice.[24]

For Bulgaria, economic rehabilitation has been difficult, although Prime Minister Zhan Videnov claimed success in early 1996 in tackling problems of inflation, unemployment, and declines in real income.[25] But the Institute of Economics at the Bulgarian Academy of Sciences painted a less than rosy picture in a report made public in March 1996, concluding, somewhat cautiously, that it was "too early to say that there are conditions for economic recovery in Bulgaria."[26] Although Bulgaria's foreign debt had shrunk from $10.4 billion in 1994 to $9.7 billion in 1995, the institute argued that only strong foreign investment could furnish the basis for stable economic growth.

Economists agreed that delays in structural reform were crippling Bulgaria's program for economic rehabilitation.[27] But by 1996, Bulgaria's economic mess was complicated by a record low wheat harvest, declining consumer demand, declining producer demand, and declines in the value of the currency.[28] Garabed Minasian, deputy chair of the Institute of Economics of the Bulgarian Academy of Sciences, put his finger on the source of the problem, noting the government's lack of decisiveness in adopting either salutory economic policies or effective measures against economic crime. Where the latter is concerned, as Minasian explained, "The inability [on the part of the government] to use all of its power given by parliament and the people to cope with unbridled street and white-collar crime speaks of either complete incompetence or total corruption."[29] As the Bulgarian treasury ran low on funds to service debts, the Greek weekly news-

Table 2.3
Percentage of the Economy
in the Private Sector (1995)

Country	% Privatized
Poland	60
Czech	virtually 100
Slovakia	60
Hungary	60
Slovenia	45
Croatia	50
Serbia	31
Montenegro	90*
Romania	40
Bulgaria	45
Albania	70

Sources: Neue Zürcher Zeitung, 4 February 1995, 15; 2
  November 1995, 2; 3 November 1995, 9; and 7 June 1996,
  11; *Balkan News and East European Report* (Athens), 28
  May–3 June 1995, 6; and *New Europe* (Athens), 15–21
  October 1995, 36; 10–16 December 1995, 36; and 5–11
  May 1996, 39.

*Figure for April 1996

paper *New Europe* warned that Bulgaria was heading toward an "economic meltdown."[30] Finally, in June 1996, the Bulgarian government began to face the necessity of closing enterprises operating at a loss, only to find angry Bulgarians taking to the street and shouting "King Simeon," in a symbolic hint of possible (though extremely unlikely) restoration of the monarchy.[31]

Of the remaining countries in the region, Albania has moved the fastest, achieving 70 percent privatization by May 1995, as shown in table 2.3.[32] In May 1996, the Tiranë Stock Exchange, with ten newly licensed traders and brokers, opened its doors.[33] By the end of 1996, the Albanian government was preparing the second round of privatization.[34] But by midwinter 1997, Albania was in chaos.

Croatian officials, who had overseen the privatization of about 50 percent of the Croatian economy by December 1995, said they hoped to achieve 70 percent privatization by the end of 1996.[35] With a foreign debt of $4.4 billion (inherited as their share of the former Yugoslav foreign debt), Croatian authorities have looked to tourism to spearhead the country's economic recovery and hoped to realize a GDP growth rate of 4 to 5 percent in 1996.[36] Loans from the

IMF and the Bayerische Landesbank of Munich announced in March 1996 promised to help with the reconstruction of hotels along the Adriatic coast and other programs of postwar reconstruction.[37] In August 1996, Croatia inaugurated a new agency charged with promoting foreign investment in the country. But despite low inflation and a favorable fiscal policy, investors responded cautiously. By October, however, investors' hesitancy had been overcome, and the Croatian stock market was surging.[38]

In Slovakia, the fortunes of privatization and economic recovery swing like a pendulum with the political fortunes of Vladimír Mečiar: when Mečiar is in office, privatization has grown languid. Even though Mečiar began his third nonconsecutive term as prime pinister in October 1994, Slovakia staged a robust 6.6 percent growth in GDP in 1995, up from 4.8 percent in 1994, while the Slovak National Property Fund promised to complete the transfer of its capital holdings to private hands by summer 1996.[39] The 1996 Slovak national budget was projected to involve a net deficit of $268.5 million, and experts said that continued state intervention in the economy would affect Slovakia's financial markets.[40] Unemployment in Slovakia declined in 1996, and despite unfavorable trends in the trade balance, the country's GDP was reported to have risen 7.3 percent in the first quarter of the year.[41] Meanwhile, in Serbia, the ruling Socialist Party scuttled plans for privatization and by late 1995 was talking in terms of "property transformation"—the exact nature of that transformation being classified, for the time being, as "top secret."[42] Montenegro, Serbia's partner in the Federal Republic of Yugoslavia, was charting a different course, however, and by May 1996 had privatized some 90 percent of its economy.[43]

The official line of the Milošević regime has been that all of the economic difficulties experienced by the Federal Republic of Yugoslavia (i.e., Serbia and Montenegro) have been due to the economic sanctions imposed on that state by the UN. However, in 1996, Dragoslav Avramović, the governor of the central bank, put at least part of the blame on the regime itself, accusing it of corruption, incompetence, economic mismanagement, and failure to reform the economy. For this criticism, Avramović was fired from his post.[44] But with inflation running at 110 percent (according to official figures), investors avoiding the country because of doubts about its fiscal and economic policies, mounting problems in the transport infrastructure and the water system, and wages paid months late, if at all, the Yugoslav economy was clearly in trouble, regardless of what official figures might boast.[45] Moreover, in November 1996, independent economists in the Federal Republic of Yugoslavia called into question the reliability of the country's official economic statistics, citing "politically charged motives."[46] Meanwhile, Milošević's economic program fostered rapidly increasing class disparities. As an unidentified American businessman told the *New York Times,* "Milošević's power is based . . . on nepotism. Those who support him get rich, really rich. Those who do not, starve. The middle class is being wiped out, and a new, powerful oligarchy rules this place like a feudal estate."[47]

Implementing Democracy

The transition from one-party socialism to some form of pluralism has necessarily required the wholesale redesign of the laws and institutions in place, including, in several cases, the passage of entirely new constitutions. In many cases, ministries have been combined or eliminated as the institutional baggage of state regulation has been trimmed. In addition, all of the countries of the region have had to take measures to depoliticize police and army and to assure civilian control (through proper channels) of the secret services. Not all have been equally successful, however. In Poland and Romania, there were charges during 1994 and 1995 that the president in each case was attempting to assert his domination over the military above and beyond what was permitted by the law.[48] In the same two countries there were also fears that the secret services were operating outside the control of appropriate supervisory bodies. As one Polish parliamentarian put it in 1995, "The secret services do not want to be controlled, they want the [Parliament's supervisory] committee to confine its activities to budgetary issues and not to have access to any information."[49]

Building New Institutions

In framing new laws and institutions, the Central and East European countries have benefited from assistance under the Central and East European Law Initiative (CEELI) program of the American Bar Association. Among other things, CEELI representatives have conducted legal education classes in several countries; consulted with local national bar associations; reviewed and critiqued draft laws regulating crime, commerce, and other sectors; and helped establish or expand law libraries. In Albania, CEELI assisted with the establishment of a magistrates' school and with the formation of the Albanian Association of Women Lawyers. Judicial reform has also been an important sector for CEELI assistance in Albania, Bulgaria, Croatia, and Macedonia, while in Bulgaria, CEELI feedback was important in drafting amendments to the labor code. CEELI representatives even conducted workshops in Sarajevo in 1995 for Bosnian justices of the Constitutional Court of the Federation of Bosnia-Herzegovina.[50] Another of the changes entailed in overhauling legal procedures has been to introduce practices associated with the Western adversarial system of justice.[51]

Western countries have also rendered assistance in other ways, such as the journalist training program funded by the U.S. Information Agency (USIA) in Budapest, the BBC school of journalism in Bucharest, and the USIA fund to stimulate the private sector in Albania.[52]

However, Western assistance has not been able to ease the tensions associated with rivalry between the legislative and executive branches. This rivalry has been the most serious in Poland under Wałęsa, in Bulgaria, and in Slovakia whenever Mečiar has been in office, although there have also been examples of such rivalry in Hungary, Romania, and in Croatia as well, albeit the rivalry there has been refracted through the prism of opposition politics within the parliament. The Czech Republic, Slovenia, and Hungary have come the closest to establishing stable parliamentary systems. Serbia (officially, the Federal Republic of Yugoslavia) and Croatia operate under de facto presidential systems—both systems witnessing the failure of a strong opposition party to emerge.[53] The remaining systems are hybrids, whether for formal or informal reasons, and whether stable or unstable.

Among these, the Romanian case is particularly interesting. As Thomas Carothers has noted:

> Although the basic forms of a democratic system are in place in Romania, significant democratic deficits exist . . . such as the incomplete transformation of the Romanian state, the poor performance of the government, the nondemocratic evolution of Iliescu's party, and the weak development of the opposition parties.[54]

Moreover, the very bureaucratic apparatus of state has been only very partially transformed since 1989, with the result that it has remained unresponsive to public needs and demands. However, with the failure of Ion Iliescu's bid for reelection and the election of Emil Constantinescu as president on 17 November 1996, the possibility opened for system overhaul in Romania.

From time to time there have been allegations of threats to judicial independence in Bulgaria,[55] while in the Federal Republic of Yugoslavia, Serbian president Milošević used various legal and extralegal measures to control the elections of December 1992.[56] In Croatia, by contrast, a controversy concerning the electoral victory of an opposition politician in 1995 and 1996 mayoral elections in Zagreb hinged not on the regime's control of the election process but on its refusal to accept the results, repeatedly invoking "national security" to veto the results of fair elections.[57] Charges of electoral fraud were also leveled in Albania's elections of 26 May 1996, in which the ruling Democratic Party of Sali Berisha claimed to have garnered 67.8 percent of the popular vote.[58] Even before the election, Albanian police were accused of destroying opposition Socialist Party campaign materials and of physically harassing Socialist Party leaders.[59] After the election, the Vienna-based Organization for Security and Cooperation in Europe and the Washington-based Republican Institute issued reports confirming that the elections had been "marred by serious irregularities."[60] A U.S. government statement suggested that, if left unremedied, these irregularities could have a negative effect on the U.S.-Albanian relationship.[61]

Similarly, in Serbia, the efforts by Milošević's ruling Socialist Party to overrule the local elections of November 1996 and block the accession of various opposition politicians into local office triggered widespread protests engulfing Belgrade, Niš, and other municipalities. Milošević was eventually compelled to back down and to acknowledge the opposition's electoral victories.

Struggles over the Press

The creation of a free press—an important precondition for stable pluralism—has been difficult, as table 2.4 reflects.

While the Czech Republic, and to a large extent Slovenia and even Poland, may boast of having succeeded in this sphere, the other states in the region still have a distance to traverse if they wish to speak of having a free press. In most cases (e.g., Albania, Bulgaria, Romania, Serbia, Macedonia, and, at this writing, also Poland), the national television station is owned and controlled by the government. This means, in practice, that the government appoints station managers, news directors, and editors and can wield the power of the purse to obtain the cancellation of programs deemed "inconvenient." On 29 December 1992, the Polish parliament passed a new law on radio and television broadcasting, establishing a nine-member National Radio and Television Council to supervise the media, designating that four of its members were to be appointed by the Sejm, two by the senate, and three by the president. But during 1994 and 1995, President Wałęsa engaged in a series of skirmishes with the council concerning licensing matters and other issues.[62] Still, in Poland the major controversy with regard to the media has not been over state regulation or supervision per se but over the Sejm's passage of a law that requires that all public media avoid any offense to "Christian" (i.e., Roman Catholic) values. Infractions of this law—as, for example, a discussion of the negative effects of the ban on abortion—are, of course, punishable. (This subject is explored in greater depth in chapter 4.)

The situation with regard to the press is quite fluid, and the line between control and influence is often fuzzy. But bearing those caveats in mind, we may use the ratings in table 2.4 to shed light on the situation as of December

Table 2.4
State of the Media in Select East European Countries
(as of December 1995)

Country	Rating
Poland	****†
Czech	*****
Slovakia	**
Hungary	***
Slovenia	****
Croatia	***
Serbia	**
Macedonia	***
Romania	***
Bulgaria	***
Albania	***

Note: I am indebted to Peter Gross, Spas T. Ralkin, and Xhevdet
Hoxha for assisting me with the preparation of this table. None
of these is responsible for the final assessments made or for the
form in which these assessments are presented.

*****	completely free
****	mostly free, but with some government interference in broadcast media
***	government control of national TV, but with at least some print media remaining independent, and with alternative radio and possibly also independent local television stations
**	mostly government controlled
*	totally government controlled
†	but with clerical influence

1995. From these ratings it is clear conditions for press freedom have been
outstandingly poor in Slovakia and Serbia. While Serbia may rightly boast that
the independent weekly newsmagazine *Vreme* is of superior quality, and while
this magazine may well claim to be one of the best in the region, *Vreme* is
beyond the pocketbook of most Serbs, and for them the Socialist Party's control of Radio-Television Belgrade has made the decisive difference. Moreover,
in February 1996, Serbian authorities shut down Belgrade's only independent
television station, Studio B, a station that had been set up only in 1989. Studio
B had regularly aired interviews with prominent opposition politicians and did
not follow the regime policy line.[63] It is also significant that under a new law
on public information adopted in Belgrade in 1993, after three court bans of
particular issues or broadcasts, the Ministry of the Interior has the right to

close down any newspaper or broadcasting station.[64] This law is tougher than the corresponding law in late-communist Yugoslavia.

In neighboring Croatia, the Tudjman government also took steps injurious to press freedom, introducing changes to the criminal code, harassing journalists of the satirical weekly *Feral Tribune* (and attempting to levy on it a special "excise tax" otherwise exacted only from pornographic publications) and shutting down in May 1996 the independent newspaper *Panorama* on charges of alleged violations of property and environmental laws.[65] Even the highly regarded independent newspaper *Novi list* (based in Rijeka) has not been able to escape Tudjman's wrath; in April 1996 it was hit with a hefty fine (the equivalent of U.S. $2.5 million) for alleged evasions of customs duties on printing equipment and further charged with tax evasion. These moves threatened to put *Novi list* out of business.[66] Then in June 1996 the ruling Croatian Democratic Community (Hrvatska Demokratska Zajednica, or HDZ) filed a libel suit against *Globus* editor Davor Butković for having alleged that the HDZ "had drawn up a blacklist of political opponents and aimed to stain their reputation through the government-controlled media."[67] That same month, *Feral Tribune* journalists Viktor Ivančić and Marinko Ćulić went on trial for having criticized President Tudjman's proposal to bury the remains of members of the World War II Ustaše regime next to its Serb and Jewish victims and for having compared President Tudjman to Spanish dictator Francisco Franco.[68] Indeed, at the rate that press freedom was being attacked and eroded in Croatia, by the end of 1996 Croatia seemed to enjoy little advantage over Serbia where press freedom was concerned.

The fluidity of the situation with regard to press freedom and diversity is well illustrated by the cases of Romania and Slovenia. In Romania, the state initially assured itself of hegemony over electronic media through a series of legislative acts enacted between 1992 and 1994, but the situation changed in the course of 1995, when the balance between public and private television began to tip in the latter's favor.[69] In Slovenia, by contrast, the problem has not been state interference so much as financial difficulties that threaten certain media with closure.[70]

Press freedom has been a subject of discussion and controversy everywhere in the region. In Slovakia, Prime Minister Vladimír Mečiar changed the law governing television broadcasting in such a way as to enable him, through the parliament, to control the appointment of all members to relevant supervisory boards; as a result, by 1996 the opposition no longer had a single representative on the governing board of Slovak Television. Since 1994, the European Union has repeatedly criticized Mečiar's government for hampering the development of free media in Slovakia.[71] As far as Hungary is concerned, for example, the International Federation of Journalists and the International Federation of Newspaper Publishers discussed the state of its media at a meeting held in Copenhagen in late 1993 and adopted a resolution asserting that freedom of the press and of information were under threat in Hungary and urging the government "to take immediate steps to restore balanced journalism in state television and radio."[72] Indeed, it was only in December 1995, after more than five years of acrimonious controversy, that the Hungarian parliament belatedly passed a bill governing broadcast media. Among other things, the Hungarian broadcast law required that two of the three terrestrial television frequencies be privatized, along with one statewide radio station and other (local) radio channels.[73] In Bulgaria, President Zheliu Zhelev told a press conference in November 1995 that he was "concerned by the attempts at censorship that we have been seeing lately . . . [in] the national media."[74] In July 1996 the Bulgarian parliament passed a draft law on radio and television. President Zhelev vetoed the law, arguing that the supervisory agency it would create to control the electronic media would be too powerful and would impair the ability of local electronic media to strike independent courses.[75] The parliament did not accept Zhelev's point, however, and on 5 September, voted 126 to 82 to override the president's veto. Given Zhelev's argument that the law is inconsistent with the Bulgarian constitution, it appears almost certain to come before the Constitutional Court.[76] And then there is Albania, which has seen allegations of political partiality in the media and police beatings of journalists of the independent paper *Koha Jone.*[77] The growth of independent media in Albania has also been encumbered by local market conditions.[78]

A Tentative Ranking

On balance, taking into account institutional development, legal safeguards, the stabilization of a pluralist party system, the independence of the judiciary, and freedom of the press, the Czech Republic, Slovenia, and Hungary seem to have made the most progress in the direction of erecting stable pluralist systems. Macedonia and Bulgaria trail at some distance. Poland, which might have been in the forefront of democratization but for the Roman Catholic Church, moved steadily in the direction of theocracy during the five-year presidency of Lech Wałęsa and thus consigned itself to a unique and rather problematic category. Whether Poland will be able to pull itself away from theocratic snares under Wałęsa's successor, Aleksander Kwaśniewski, remains to be seen. Democratization has been slower in Romania and has been roadblocked in Croatia. Albania had seemed, well into 1994, to offer some prospects for democratization, the extralegal behavior of Albanian police reported in late 1994 notwithstanding.[79] But the miscarried elections of 26 May 1996 and widespread losses in pyramid schemes led to widespread civil disorder, looting, and chaos by late winter 1997. Finally, in Serbia and Slovakia, although they are under different social and economic conditions, one cannot even speak of democratization at all; there are, however, some currents within Montenegro, albeit dependent upon expanding local autonomy, in the direction of a more open system than that prevailing in Serbia proper.

Problems

As Ghia Nodia has argued, "the democratic enterprise, supposedly the epitome of rationality, rests unavoidably on a nonrational foundation."[80] That foundation is the assumption that a collectivity of people defining themselves as a community has the right to set rules for all persons living on the territory claimed by that collectivity, even if those rules harm the individual or collective interests of some of those concerned. Nationalism figures, inter alia, as the most common ideological and mythological justification for this claim, but it in turn sets into motion forces that may be dramatically at variance with any concept of democracy. Thus, although wedded to democracy, nationalism also poses the most serious threat to democracy, at least while a democratic system is still in its early stages.

Ethnic Hatreds

In Central and Eastern Europe, as table 2.5 makes clear, there are at least nine zones afflicted by ethnic hatred and intolerance. Of these, the most serious to date has been the case of Bosnia (a case I have discussed at length elsewhere).[81] Close behind, in terms of the intensity of frictions and the degree of discord, is Kosovo, where local Albanians, who constitute more than 80 percent of the local population (more than 90 percent prior to the recent exodus of Albanians), have been subjected to systematic policies of apartheid, harassment, beatings, dismissals from work, and deprivation of education. (The case of Kosovo is discussed at greater length in chapter 6.) Aside from these, the greatest potential for hostilities can be identified with problems of discrimination against the Hungarian minority in southern Slovakia and Romanian Transylvania. In both cases, national regimes have discriminated against local ethnic Hungarians, depriving them of the right to use their native language for official business; taking steps to reduce the use of Hungarian as a language of instruction in local schools; and, in the Slovak case, removing Hungarian street signs from villages populated entirely by Hungarians, replacing them with Slovak-language signs. Slovak authorities even went so far as to pass a

Table 2.5
Flashpoints for Ethnic Hatreds in Eastern Europe

Case	Rating	Date of Genesis
Bosnia (Muslims, Serbs, Croats)	*****	1918
Kosovo (Albanians, Serbs)	****	1913
S. Slovakia (Hungarians, Slovaks)	***	1918/20
W. Macedonia (Albanians, Macedonians)	***	1878
Transylvania (Romanians, Hungarians, Germans)	***	1920
Vojvodina (Serbs, Hungarians, Croats)	***	1918/20
Bulgaria (Bulgarians, Turks)	**	1878
S. Albania (Albanians, Greeks)	*	1913
S/W Poland (Poles, Germans)	*	1945

*****	intense
****	very serious
***	serious
**	clearly polarized
*	partially polarized

law requiring that a Hungarian woman marrying a Hungarian man add the suffix "-ova" to her name, as is the custom among Slovaks. Hungarians have rebelled against the prospect of such amalgams as "Nagyova," "Bartokova," "Kodályova," and "Petöfiova." (The situation of Hungarians in southern Slovakia is discussed at some length in chapter 5.)

In Romania, when the Romanian Senate passed a draft education law in June 1995, the Democratic Union of Hungarians in Romania issued a communiqué protesting that the law "unequivocally curbs the rights of ethnic minorities and is at variance with both the Constitution and the European integration requirements."[82] The German Democratic Forum (the organization of ethnic Germans in Romania) agreed with this assessment and joined representatives of local Czechs and Slovaks in protesting against the law.[83]

None of these hatreds is of "ancient" vintage, and none of them arose purely on the basis of indigenous forces. On the contrary, *all of these hatreds* are the products or by-products of Western-supported annexations or Western-sponsored treaties, as shown in table 2.5. The problems in Macedonia and Bulgaria, for example, can be traced to the ill-conceived and shortsighted Treaty of Berlin (1878) that overthrew the more farsighted Treaty of San Stefano (drafted six months earlier), which would have united all Bulgarians into a single state. The problems relating to Albanians in Kosovo and southern Montenegro can be dated to the Treaty of London (1913), through which Britain, France, and Russia took land claimed by Albania and inhabited by a majority

Albanian population from newly independent Albania, Austria's friend, and turned it over to Serbia, *their* friend. The previously relatively low-key tensions between Muslims, Serbs, and Croats in Bosnia escalated dramatically after 1918, when Belgrade, with the approval of Britain and France, annexed the province and imposed a centralized regime on the country. The continued injustices perpetrated against ethnic Hungarians in southern Slovakia, Vojvodina, and Transylvania date from the Treaty of Trianon (1920), when Britain and France sacrificed the preference of the local populations to their own insatiable hunger for vengeance. And the less voluble frictions between ethnic Germans and Poles in the southwestern corner of Poland date from 1945, when the Western allies acquiesced in Polish control over stretches of land populated entirely or almost entirely by Germans. Far from being an ancient problem, the ethnic hatreds that plague Eastern Europe are a relatively recent "gift" of sorts from the great powers.

Economic Inequality

A second problem specifically associated with the democratic project has been the deepening of inequality along a number of axes. Although some may agree with John Mueller's neoconservative definition of democracy as "a form of government in which the individual is left free to become politically unequal,"[84] for ethnic Albanians of Kosovo who are jailed and beaten only because they are Albanians, or ethnic Hungarians in southern Slovakia getting married in a Hungarian church in front of a totally Hungarian congregation who are compelled to exchange their vows in Slovak, using an interpreter if necessary, inequality does not seem to correspond to anything one might call democratic, and most certainly not to *their* idea of democracy.

Inequality manifests itself in other spheres as well. Where the communists made it a point of pride to promote women to positions of responsibility, Eastern Europe's "democrats" have self-righteously pushed women out of such positions, often demanding a "return" to so-called traditional values. The result is that the representation of women in the parliaments and governments of the region has fallen noticeably since 1989.[85]

Class inequality has also widened and deepened. As of 1994–95, at least 20 percent of Slovak households were living below the poverty line, while 60 percent of Romanians and about an equal proportion of Serbs lived below the poverty line.[86]

Discontent with these inequalities, as well as with falling living standards, was expressed in repeated workers' demonstrations in Romania in 1994 and 1995,[87] as well as in the electoral victories of reformed communist parties in Hungary (1993), Bulgaria (1994), and Poland (1993 and 1995), not to mention the participation of reformed communists in parliamentary coalitions in Slovenia and Macedonia.

Religious Zealotry

Two other problems have arisen in the postcommunist transition. The first, which is most clearly displayed in Poland, is religious zealotry (described in chapter 4). In a word, the Roman Catholic Church has dictated its terms on abortion to the entire country, has introduced supposedly voluntary (but de facto quasi-mandatory) Catholic religious instruction in state schools, has secured a legal requirement that broadcast media respect Catholic values (as noted above), and has engaged in a still unfinished struggle to incorporate into the preamble of the Polish constitution a clause describing Poland as a Catholic nation. As *Gazeta Wyborcza* noted in 1995, "Public opinion polls indicate that most Poles oppose the Church's political involvement. Some politicians and observers believe that the bishops are breaking the democratic principles."[88] That the theocratic impulse is simultaneously disrespectful toward non-Catholics of all stripes and hostile to democratic principles should, indeed, be completely obvious.

Increased Crime

The final problem that has accompanied the postcommunist transition has been a proliferation of crime of all kinds, especially the growth of organized crime throughout the region. Between 1989 and 1995, the crime rate doubled in Poland, Hungary, and Slovakia, tripled in the Czech Republic,[89] and sky-rocketed in Serbia, but it has reportedly nowhere been as serious as in Bulgaria, where about half of all robbery victims are foreigners.[90] Poland, the Czech Republic, Slovakia, Hungary, Romania, Macedonia, Bulgaria, and Albania have all seen a dramatic upturn in drug smuggling and substance abuse.[91] Organized crime in Serbia has played a large role in the illegal drug trade, although statistics for drug abuse among Serbs are not readily available.[92]

Some 74 percent of Poles and 87 percent of Bulgarians say they do not feel safe on the streets of their own towns.[93] Violent crimes, extortion, and smuggling of arms, fuel, illegal drugs, and uranium have led the way in the recent crime wave. In Macedonia, Bulgaria, and Serbia, the UN embargo against the Federal Republic of Yugoslavia (suspended in November 1995) closed off legal channels for trade and provided a tremendous impetus for organized crime to step into the breach. In several countries, including Poland, Hungary, Serbia, Macedonia, Bulgaria, and Serbia, there have been allegations that organized crime has infiltrated and subverted some of the echelons of government;[94] indeed, in the case of Bulgaria, it has been reliably reported that many members of the old communist *nomenklatura* had made big money by 1993—some through drug trafficking, prostitution, and blackmail.[95] In the Czech Republic, Russian and Ukrainian mafia chiefs were said to have attempted to infiltrate government institutions.[96] "What is the most dangerous thing about organized crime is not that it makes a lot of money," according to Vladimir Shuman, head of the Czech Republic's parliamentary committee for security, "but that it has the tendency toward power."[97] The problem is that, in its own perverted way, crime is the quintessential expression of the principles of free enterprise and laissez faire, the twin pillars of the free market economy. That is one of the reasons the transition to a free market economy has brought with it an irrepressible surge of criminal activity. On the other hand, the proliferation of crime of any kind is incompatible with the rule of law, an essential element in liberal democracy.

Politicians have proposed alternative schemes to combat organized crime. Prime Minister Gyula Horn of Hungary has, for example, pushed for the creation within Hungary of a "rapid-reaction Super-police,"[98] while President Kwasniewski of Poland, noting that there were some 293 organized crime groups operating in Poland as of mid-1995,[99] urged the signing, under UN auspices, of an international anticrime convention "to enhance inter-state cooperation and facilitate the work of law enforcement agencies in fighting transnational organized crime."[100]

Challenges and Trends

All of the new elites in Eastern Europe, even Serbia, have expressed a strong interest in joining NATO and the European Union.[101] With the establishment of a U.S.-NATO air base at Gjadër, 150 kilometers north of Tiranë,[102] Albania appeared to enjoy NATO Secretary-General Javier Solana's support in its quest to be admitted to NATO. President Sali Berisha of Albania has adopted a forthrightly pro-U.S. posture[103] and enjoys the advantage of offering a key strategic location in the vicinity of unstable Bosnia. The United States and Albania conducted nine joint military exercises in 1995 and announced plans to conduct twelve such exercises in 1996.[104] Moreover, when NATO Secretary-General Solana arrived in Tiranë on 1 May 1996, he said that "Albania will be treated as a priority in the group of Eastern European countries which have asked for NATO membership."[105] Later that year, he was quoted as saying, "Albania is de facto [already] in NATO."[106] The disintegration during February and March 1997 may affect at least the timetable for Albania's admission.

Of the other countries in the region, Poland, Hungary, the Czech Republic, and possibly Slovenia have the best prospects for early admission to NATO, although NATO officials have avoided explicit guarantees.[107] Hungary endeavored to ingratiate itself with NATO by providing facilities and logistical support for U.S. peacekeeping troops on their way to Bosnia in 1995 and 1996 but was given no guarantees at the time. Hungarian officials were given some encouragement in April 1996, however, when Secretary-General Solana stopped briefly in Budapest.[108] Poland, whose leader (whether Wałęsa or Kwaśniewski) has been impatient to obtain admittance to the alliance, is arguably the most pivotal country in the region. In spite of Russian opposition to Polish integration into NATO,[109] Warsaw has remained optimistic about Poland's eventual membership and has set 1999 as its target date.[110] As for the remaining countries in the region (Slovakia, Romania, Bulgaria, Croatia, Serbia, Macedonia, and—if one may speak of it as if it were a state—Bosnia), only one, Macedonia, appears reasonably well positioned for NATO membership at this time, although that would require Greek assent. It is unlikely that Slovakia, Romania, Serbia, or Bosnia will be admitted in the foreseeable future. Some twenty-two countries sent troops to take part in NATO military exercises in August 1996; among the participating states were Poland, Hungary, Slovakia, Romania, Bulgaria, and Albania. The Czech Republic sent observers.[111] Croatian membership could possibly encounter resistance from Britain and France, which both tilted toward Serbia in the Yugoslav war of 1991–95, while the Bulgarian leadership was said to be internally divided as of May 1996 as to whether membership in NATO was even desirable.[112]

Where the European Union is concerned, the front-runners are virtually the same, except that Albania is less well situated for admission into that body. Among the East European states, Poland hoped for admission into the European Union by the year 2000.[113]

Meanwhile, Russia has been actively wooing its former satellites, concentrating its efforts on Slovakia and Bulgaria, and, to a lesser extent, Romania and Hungary. In February 1995, as a token of Moscow's interest, Russian prime minister Viktor Chernomyrdin paid an official visit to Bratislava, signing twelve important agreements with Slovak prime pinister Mečiar.[114] The Bulgarian-Russian relationship was subjected to strains in 1996, however.[115] Russian foreign minister Yevgeny Primakov also visited Bratislava in March 1996. He used the occasion to express Moscow's firm opposition to the integration of its former East European satellites into NATO.[116] While Slovakia's Mečiar has been more cryptic about his intentions,[117] President Iliescu of Romania explicitly rebuffed Moscow's remonstrations and insisted on Romania's right to join the international organizations of its choosing.[118] Slovakia's chances for NATO membership are, in any event, reduced as a result of questions about its respect for human rights and the character of its system.[119]

Chernomyrdin signed sixteen agreements for economic cooperation with Bulgaria in May 1995, including an agreement to establish a natural gas joint stock company.[120] Russia has also signed significant military and economic agreements with the Federal Republic of Yugoslavia.[121]

Conclusion

As was noted in the preceding chapter, the political configuration of Eastern Europe in the 1990s appears in some ways to replicate patterns of the 1920s. Among the parallels, one might note in particular the heightened tensions associated with ethnic and religious differences. Claims made on behalf of specific ethnic and religious groups (e.g., on behalf of Romanian Orthodox believers by Corneliu Codreanu's League of the Archangel Michael) in the interwar era were harnessed by fascist parties in bids for absolute power. These claims thus were used as instruments in a battle against democracy. As we shall see, similar claims on behalf of the "collective rights" of ethnic and religious communities in the 1990s have likewise proved injurious to democratic principles and practices. The doctrine of collective rights does not regard the democratic principle as prior and superordinate but, on the contrary, asserts its own claim to primacy—and therein lies the core of the problem.

3

The New Ethnarchy and Theories of Rights

Central Eastern Europe has emerged as a seedbed of a virulent form of collective rights, to which G. M. Tamás has given the name ethnarchy. According to Tamás, this new species of politics is characterized by the supposition that power should be vested not in all citizens of a state (the presupposition of Western democracies such as Britain, France, Germany, and the United States) but in a subgroup of that citizenry, defined by ethnic, racial, and/or religious homogeneity. The claims for ethnarchy are, in turn, as Tamás notes, applied "within any arbitrarily given territory that may or may not belong to a state, that may or may not be under the authority of a legally constituted government," with the attendant claim that states can and should "be reshaped at will, regardless of ancient ties between different linguistic, religious, or other groups through centuries. Only natural identity counts, an identity based on a 'nature' that cannot be approached rationally."[1] Moreover, where the nineteenth-century advocates of Magyarization and Russification believed that by changing the language, religion, and culture of non-Hungarians and non-Russians, one could assimilate them to the dominant nation—a supposition inherited by the Stalinists—the new ethnarchs "do not believe that anybody from a different cultural background, racial origin, or religious creed can be or ought to be assimilated, made into a citizen or a new political community."[2] On the contrary, expulsion or extermination is thought to be a more suitable means of resolving the "dilemma" posed by heterogeneity.

Separatism, autonomism, and imperialism, insofar as they may be based on claims derived from the doctrine of collective rights, are all species of the same political phenomenon, a phenomenon that, although it has pre-Napoleonic antecedents, received a strong boost from the Napeolonic Wars and from the peace that followed. In particular, the concept of territorially defined autonomy for ethnically defined groups can be traced in modern times to the *Kongresówka* in the Russian Empire after 1815[3] and to *Ausgleich* Hungary. By contrast, the Vojna Krajina (Military Frontier) of Habsburg Croatia is not a true precedent, because its raison d'être was not ethnicity or collective rights, but military security; indeed, the Slavs (Serbs) living there had been brought there specifically to perform military functions.

But even before the Ausgleich, which split Habsburg Austria into two administrative units—the Austrian "empire" and the Hungarian "kingdom"—the abortive Kremsier Constitution of 1849 marked a milestone in recognizing the emergence of the doctrine of collective rights, offering an alternative. In particular, this draft constitution affirmed, "Each people has an inviolable right to preserve its nationality in general and its language in particular. The equality of rights in the school, administration and public life of every language in local usage is guaranteed by the state."[4]

But, as already noted in the introduction, the doctrine of collective rights emerged within a moral framework—indeed, within the context of changes in the dominant moral paradigm. In medieval times, the dominant moral paradigm was universalism (the belief that the same moral rules applied to all people) with divine law seen as revelatory of inherent moral principles. Consistent with this view of the moral universe, the medievals understood the purpose of the state to be the fostering of the moral life of the community. Social differentiation was based, in the first place, on class (noble versus burgher versus artisan versus peasant versus serf).

In Reformation-era Europe, the dominant moral paradigm was still universalism, but with the important modification that Divine Law was given a preeminent place as the fountainhead of all moral law. In other words, for Reformation-era Europe, God was placed clearly and unmistakably above the moral law. This difference notwithstanding, ideologies of Reformation-era Europe agreed with the medievals that the purpose of the state was the fostering of moral life. The organization of Calvin's Geneva is a quintessentially clear illustration of this principle. In this era, given growing religious heterogeneity (a result both of the Reformation and of the expansion of the Ottoman Empire to the Danube River), social differentiation came to involve a greater emphasis on religion. Hugo Grotius (1583–1645) was the last great exponent of the medieval approach to Natural Law, which emphasized "the correspondence of the law of nature to a nature understood as divine order."[5]

The Enlightenment made decisive changes to all three parts of the moral formula. To begin with, the Enlightenment (centered in Britain and France, with important voices also in the Netherlands and Germany), while still subscribing to universalism, scuttled the appeal to Divine Law, appealing instead to a secularized Natural Law (Universal Reason). As Bobbio notes, the modern theory of Natural Law was born with Thomas Hobbes (1588–1679), who, however, qualified it in important ways.[6] John Locke (1632–1704), Benedictus de

Spinoza (1632–77), and Freiherr Samuel von Pufendorf (1632–94) further developed the concept, which also underpinned the writings of Immanuel Kant (1724–1804).[7] The leading prelates of the seventeenth century understood full well that the concept of Universal Reason rendered Divine Law unnecessary as a source of morality. It was this realization, along with the nature of Hobbes's minimalist concept of Christianity and his alleged "nonchalance" in regard to the Scriptures,[8] that accounted for the strong critique made by Church prelates of the day of Thomas Hobbes's *Leviathan*. Onto this secular concept of moral universalism, the Enlightenment thinkers grafted a new concept of the state; for them, the purpose of the state had nothing to do with moral life, nor even with Universal Reason, but with the protection of property and life, usually in that order. G. W. F. Hegel, as is well known, rejected this Enlightenment recasting of the state and insisted on holding onto a construal of the state as inextricably bound up with Universal Reason (sometimes translated as "Absolute Knowledge"). Indeed, Hegel undertook a highly original task—to synthesize major constructs of both traditional and Enlightenment theories of politics into a practical philosophy that both preserves and transforms the constructs it takes over. From traditionalism Hegel took his concept of the state as an ethical community entrusted with moral tasks and moral responsibilities, as well as the interactive dyad, family-state. From Enlightenment theories Hegel drew his dyadic concept of nature–civil society and a reconstructed notion of Universal Reason.[9] Far from being a precursor of authoritarianism, as he is sometimes depicted, Hegel was working within the democratic tradition, endeavoring to purify and refine its central principles. The Enlightenment era also saw the preeminence of a new category of social differentiation: membership in the nation, *defined in terms of citizenship*. For the Enlightenment, the state, therefore, was supposed to be a citizens' state (*gradjanska država,* in Serbo-Croatian), protecting the rights of all citizens equally.

The modern and postmodern eras have been characterized by an obscuring of vision, so that moral law can no longer be discerned except through a fog. Recognizing no moral law, moral relativists of the so-called postmodern era abandon universalism, deny the existence of any moral absolutes (thus paving the way for a "moral," or rather amoral, validation of genocide), and sometimes refer all moral questions to considerations of convenience and profit. Moral relativism thus shows itself to be not much above the level of the "morality" of organized crime. It is, therefore, not surprising to find that moral relativism owes something to the writings of Georges Sorel, a French publicist generally credited with being a precursor of fascism,[10] or that the rejection of universalism constitutes a key presumption for all forms of extreme nationalism.[11]

The moderns and postmoderns have by and large retained the notion that the purpose of the state is to protect property and life, although the fascists added much to this concept (as is well known). The moderns and postmoderns have also transmogrified the Enlightenment concept of *nation,* wielding it still as the prime measure of social differentiation but construing it, not in terms of citizenship, but in terms of membership in a specified ethnonational group. This reconstrual of nation—which was largely accomplished in the years 1880–1914[12]—was thus divisive rather than unifying. For many postmoderns, the state is seen as ideally constituting itself as the state of a specified people—not a citizens' state, but a national state (a *nacionalna država,* in Serbo-Croatian).

I have noted the Serbo-Croatian terminology for two key terms of debate because it was in moribund Yugoslavia that one saw a fierce debate coming into full bloom between advocates of the concept of *gradjanska država* (such as Ante Marković and Branko Horvat) and advocates of the concept of *nacionalna država* (such as Slobodan Milošević and Franjo Tudjman). As long as a society is defined as a citizens' state, it remains at least potentially an open society, with open membership. When a state is declared, as Croatia is, to be the state of the a specified nation (the Croatian nation here), the implication is that those citizens not of the titular nationality (in this case, non-Croats) are intended to enjoy fewer rights than other citizens. Three of the Yugoslav successor states (Serbia, Croatia, and both halves of divided Bosnia) have functioned as national states, rather than as citizens' states, although Macedonia is nominally also a national state—a fact that inspired Robert Hayden to argue that Gligorov's Social Democrats and even Slovenia's DEMOS coalition "had based their election campaigns largely on chauvinism."[13]

Closely associated with the national state concept is the concept of "state-forming nations" *(državnotvorni narodi),* as the titular nations have come to be called. Typically, the members of declared state-forming nations have felt that there could be no significant changes to the system or boundaries or affiliation of their given state, even if that state was only a federative constituent republic within Yugoslavia, without their consent. What is not always recognized by foreign observers, most especially by those eager to point fingers at Bosnian president Alija Izetbegović for having agreed to conduct a referendum on the future of Bosnia 29 February–2 March 1992, is that the concept of state-forming nations is an antidemocratic and antiliberal notion, the scuttling of which was presupposed in any aspiration to move in the direction of creating a liberal democratic state. Where liberal democracy operates on the basis of majority vote (whether simple majority, two-thirds majority, or some other rule), the concept of state-forming nations rejects the majoritarian principle and requires that each constituent state-forming nation give its consent and that no measure may be considered to have been approved, even if it should gain 90 percent of the popular vote, if the representatives of a designated state-forming nation decline to give their assent.

It cannot be said that ethnarchy and the concept of the national state are atavistic, as implied in the equation of contemporary nationalism with some sort of "new tribalism," a term popularized by Michael Walzer.[14] On the contrary, they are paradigmatically modern (or "postmodern") construals. Indeed, the blossoming of ethnarchy, as of the doctrine of collective rights, has presumed, indeed required, the erosion of moral universalism. Similarly, the concept of the state-forming nation is relatively new, tracing its antecedents back to the modus operandi of the Habsburg Empire in the nineteenth century.

Contemporary states have reached a moral dead end, which in turn may generate avoidable political impasses. But if the modern/postmodern formula has proved pernicious both in spirit and in its effects, there can also be no return to the superseded formulas of the past. What may be needed is a new formula, one that combines the Enlightenment-era apotheosis of Universal Reason and the Enlightenment understanding of citizenship with a secularized version of the medieval concept of the state as existing for the purpose of fostering moral life. In the twentieth century, this understanding of politics has most commonly been referred to as Wilsonianism, in tribute to Woodrow Wilson, a latter-day Kantian. Such a formula would also be able to trace its genealogy back to Hegel, for reasons I have suggested above.[15]

Critics of the tradition of Universal Reason abound. Their objections range from claims that there can be no law without a lawgiver and that there is no lawgiver available,[16] to avowals that the Natural Law tradition is incoherent and logically indefensible,[17] to intimations that the concept of Universal Reason may not be "useful."[18]

Other theorists argue, on the contrary, that a paradigm of human action shorn of universal moral law is itself incoherent and self-contradictory. On this premise, Virginia Held argues:

> If one imagines a system of rules all of which are incompatible with valid moral principles [i.e., with commonly accepted notions of Natural Law], it is doubtful that any of us would be willing to call it a legal system, though a straightforward legal positivist might be able to offer a few arguments for . . . doing so, as long as the system was effective.[19]

Indeed, a system in which bank robbery and murder were rewarded with medals and in which kindness was punished by flagellation and imprisonment—to take Held's dystopia to its logical conclusion—would not only seem "inconvenient" (the term of favor among moral relativists) but would likely strike all except sociopaths as self-contradictory; that is, there is something irrational about constructing a legal system that systematically flies in the face of Natural Law. Universal Reason is, in the first place, a dimension of reason. As related to the politics of human rights, the difficulty is that if there is no moral universalism, then it may well be that there are no universal human rights.

There are four traditional ways in which philosophers derive rights, known respectively as theories of natural rights, contractarian rights, conventional rights, and consequentialist rights. Of these four theories, the theory of natural rights is the only one to derive rights from duties, indeed, to treat the concept of right largely as an entitlement to the performance of a duty by someone else (e.g., an individual's right to life and liberty would be derived, on this account, from the duty of others to respect the life and liberty of the given individual). According to the theory of natural rights, moral rights are objective but derivative; they cannot be basic, because they are derived from duties that are, in turn, derived from Universal Reason. Indeed, as Sumner notes, "Moral rights cannot be both objective and basic. [This realization leaves] . . . two possibilities open: either such rights are subjective or they are derivative (or both)."[20] (See table 3.1.)

Contractarian theories ground rights in one or another contract. On the face of it, this would seem to require a view of rights as derivative and perhaps also as "subjective." But Sumner identifies four alternative currents among contractarian theories. According to him, the moral structure of a contractarian theory may assume any of the following forms: "(1) it may contain no rights whatever; (2) it may contain rights but treat none of them as basic; (3) it may treat rights as basic along with some other items; [and] (4) it may treat nothing but rights as basic."[21] Most contractarians consider all rights to be subjective,[22] and all of them seem to share an understanding of rights as emerging from collective choice, that is, as artifacts of human design. Not only that, but as Sumner explains, contractarians "appear to be committed to the view that there are no objective values."[23] This position, however, brings contractarians close to Max Stirner's Union of Egoists and to his repudiation of all values,[24] suggesting that contractarians are not so much relativists as moral nihilists. But even for those who might be willing to embrace moral nihilism, there is a further problem with contractarianism, that is, its reliance on a purely mythical model of collective choice. To suggest, as contractarians must, that human rights of life and freedom of movement derive from some mythic contract to which "all people" have subscribed reminds one of theories of the origins of intelligent life on this planet that solve the mystery by declaring that it came ultimately from another planet, leaving unanswered the question of how intelligent life developed, in that case, on that other planet.

Table 3.1
Political Correlates of Alternative Moral Theories

Moral Theory	Corresponding Values	Assumption	Moral Character	Political Posture
Universal Reason (Natural Law)	Objective rights & values	Gov't. must be moral	Moral universalism	Idealism
Contractarianism	Subjective rights & values	Mythical model of collective choice	Moral nihilism	Isolationism
Conventionalism	Rights & duties derive from specific laws, conventions, & agreements	Only positive law is real	Moral relativism	Realism
Consequentialism	No a priori morality or values; pleasure is the measure	Results must be good	Moral hedonism	Short-term thinking
Theocracy	Moral laws are created by God and discernible only through revelation	Gov't. must enforce the approved religious faith & practice	Justification by faith, not works; conformism & obedience	Hegemonism

Conventional rights theories avoid the conundrum of the contractarians by tracing rights to specific laws and conventions. This avoids the mythical abstraction of contractarianism, but opens the door to complete moral relativism. On the conventionalist account, human rights may vary from society to society and within the same society over time. Or to put it another way, conventional rights theories do not distinguish between human rights and interpretations of human rights.

Consequentialist theories of rights are certainly more subtle than either contractarian or conventionalist theories, in that they return the focus to human actions, rather than to agreements, contracts, and conventions seen as preceding those actions. For consequentialists, actions are to be judged by their consequences, rather than by their intention or character, let alone according to the criterion of whether they accord with certain contracts and conventions. Consequentialism appears to be a reincarnation of what used to be called situation ethics, or the notion that there are no a priori rules of moral behavior and that each individual must judge for herself what action appears likely to produce the most satisfactory results. This result-oriented view gives consequentialism a character of hedonism, whether egoistic or altruistic.

On my account of things, natural rights theories can be understood as tantamount to moral universalism, contractarian theories to moral nihilism, conventionalist theories to moral relativism, and consequentialist theories to moral hedonism. Theocracy, noted in table 3.1, will be discussed in the next chapter.

I have spent some time elaborating these approaches and setting them in context because I am convinced that only moral universalism can provide a moral bedrock for concepts of human rights and tolerance, themselves prerequisites for liberal democracy. Contractarian and conventionalist theories provide no basis for criticizing the doctrine of collective rights, even when it may give rise to repressive actions. Consequentialism would appear, at first sight, to offer better prospects of guidance, but it suffers from various debilities, including the requirement that the consequences of a given action be known in advance if a moral judgment is to be available concerning an action in preparation. It also appears that consequentialism approaches the contention that the end justifies the means—a notion that inspired the Stalinist model in Russia and Eastern Europe. Where the doctrine of collective rights is concerned, it is clear that consequentialism/hedonism will serve its purposes much better than moral universalism, in that consequentialism may open the door to emphasizing the pleasures afforded to the designated group to be privileged, at the expense of pains to be served to other groups.

The doctrine of collective rights, a doctrine fully incompatible with any notion of Universal Reason or moral universalism, has figured prominently in recent political discourse in Central and Eastern Europe. In the following pages, I shall examine five cases in which that doctrine has been invoked with ill effect. These cases are the Hungarians of Transylvania, the Turks of Bulgaria, the Albanians of Macedonia, the Serbs of Croatia, and post-Dayton Bosnia-Herzegovina. The first of these has been expressed largely in ethnic-national terms; the remaining four cases all display both ethnic and religious dimensions. All five have been correlated with economic and social competition between groups.

The Hungarians of Transylvania

At the end of 1918, Transylvania, a traditional component of the Crownlands of St. Stephen of Hungary for more than nine centuries, was annexed by Romania, in fulfillment of a secret treaty signed between Romania and the Entente powers of World War I. Although the majority of the population of Transylvania was Romanian (2,830,040 out of a total of 5,263,602 inhabitants in 1910, or 53.8 percent of the total), the Hungarians constituted a large minority (1,664,296, or 31.6 percent of the total), many of them situated in compact areas near the Hungarian frontier.[25] No referendum was conducted in any portion of Transylvania, so that the much touted principle of national self-determination, in the name of which the framers of the Treaties of Versailles and Trianon congratulated themselves, was never actually put to the test where Transylvania was concerned.

The new Romanian authorities subscribed to an ideology that equated the Romanian nation to a large extent with the peasantry. Since it was in the cities that especially large concentrations of Jews, Germans, and Hungarians were to be found, this equation added an urban-rural antipathy to Romanian nationalism, simplifying its incarnation as xenophobia. As Livezeanu notes, 72.7 percent of the urban population of Transylvania in 1910 consisted of Hungarians and Jews, 19.7 percent of Romanians, and 15 percent of Germans.[26] The Romanian authorities sought to cope with the non-Romanian character of Transylvania's cities and much of its countryside by twin policies of "reconverting" Széklers (who were said to be Magyarized Romanians) back to Romanian culture[27] and of encouraging the assimilation of Hungarians by compelling schools and universities with Hungarian as the language of instruction to switch to Romanian. Székler children were therefore sent to Romanian summer camps in order "to awaken them to a new life" as Romanians.[28] Even the Churches were put to work to serve the national cause, with the establishment of new Uniate and Orthodox parishes in Székler areas after 1918.

The most important bastion of Hungarian culture in Transylvania was the University of Koloszvár (Cluj), which could trace its history to 1581. The protests of the faculty and two thousand ethnic Hungarians attending that university were unavailing. Onisifor Ghibu, like many in the Romanian state establishment, felt that the Romanians had too long been history's "victims" and wanted to see a redressing of the balance. "We are today the cultural invalids of an unequal war that has lasted for one thousand years," Ghibu declared. "The Romanian state cannot worry now about the healthy ones; it must take to heart its own invalids."[29] The university was Romanianized as of 1 October 1919, and all faculty were replaced.

The resentment felt by local Hungarians was tangible and was one of the factors that inspired the transfer of portions of Transylvania back to Hungarian rule in 1940 in the so-called Second Vienna Award. This restoration of Hungarian sovereignty in parts of Transylvania did not survive the end of World War II. The Romanian coalition government passed a nationality statute as early as 6 February 1945 guaranteeing equality with regard to nationality, language, and religion; but when the communist-supported land reform was implemented the following month, it targeted non-Romanian landowners first for expropriation.[30] There were, however, some reassuring measures adopted in the early postwar years; during the prime ministership of Petru Groza (1884–1958; prime minister, 1945–52), a Hungarian medical college was established in Marosvásárhely, the Bolyai University of Science was inaugurated in Cluj (Kolozsvár), and, for a while, Catholic Hungarian schools and teachers' colleges received a government subsidy. A Székely theater was established in Marosvásárhely and a Hungarian one in Nagyvarad, alongside a Hungarian music and drama college in Cluj.[31] Hungarian journals and opera (at Cluj) were also allowed to reopen. But even in those days, communist policies were mixed. In 1947, meetings of local Hungarians were regularly broken up by groups of Romanians,[32] and clergy of the Roman Catholic, Calvinist, Lutheran, and Unitarian Churches were imprisoned or sent to forced labor camps.

In 1948, the Romanian communist authorities passed an educational reform that mandated a radical rewriting of the history syllabus.[33] In 1952, Bucharest took a significant step by establishing an Autonomous Hungarian Region in the Székely area of Transylvania, with Marosvásárhely (Tirgu Mures) as its capital. This step provided a few benefits, such as bilingual street signs, and although the grant of autonomy was for the most part merely formal, it served as a potentially important symbol to local non-Romanians. It also confirmed that the Romanian communists subscribed to a variant of the doctrine of collective rights, insofar as Hungarians were now promised "special" rights within the autonomous zone but were denied those rights elsewhere in Romania. The notion that an individual's rights may vary from one part of the country to another is not compatible with liberal democracy or with internally consistent concepts of individual and societal rights, but it fully reflects the doctrine of collective rights.

In 1959, the Hungarian-language Bolyai University in Cluj was compelled to merge with the Romanian-language Babeş University, becoming the Babeş-Bolyai University; this was an important step in the Romanianization of higher education in Transylvania. Parallel processes of educational "merger" succeeded in eliminating all technical education in minority languages.[34] In 1960, the Hungarian Autonomous Region was gerrymandered and redesignated the

Mureş-Maghiar Autonomous Region.[35] Finally, in February 1968, the Mureş-Maghiar Autonomous Region was eliminated, and all pretense of Transylvanian autonomy came to an end. The region had not been granted a statute of any kind at any point during the sixteen years of its existence.[36]

After 1968, pressures on the Hungarian population in Transylvania increased. Széklers were pressured to convert to the Romanian Orthodox Church and to assume Romanian language and culture.[37] Hungarian-language newspapers were allocated smaller supplies of newsprint after 1974, and censorship was tightened.[38] Non-Romanians enjoyed more restricted travel opportunities than ethnic Romanians, minority theaters experienced a drastic curtailment of their opportunities for foreign tours, minority Church archives were plundered, and libraries catering to the Hungarian population found it impossible to obtain specialized texts. Moreover, Hungarian students and scholars were systematically prevented from obtaining access to documents and other materials that would have informed them about the real history of Transylvania.[39]

Population shifts also occurred during the Ceauşescu era (1965–89), involving, inter alia, the migration of ethnic Romanians into traditionally Hungarian districts in connection with the creation of industrial jobs in those districts. A similar policy was pursued in Kosovo, where industries were sited in purely Albanian municipalities for the purpose of introducing Serbian workers into the region. At the same time, other policies were designed to bring about the migration of the Széklers into predominantly Romanian regions, thus "drowning" them in a Romanian sea.

To the extent that Nicolae Ceauşescu thought in moral terms, it would seem that he would have had to plead either conventionalism (socialist legality) or consequentialism (the glorious socialist future being built) to provide a moral justification for his actions.

With the fall of the Ceauşescus from power in December 1989, politically active Hungarians in Transylvania were impatient for a change in policy. One of the central demands of politically active Hungarians was the restoration of a separate Bolyai University, and in March 1990, ethnic Hungarian leaders collected some fifty thousand signatures on a petition in support of this demand.[40] Interethnic violence (between local Hungarians and Romanians) erupted in Tirgu Mureş on 19 March 1990, following minor scuffles on 16 March.

The leading political party among Romania's Hungarians is the Democratic Alliance of Hungarians in Romania (DAHR), which, in the parliamentary elections of 20 May 1990, obtained 7.22 percent of the vote, even though Hungarians constitute only 7.1 percent of Romania's population. The Alliance therefore elected 20 deputies to the 396-member Chamber of Deputies and 12 senators to the 119-member Senate.[41] In the subsequent elections of 27 September 1992, the DAHR increased its share of the vote to 7.52 percent, thus obtaining 27 deputies in the now 341-member Chamber of Deputies, while increasing its share in the Senate as well.[42]

The Romanian government of President Ion Iliescu announced that it would recognize individual rights but not ethnic (collective) rights, thus signaling its intention to create a citizens' state rather than a national state.[43] But spokespersons for the Hungarian community have repeatedly complained that Romania does not observe the Council of Europe's norms with regard to minority rights, however conceptualized.[44] For example, Bishop László Tökés of the Hungarian Reformed Church in Romania has claimed that Hungarians suffer systematic discrimination in employment in the state administration, including railways, health care facilities, the postal service, and other offices at both the local and national level; according to Tökés, moreover, there are almost no Hungarian judges or lawyers in the country—a fact that he blames on discrimination.[45] Furthermore, although the Romanian law on education guarantees non-Romanians the right to education in their native languages at all levels of education, while providing that classes in the history and geography of Romania be taught in Romanian, not only Hungarians but also ethnic Germans and Roma (Gypsies) have expressed their dissatisfaction with the law.[46] Among the points in contention are Hungarian demands that state-funded hostels or boarding schools be provided (together with appropriate transportation) for children scattered in numbers below the legally specified minimum required within a given municipality, that diplomas of higher education obtained abroad (Hungary being the relevant calculation here) be recognized as equivalent to Romanian degrees, that religious organizations recognized by the state be free to organize schools at all levels, and that state and local authorities provide financial support for private educational institutions, including those offering instruction in languages other than Romanian.[47]

Spokespersons for the Hungarian community in Romania also complain that their people have been defamed in the press and broadcast media. Indeed, it is this facet of Romanian life that Bishop Tökés chose to highlight in an interview conducted in November 1995. He argued at that time that, for Hungarians living in Romania,

> the most serious problem is that verbal aggression, which is directed constantly against Hungarian minorities. It reminds us of the anti-Semitic propaganda that took place in the 1930s before the Second World War. . . . The Hungarian minority is victimized for everything. We can call it the scapegoat mechanism. For everything, the Hungarians are responsible. . . . [And] the intimidation against Hungarians is going on not only on a verbal level. The visible everyday presence of the army [in mostly Hungarian-populated localities] is an indirect threat. . . . [In territories with local Hungarian majorities] army exercises are

quite often being organized and these have a bad and intimidating effect on the Hungarian population.[48]

The tensions thus stimulated between the Hungarian minority and the Romanian government were transferred to the international plane, holding up agreement on a Hungarian-Romanian treaty of cooperation until late 1996.

The Turks of Bulgaria

In a study of Romanian historiography published in 1976, Elemér Illyés observed, "The later a nation acquires political, economic, and cultural independence, [and] the later it becomes a national state with a developed national consciousness, the more pronounced will be the nationalist character of its historiography."[49] To this, Andrew Ludanyi added, "The less developed, [and] the less politically mature [a nation], the more likely is nationalist assertion to become a cover for a sense of uncertainty or even inferiority."[50] If these principles applied to the Romanian case, they applied equally well to the case of Bulgaria at the point at which it obtained its independence. As Kemal Karpat has pointed out:

> Bulgaria was not a nation in the modern cultural, ethnic, or political sense of the word at the time the Russian army made the newly created Principality autonomous in 1878. The fledgling state felt the urgent need to develop immediately a national-historical raison d'être and thus adopted the idea of an absolute ethnic-national homogeneity as its principle for nation formation. Thereafter, the government worked to either assimilate or liquidate all of its national minorities.[51]

Before achieving independence, Bulgaria was ruled for about five centuries by the Ottoman Sultanate in Istanbul. During this period, conversions to Islam in the Balkans assumed significant proportions only in Bosnia-Herzegovina and Albania. As L. S. Stavrianos has noted, although "at least two sultans, Selim I and Murad III, did consider seriously the mass extermination of all Christian subjects who refused to embrace Islam," ultimately a kind of tolerance prevailed, and "Balkan Christians were never subjected to systematic and sustained proselytism" comparable to what Muslims were to experience in Christian Spain.[52]

Even so, there were some conversions among the Bulgarian population, said to have coincided with sporadic waves of violence in 1422, 1512, 1512–20, and 1666–1700.[53] As a result of these conversions as well as of immigration by Turks, at least one-third of the population of the region that makes up Bulgaria today was, as of the mid-nineteenth century, Islamic, mostly Sunnis of the Hanafite rite, with some Shiites near Razgrad and Rusé. The Muslims of Bulgaria at the time were divided into four ethnic groups: Turks, Pomaks (Bulgarophones), Tatars (recent arrivals, at the time, as refugees from czarist expansionism), and Roma (Gypsies).[54] Large numbers of Muslims left Bulgaria in connection with the war of 1877–78, however. After the war, the Turks of Bulgaria lost their privileges and were confronted with a dramatically altered social and political situation; as a result, the emigration of Turks— among them many well-to-do Muslim landowners—from Bulgaria continued through the 1880s. By the time the census of 1 January 1893 was taken, of the 3.2 million inhabitants of Bulgaria, only 569,728 were Turks, while the census recorded 2.5 million ethnic Bulgarians. No other group could count more than 62,000 members.[55] The steady stream of Muslims leaving Bulgaria was the result, not merely of the change in political suzerainty, but also of systematic government policy. As R. J. Crampton notes:

> The governments of Sofia and, even more so, of Plovdiv indulged, consciously and unconsciously, in the politics of disincentive. There was to be no outright discrimination against or restriction of Turk or Muslim, but the latter's established cultural and social attitudes and behavior were to be frustrated and sometimes affronted. Gradually many came to the conclusion that the new Bulgaria and Eastern Rumelia were not places in which Muslims could live in quiet and contentment. This policy evolved over a number of years and was pursued and applied with varying degrees of intensity at different times.[56]

But for all that, the Turks were granted cultural and religious autonomy. Beginning in 1885, they operated their own schools, which, although autonomous, benefited from state financial subventions.[57] Moreover, changes in political system are often accompanied by changes in the names of municipalities, streets, and plazas, and post-Ottoman Bulgaria was no exception. Indeed, between 1878 and 1912, a total of 114 changes of place names were recorded in Bulgaria and Rumelia.[58]

The number of Turks declined in absolute terms, sinking to 465,641 as of 1910; that same year, the number of ethnic Bulgarians residing in Bulgaria was set at 3,518,756.[59] The de-Turkification proceeded more rapidly in urban centers than in the countryside.[60] In addition, population exchanges negotiated between Bulgaria and Turkey after the Second Balkan War and again after World War I resulted in further declines in the Turkish population of Bulgaria; these exchanges did not affect the bulgarophone Pomaks, however. Turkish emigration continued throughout the interwar period, and between 1925 and 1940, an average of 10,000 to 12,000 Turks emigrated from Bulgaria annually.[61]

Muslims and other non-Orthodox citizens were guaranteed freedom of conscience and worship in the Turnovo Constitution of 1879, but for the first thirty years of Bulgarian independence, the muftis (religious officials responsible for mosques, Muslim educational institutions, and the administration of justice within the Islamic community) were nominated and paid by the Bulgarian government. In 1909, however, as a result of the Turco-Bulgarian convention of 19 April 1909, muftis were henceforth elected by their own local Muslim communities, their election to be confirmed, not by the Bulgarian government, but by the Sheik-ul-Islam in Istanbul. Other changes introduced by the convention of 1909 entailed parallel changes to Bulgarian legal codes, and it was only on 23 May 1919 that the Law concerning the Establishment and Administration of the Mohammedan Religious Community in the Kingdom of Bulgaria was finally passed. The law granted Muslims extensive autonomy in their internal affairs and remained the basis of claims of Muslim communal rights until after World War II.[62] The law of 1919 also established Islamic religious *(shariat)* courts, with the final court of religious appeal designated as the Supreme Tribunal in Sofia, headed by the Grand Mufti.

By contrast with the interwar Romanian authorities, the Bulgarian authorities of the interwar era were liberal in authorizing the use of minority languages (chiefly Turkish and Greek). As early as 1891, a law on education provided that non-Christian children might be educated in their native language—a wording that favored Turks but discriminated against Greeks and grecophone Gagauzes. As R. J. Crampton notes:

> the major problem in Muslim and Turkish education was not the hostility of the authorities but the backwardness, the remoteness, and the cultural exclusiveness of many Turkish communities. Put simply, the Turks did not attend school in sufficient numbers. In 1905, 47 percent of adult Bulgarian-speakers could read and write, but only 6 per cent of Turks; and for the Pomaks, the literacy figure was 4 per cent; for gypsies, 3 per cent.[63]

Where higher education was concerned, it should be noted that by the late 1930s a large number of Turks were enrolled at Sofia University. In addition, a grand medresse, or Islamic religious school, Medresse-i Nuvvab, was established in Shumen in 1922, teaching Arabic and Turkish, as well as Islamic theology. The medresse attracted students not only from within Bulgaria but also from Romania.[64]

A Turkish-language press flourished, with more than sixty different Turkish newspapers and journals appearing during the interwar years. There was a

Turkish printing press in Shumen, which put out a steady supply of Turkish-language books and other materials. The Turks and other Muslims of Bulgaria enjoyed political and cultural rights, and Turks were represented in every parliament from 1879 to 1947. In 1923, for example, there were ten Turkish deputies in the Bulgarian parliament.[65] In general, as Crampton points out, the Turks of Bulgaria during the years 1878–1944 enjoyed "communal and civil rights that would have been the envy of the many other minority groups" in Eastern Europe.[66] This was accomplished, not by creating autonomous zones in which Turks and/or Pomaks were to enjoy rights they did not enjoy elsewhere in the country, but by endeavoring to guarantee all citizens of Bulgaria certain basic rights and prerogatives, without regard to differences in religion or language.

The rather favorable circumstances of Bulgarian Turks worsened after the military putsch of 19 May 1934, when their organizations were proscribed and their publishing activity was restricted.[67] The Turkish cultural organization Turan was also forced to dissolve that same year. Conditions for the Turks of Bulgaria did not improve in subsequent years; on the contrary, they further worsened after the communist takeover, in part as an epiphenomenon of generalized communist hostility to religious creeds and landownership, the latter affecting some prosperous Muslim landowners in Dobrudja, for example. Turkish emigration resumed, with some 140,000 Bulgarian Turks leaving Bulgaria, under pressure, between August 1950 and November 1951.[68] The communist authorities were especially interested in witnessing the departure of Islamic clergy. Indeed, between 1956 and 1965 alone, the number of Turkish ulema declined from 2,393 to 462, the number of Pomak ulema from 322 to 95.[69] In 1958, the separate Turkish-language schools, which had been operated in accordance with a constitutional guarantee, were fused into Bulgarian-language schools; the teaching of the Turkish language in Bulgaria's elementary and secondary schools continued for a few years, until 1974.[70] Further, on 17 July 1970, in a sign of things to come, the party issued a decree calling for "patriotic education" to "persuade" Pomaks to change their names to more Slavic-sounding equivalents. The following year, a Bulgarian publication admitted that atheization was intended, among other things, to contribute to the "Bulgarianization" of Turks, Pomaks, and Tatars alike. In 1974, Bulgarian communist authorities terminated all Turkish-language teaching, shutting down the Department of Turkish Studies at Sofia University; Turkish schools and newspapers were also closed in quick succession.[71]

It was only in 1984, however, that the Bulgarian regime officially extended the program of Bulgarianization of personal names to the Turks. The campaign started in August 1984 with a local ordinance in Stambolovo, and it was only in December of that year that pressures on Bulgaria's Turks to Bulgarianize their names became widespread. At the same time, mosques and Koran schools were demolished, copies of the Koran were burned, and Muslim women and men were detained in police camps.[72] "In early 1985, the longtime bilingual (Bulgarian/Turkish) newspaper *New Light [Nova Svetlina/Yeni Isik]* stopped publication in Turkish. Turks were ordered to adopt Bulgarian (Christian) names, and some Muslim villages were surrounded by tanks to compel 'Bulgarianization.. By the end of 1985, Muslim culture in Bulgaria [had been] shattered."[73] It became illegal even to speak Turkish in public places, and penalties of up to two years in prison, as well as fines, were mandated for infractions of this law.[74] It may come as a surprise that the number of Turks in Bulgaria was greater in the mid-1980s, at the time of these repressions, than in interwar Bulgaria, during an era of relative tolerance. In 1956, for instance, official Bulgarian statistics recorded the presence of some 860,000 Turks and Pomaks in Bulgaria; in 1984, the Turkish population of Bulgaria was officially estimated at 900,000.[75] Kemal Karpat offers a higher figure, suggesting that there may have been as many as 3 million Muslims (mainly Turks) living in Bulgaria in 1985.[76]

Amnesty International obtained the names of more than 250 ethnic Turks who had been arrested between December 1984 and March 1985 in connection with the Bulgarianization campaign and indicated that it had received numerous reports of imprisonment and judicial murder.[77] In a statement issued on 20 October 1988, Eduard Genov, spokesperson for the unofficial Independent Association for the Defense of Human Rights in Bulgaria, declared that

> the Bulgarian citizens of Turkish origin are not only deprived of their right to self-affirmation as such, [are] not only deprived of their family names, but also they are subject to severe repression if they use their maternal language or practise their religion. Additionally, in some large cities, mosques have been closed or destroyed. Even cemeteries have been destroyed, something that has previously always been considered profane. Several hundred of them are still imprisoned and many more assigned to [compulsory] residence.[78]

Following repeated international protests, Bulgarian authorities allowed a delegation from the Organization of the Islamic Conference to visit Bulgaria in June 1987, but there was no immediate sign of amelioration.

The collapse of the communist party monopoly in 1989 and 1990 reshuffled the political deck in Bulgaria as elsewhere, but it is noteworthy that the most vociferous protests in the early months of the Bulgarian political transformation came from rural Bulgarians protesting against promises from the government to assure the Turks of equal rights.

Unlike their counterparts in Slovakia, Romania, Serbia, and elsewhere in

Central and Eastern Europe, the postcommunist authorities in Bulgaria ruled that political parties could not be organized along ethnic or confessional lines. The emerging Turkish party therefore took the name Movement for Rights and Freedoms and announced that it would be happy to admit Bulgarian citizens of all ethnicities and religious orientations. The government argued that the party was unconstitutional and took the case to the twelve-member Constitutional Court, which, on 21 April 1992, split six to six, thereby failing to proscribe the party.[79] In parliamentary elections of 1990, 1991, and 1994, the party garnered fluctuating shares of 6 percent, 7.6 percent, and 5.4 percent respectively.[80] Today there are about 800,000 ethnic Turks living in Bulgaria, as against 7.2 million Bulgarians. Counting members of other nationalities as well, the population of Bulgaria came to 8.38 million in 1995.[81] There were reportedly 945 mosques in operation throughout Bulgaria as of August 1996.[82]

Although recent survey data show a high degree of interethnic and interconfessional tolerance in spite of anti-Turkish incidents in Kurdzhali and elsewhere,[83] discontent in the villages is said to have been on the rise, owing to a combination of economic and social factors.[84] The restoration of Turkish-language schooling has been slow in coming;[85] perhaps as many as 90 percent of Turks were unemployed as of 1996, according to a report prepared by an Islamic movement,[86] and matters have hardly been helped by the energetic missionary work being conducted among Muslims by Father Boyan Saruev, with his so-called St. John the Baptist Movement.[87] The constitution explicitly rules out the grant of territorial autonomy to any group for any reason, but an association calling itself the Islamic Defense Movement has nonetheless been demanding the creation of such an autonomous region. In that movement's conception, the autonomous zone should be responsive to the needs of Turks, Pomaks, and Roma. In late 1996, the movement drew up a letter for distribution to all embassies, the president, and the media, warning against campaigns to convert local Muslims to Christianity, expressing forebodings about the prospect of ethnic hatred pushing Bulgaria into a Bosnia-type syndrome, and declaring itself prepared to overthrow the Bulgarian government by force.[88] The Islamic Defense Movement is, rather obviously, illegal and has operated clandestinely, concealing the location of its headquarters and other vital information.

But if Muslims have been concerned about Christian proselytization, so too have Bulgarian Christians been concerned about the geographic spread of Islam, alleging that Turkish émigré organizations were trying in 1996 to establish Muslim settlements in areas inhabited by Pomaks.[89] Christians of Belitsa and Yakoruda have also cited Bosnia as a dread example, warning that the Pirin and Rhodope regions could dissolve into fratricidal war if appropriate measures are not taken to calm interconfessional relations. There have even been reports of a videocassette circulating in the Yakoruda district that allegedly calls on Muslims to "declare war on the other religions."[90] One cannot discount the proclivity of political activists to make rhetorical exaggerations for the purposes of provoking concern, and hence one should be wary of interpreting these comparisons with Bosnia as predictions with any particular refinement. On the other hand, the fact that these comparisons can be made publicly without their authors looking like fools suggests that the problems besetting Bulgarian-Turkish relations have remained quite serious.

The Albanians of Macedonia

In Albania one finds Albanians of three major religious communities: Islam, Orthodoxy, and Catholicism. In Macedonia, however, most of the Albanians are Muslim. This fact significantly increases the ethnic distance between Macedonians and Albanians and contributes to distrust and misgivings between the two groups. The Albanians constitute about 20 percent of the population of Macedonia according to official statistics, although Albanian party spokespersons claim that the true figure would be closer to 40 percent, with large concentrations of ethnic Albanians in the towns of Tetovo, Gostivar, Kičevo, and Debar.

As L. S. Stavrianos notes, the Albanians of the Balkans remained politically quiescent, even unconscious, until the shocks associated with the 1878 Treaties of San Stefano and Berlin. The apprehensions that the Albanian communal leaders felt as Europe's diplomats sat down in Berlin led directly to the formation on 1 July 1878 of the Albanian League for the Defense of the Rights of the Albanian Nation.[91] The Albanians subsequently resisted the assignment of the towns of Podgorica and Antivari (Bar) to Montenegro and opposed the cession of any part of Epirus to Greece. On 28 November 1912, delegates from sundry Albanian communities met at Vlorë and proclaimed an independent Albania. Their territorial aspirations extended to Kosovo, as well as parts of what are today Montenegro and Macedonia, but the great powers, meeting in London the following year, assigned Albania more modest borders, corresponding roughly to its current boundaries.[92] After World War I, the Albanian government tried once more to obtain what it considered its legitimate boundaries and proposed that it be allowed to take possession of sections of western Macedonia, southern Montenegro, and southern Kosovo; the areas claimed by the Albanian government included the towns of Bar (Tivari), Podgorica, Peć, Priština, Debar, and Ohrid.[93] These aspirations were largely realized during World War II when, in April 1941, Italian-occupied

Albania was assigned territories corresponding closely to the demands of 1919.

After World War II, the communist authorities granted autonomy to the Albanians of Kosovo but wanted to avoid extending a similar arrangement to the Albanians of Macedonia or Montenegro. Instead, the Albanians were recognized as a nationality *(nacionalnost),* which was understood, in Yugoslav communist jargon, to signify a second-class ranking below those groups recognized as nations *(narodi).* Even so, this recognition brought some benefits, and by 1951 the Albanians of Macedonia enjoyed more than 200 elementary schools with instruction in Albanian, catering to some 26,000 pupils.[94] As of July 1981 there were some 287 Albanian-language elementary schools in the Socialist Republic of Macedonia, with about 3,000 teachers and more than 74,000 pupils. Some 2,365 students of Albanian nationality were enrolled at institutions of higher education as of 1980, while many cultural associations, theater groups, sports clubs, and so forth had been created in Macedonia for the local Albanian population.[95] Macedonia's Albanians did not have an Albanian-language university in Macedonia but could enroll at the University of Priština in the neighboring province of Kosovo. The Macedonian political establishment also saw to the creation of a state-funded Albanian newspaper, *Flaka e Vëllazërimit;* an Albanian magazine for children, *Fatosi;* and Albanian television and radio programs.

Late in 1968, demonstrations in Kosovo spread to the Albanian areas of Macedonia, especially Tetovo and Gostivar, where demands were heard for the attachment of the Albanian areas of Macedonia to Kosovo and their joint reconstitution as a seventh republic of Yugoslavia. The authorities rejected this demand and instead authorized the revision of syllabuses and textbooks in order to curb what it called "the penetration of Albanian nationalistic, irredentist and counter-revolutionary tendencies through printed textbooks and other literature."[96] Associated with this, the Commission for Intra-National Relations of the Macedonian Assembly called for an increase in the number of hours devoted to teaching Macedonian in Albanian-language schools.

A central worry of Macedonian authorities was (and remains) the high birthrate of the Albanians. In 1988, there were charges that Macedonian authorities were using various devices to restrain the Albanian birthrate, in particular by requiring that families pay for any and all medical services required by any children after the first two.

Some one hundred officials of Albanian nationality were dismissed from their posts in the Macedonian state administration in October 1987 as a result of "ideological differentiation."[97] These and other measures fueled resentment among the Albanians of Macedonia. Indeed, in early 1988, Azem Vllasi, then president of the League of Communists Provincial Committee of Kosovo, took it upon himself to criticize Skopje's treatment of the Albanians. The Macedonian Assembly did not react well to this, however, and in February of that year agreed on legal measures designed to prevent Albanians from buying property from Macedonians.[98]

The resultant intercommunal frictions reached fever pitch in August and October 1988, when young Albanians in Kumanovo and Gostivar staged demonstrations to protest these measures and to demand the rights that they were guaranteed under the constitutional system of 1974. Police arrested 128 persons in Kumanovo and an additional number in Gostivar. Of these, 20 were ultimately imprisoned, with terms of up to eleven years.[99] But in 1989 and 1990, while tensions were escalating in other parts of Yugoslavia, interethnic relations in Macedonia calmed down, perhaps in part because the Albanians were allowed to organize ethnic Albanian parties. The first, and most important, of these was the Party for Democratic Prosperity (PDP), founded on 14 April 1990 under the leadership of Nevzat Halili, an English teacher from Tetovo. The National Democratic Party (NDP) was established in Tetovo only two months later, on 24 June 1990. Other parties and associations among Macedonia's Albanians include the Democratic Alliance of Albanians–Liberal Party (under the presidency of Dzemil Idrizi), the Union of [Albanian] Intellectuals, and the Association of Albanian Women.

In the first multiparty elections, held in 1990, the PDP and NDP together obtained 23 seats in the 120-deputy Macedonian parliament (22 for the PDP, 1 for the NDP), but Albanian spokespersons complained, "Every time ethnic relations came before the parliament, we faced a democratic tyranny of the majority, because the 23 Albanian deputies were outvoted every time by the non-Albanian MPs."[100] Macedonia's second pluralist elections were conducted in 1994, and on this occasion, as a result of their political fragmentation, the Albanian politicians obtained only 19 seats in the parliament. The PDP joined in the government coalition together with the Social Democratic Party (SDP) (former communists), the Liberal Party (LP), and the Socialist Party (SP). Four Albanians were given cabinet posts, and the vice presidency went to an Albanian. The army officer corps, police, administrative apparatus, and diplomatic service were also opened up to increased Albanian participation. A policy of affirmative action was also introduced at Macedonia's universities. As Mirče Tomovski reports, "In addition to the equal opportunity for studying at any of the university faculties, an additional quota of 10 percent has been established, under which Albanian students, as well as other [non-Macedonian] nationalities, can enroll in the universities."[101] But Albanian enrollment in university remains disproportionately low, even if it has inched upwards from 4 percent in the 1992–93 school year to 6 percent in 1993–94, and 6.5 percent in 1994–95.[102]

The chief controversies relating to interethnic relations within Macedonia since 1990 have been the questions of statehood, autonomy, and education. Regarding statehood, the controversy has revolved around the demand registered by certain Albanian politicians (in particular, members of the PDP) that the Albanians be declared a "constituent nation" of the Republic of Macedonia and be so designated in the constitution.[103] In this regard, the Albanian politicians were thinking of the preamble to the Macedonian constitution, which declares that it takes as its point of departure "the historical, cultural, spiritual, and statehood heritage of the Macedonian people and their struggle for centuries for national and social freedom as well as for the creation of their own state."[104] But the concept of a constituent nation, as noted at the beginning of this chapter, presumes that the given state is constituted as a national state. And here, despite the introductory sentence, the preamble goes on to stipulate that "Macedonia is established as a national state of citizens." Moreover, article 48 adds, "The Republic guarantees the protection of the ethnic, cultural, linguistic, and religious identity of the nationalities."[105] Thus, it appears that Macedonia is not a national state at all, but a citizens' state, in which the concept of constituent nation is irrelevant.

Autonomism was, at first, a more vexing problem and may still be on the political agenda. Socialized in Tito's Yugoslavia and thus taught to believe that autonomism and federalism are the key to solving all interethnic dilemmas, Macedonia's Albanians displayed autonomist sentiments soon after the republic achieved independence. As early as January 1992, the two thousand inhabitants of the village of Vevčani voted to form an independent Republic of Vevčani and to "affiliate" with a federalized Macedonia. Three months later, Albanian activists in Struga proclaimed the founding of the "Republic of Ilirida."[106] Although these initiatives were stillborn, Muhamed Halili, the coordinator of the PDP's parliamentary group in the parliament, confessed to a Bulgarian newspaper journalist that his party still sought to achieve autonomy and added that "autonomy is only the first stage in the option of a two-nation state. Federalization represents a complete realization of the idea."[107] The leading figures of the SDP, LP, and SP wanted to sweep this issue under the carpet, but both leading Albanian parties continued to raise the issue. In June 1994, for example, the NDP resolved that "the Ilirida autonomy is the minimum which the Albanians [of Macedonia] should realize."[108] Four months later, Aburahman Aliti, president of the moderate branch of the now-split PDP,[109] warned that "all the Macedonian politicians, including the current President Kiro Gligorov, are wrong when they think that the option of autonomy for the Albanians does no longer exist."[110]

Closely connected to the controversies concerning both statehood and autonomy is the dispute about the census. After all, the larger the proportion of Albanians, the better their claim, arguably, to constituent-nation status and autonomy. An official census conducted in March 1991 found that Macedonians constituted 64.6 percent of the population, while the Albanians constituted 21.0 percent; no other nationality represented even as much as 5 percent.[111] The Albanian politicians, who had called on their fellow Albanians to boycott the census, now claimed that the census underestimated their true numbers. In response to persistent criticism, Macedonian authorities agreed to conduct a second census in June and July 1994. Once again, Albanian political leaders called on their coethnics to boycott the census (thus enabling them to challenge the results later), and the results were similar. In the 1994 census, Macedonians were found to constitute 66.9 percent of the republic's population and Albanians to number 22.6 percent, with no other nationality representing even as much as 4 percent of the republic's total population.[112] These figures remain in dispute.

The third controversy that has bedeviled interethnic relations in postcommunist Macedonia concerns education. The Albanians have demanded that a state-funded university, with instruction in Albanian, be established in Tetovo. Under article 45 of the constitution, all "citizens have a right to establish private schools at all levels of education, with the exception of primary education, under conditions specified by law."[113] But the Albanians lacked sufficient private funding to cover the costs of maintaining a university beyond an initial transition period. They therefore approached the government with their proposal, which became bogged down as a result of a combination of Macedonian antipathy to the proposal and sheer red tape. Macedonian law prescribes fixed procedures for the creation of state universities, but the Albanians, despairing of the legal procedures, took matters into their own hands and declared the establishment of a state university at Tetovo in mid-December 1994. The Commercial Court in Skopje turned down the request for the registration of Tetovo University,[114] and the state authorities sent in police, who broke into the university's premises, removed its effects, and sealed the facility. Leaders of the PDP and NDP proceeded with plans to establish the University of Tetovo, and on 15 February 1995 the university was for the second time declared open. Instruction began at the faculties of philology and philosophy the next day. Once again, on 17 February, police were sent in, this time with bulldozers. All but one of the buildings that had been turned over for university use were demolished, the five leading organizers were jailed, twenty-eight Albanians were wounded in scuffles with the police, and one died. As authorities initiated criminal proceedings against the university's organizers, the parliamentarians of all the Albanian parties protested by boycotting sessions of the parliament.

Authorities in Skopje have feared that the establishment of a purely Albanian university could fuel separatism and whittle down their small state even further. At the same time, they have recognized the legitimacy of the demand for higher education in Albanian. They have therefore provided for Albanian-language instruction in certain classes at the Cyril and Methodius University in Skopje as well as at St. Kliment University in Bitola.

Although the University of Tetovo has a high visibility in political discourse in Macedonia, there have also been controversies concerning secondary education in Albanian. Ethnic Albanian leaders claim that they established a private secondary school with Albanian as the language of instruction (as permitted by the constitution) in Ladorisht and that the police were sent to close it; the leaders attribute the closure to the government's allegedly anti-Albanian policy.[115] But officials at the Ministry of Education claim that the closure was not ethnically motivated and argue that the village of Ladorisht did not need its own secondary school, adding that no village in Macedonia has its own secondary school. Moreover, ministry officials pointed out that six schools with Macedonian as the language of instruction, which had been set up on private initiative, had also been closed, because they had not met the ministry's set curriculum.[116]

Meanwhile, after the PDP left the government coalition and formed a coalition with Ljupčo Georgievski's opposition party, the Internal Macedonian Revolutionary Organization–Democratic Party for Macedonian National Unity,[117] police and judicial authorities allegedly began to harass the leadership and active cadres of the PDP.[118] As 1996 drew to a close, Macedonian-Albanian ethnic relations remained tense, with concern over food poisoning affecting more than one thousand Albanian children in Tetovo[119] and frustration among Albanian parliamentary deputies at the Macedonian majority's rejection of all Albanian-proposed amendments to a new bill concerning the system of administrative districts in the country.[120]

The Serbs of Croatia

The presence of Serbs in the territory of Croatia can be dated to the mid-sixteenth century, when Balkan refugees crossed into Habsburg lands and entered into Habsburg service. The Military Frontier (*Militärgrenze* in German, *Vojna Krajina* in Serbo-Croatian) was established by Kaiser Ferdinand I of Austria, beginning in the years after 1522, and more formally after his election of Hungary and Croatia in 1527.[121] By 1538, the Military Frontier was organized into two zones: the Croatian Frontier *(Krabatische Gränitz)* and the Slavonian Frontier *(Windische Gränitz)*. The idea was to create a militarized frontier as a buffer against Turkish military incursions, and for this purpose immigration was encouraged. Military colonists were granted small tracts of land, exempted from the usual manorial obligations, and authorized to retain a share of all war booty. They were also allowed to elect their own captains *(vojvode)* and magistrates *(knezovi)*. All Orthodox settlers were promised freedom of worship.[122] For the first century, there were constant Turkish military probings of the border. In 1553, Kaiser Ferdinand appointed a general officer with full authority over both civil and military affairs within both the Krabatische Gränitz and the Windische Gränitz. This effectively divided the empire into separate civil and military zones.

Perhaps inevitably, the Hungarian Diet and Croatian nobles were displeased with the removal of the frontier from their authority and tried from time to time to whittle down the Frontier's autonomy. But the *Grenzer* (frontiersmen) knew that if they were incorporated into civil Croatia, they would be reduced to the status of ordinary peasants, thereby suffering a clear loss of status and prerogative. In the 1620s, the Croatian Sabor and Croatian Ban appealed to Kaiser Ferdinand II to abolish the special status of the Frontier and to authorize its incorporation into civil Croatia.[123] In 1627, the Warasdiner Grenzer told the Habsburg authorities that they "would rather be hacked into pieces than be separated from their officers and become subjects of the Croatian nobility."[124] In response to this and other petitions from the (Serb) Grenzer, the Kaiser issued a statute on 5 October 1630 defining the rights and obligations of the frontiersmen and setting up the first formal administrative organization for the Military Frontier, thereby confirming and placing on firmer institutional footing its administrative detachment from civil Croatia.[125] The Ottoman Empire was still in its prime and laid siege to Vienna (for the second time) in 1683. But the Austrians eventually lifted the siege and drove the Turks out of Austria and halfway across the Balkans; on 6 September 1688, Austrian troops captured Belgrade, and a year later, Skopje. But the Austrian forces were unable to hold this position, and an Ottoman counteroffensive drove the Austrian forces out of Serbia. It was at this time that some thirty-five thousand Serbs, led by Patriarch Arsenije III Čarnojević, resettled in Habsburg lands, withdrawing together with the Austrian troops. Kaiser Leopold I granted these refugees permission to settle in the empire and the right to practice their religion and maintain their customs. These privileges were formally extended on 21 August 1690.[126] Confirmed in 1691, these concessions considerably expanded the scope of concessions granted earlier by Ferdinand I.[127]

Under the Treaty of Karlowitz (1699) the Ottomans ceded Lika, Krbava, Bačka, and parts of Slavonia, Srem, and the Banat to the Habsburgs; these new acquisitions were incorporated into the Military Frontier, which would now stretch for a thousand miles, with a depth of twenty to sixty miles. The Austrian-Turkish border shifted back and forth in the early decades of the eighteenth century, and as a result of the Austro-Turkish war of 1736–39, thousands more Serbs, led by Patriarch Arsenije IV Jovanović Šakabenta, migrated to Austrian lands. As Wayne Vucinich notes, "The eighteenth century witnessed many other administrative reforms that gave the Military Frontier . . . a more unified organization."[128] In spite of these formal guarantees, however, Catholic proselytization was pursued energetically; indeed, repeated violations of the religious rights of the Grenzer resulted in a decline in the morale of the border units in the first half of the eighteenth century and provoked a series of rebellions and disorders all along the Military Frontier. As a result of these problems, the Habsburgs authorized the first of a series of administrative reforms of the frontier.

In 1740, Maria Theresa succeeded to the Habsburg throne, and the War of Austrian Succession broke out. The frontier raised more than forty-five thousand men to fight for the empress, twenty thousand of these fighting in Silesia.[129] The frontiersmen fought fiercely and quickly won a reputation as the best irregulars in Maria Theresa's army.[130] But as the military pressures subsided, the Habsburg authorities once again showed too little regard for the religious sensibilities of the Orthodox population of the frontier.[131] Maria Theresa and Josef II continued to allow the Orthodox population to use the Julian calendar, but the Illyrian Regulation, proclaimed in September 1770, curtailed the functions of the Orthodox hierarchy and provided for the strict control of the religious schools and of the printing of religious literature. Protests from the Serbian Orthodox Church were unavailing.

The nineteenth century saw the spread of nationalism among the frontiersmen, via civil Croatia.[132] But what is striking about these years is that the growth of nationalism did not, at the time, divide Croats and Serbs; on the contrary, they felt themselves to be collaborators in an Illyrian or South Slav project. As Gunther Rothenberg observes:

> Although the [South Slav] national movement on the border became divided by two centers of attraction, one in Zagreb and the other in Belgrade, there always had been a good deal of common feeling between Catholic and Orthodox Grenzer. Then, too, the events of 1848 also had created considerable sentiment for South Slav cooperation in civil Croatia and Serbia which cut across divisive religious loyalties.[133]

Indeed, Ausgleich-era Austria-Hungary was witness to increasing currents of cooperation between Serbs and Croats, both before and after the 1881 administrative abolition of the Military Frontier. The Hungarian-appointed governor of Croatia between 1883 and 1903, Count Károly Khuen-Héderváry, tried to obstruct Croat-Serb cooperation, but in spite of the efforts of Khuen-

Héderváry and his successors, Serb and Croat political leaders negotiated a program for collaboration, resulting in the formation of the so-called Croatian-Serbian coalition in 1905. This coalition remained the most important political force in Croatia until 1918 and drew several Serbian parties into cooperation with Croatian parties.[134] As of 1910, about 611,257 Orthodox lived within the present-day territory of Croatia, representing 18.21 percent of the population. As a result of wartime casualties during World War I, an outbreak of Spanish flu, and variable rates of natural increase, the Orthodox population of Croatia (which, in addition to Serbs, also included some Russian immigrants) represented 17.8 percent of the same region in 1931.[135]

During the interwar years, 1918–41, Croatian Serb politicians behaved in conformity with the spirit of cooperation established earlier, and against the Greater Serbian hegemonism of certain circles associated with Belgrade, the leading Serb politicians in Croatia were inclined to an accommodationist stance.[136] But, according to Ivo Banac, ordinary Serbs of interwar Croatia were susceptible to the more hegemonist pretensions emanating from Serbia.[137] Gradually, suspicions undermined Serb-Croat dialogue, and Milan Pribičević was accused of promoting the secession of Lika and Banija from Croatia and seeking their unification with Serbia. Pribičević's denials did little to allay such fears.[138] But despite certain policies of *divide et impera* on Belgrade's part,[139] Croatian Serbs and Croats found some common interests and joined forces to push for a standardized taxation schedule throughout the kingdom—a campaign that bore fruit in 1928.[140]

Hence, despite problems that should probably be considered normal in a newly constituted state, the Serbs and Croats of Croatia by and large maintained civility in their relations until the Nazi invasion in April 1941 and the creation of the fascistic Independent State of Croatia (NDH). Bogoljub Kočović, a Serbian scholar, has calculated that about 334,000 Serbs lost their lives in the NDH in the years 1941–45.[141] Counting casualties in other parts of Yugoslavia, altogether some 530,000 Serbs died in World War II, out of a total of 1,027,000 Yugoslavs who lost their lives during those years.[142] Untold numbers of Serbs living in Croatia were forcibly converted to Catholicism.[143] The horrors of World War II have been ably recounted by other scholars;[144] what is important for my purposes here is that the atrocities perpetrated by the *Ustaša* in the NDH deeply scarred the Serbs throughout Yugoslavia and left them with psychological pain that would be difficult to relieve.

The communists appreciated the difficulty of the problem created by Ustaša atrocities, and during World War II, Moše Pijade, together with some Serbian communists, proposed the creation of a Serbian Autonomous Region within postwar Croatia. But the Serbs were dispersed across much of Croatia, rendering any such solution rather complicated, and, in any event, Tito feared that the adoption of such a proposal would alienate Croats from the new order being created by the Communist Party of Yugoslavia (CPY).[145]

At the end of World War II, Serbs constituted a disproportionate element in the Croatian branch of the CPY. This set the stage for a disproportionate representation of Croatian Serbs in the Croatian party apparatus and Croatian police in years to come, in turn providing grist for Croats fearful of Serbian influence. Drago Roksandić cites the following figures: In 1945, Serbs constituted 41 percent of the membership of the Croatian communist party organization; after Croats began to be recruited into the party, the Serbian representation declined to 28.3 percent in 1948, a figure still markedly higher than the Serb proportion of the republic's population; and even as late as 1984, Serbs still accounted for 22.6 percent of the membership of the Croatian party, as against 11.5 percent of the population of Croatia. Within the central committee of the Croatian party organization, Serbs constituted 26.3 percent in 1948 and still held onto 21.6 percent of the seats as late as 1986.[146]

With the creation of communist Yugoslavia, the stage was set for interrepublic migrations. In the 1960s, large numbers of Croats began to seek employment in Germany and Austria as *Gastarbeiter,* and a certain number of Serbs obtained employment along the Dalmatian coast. These trends continued into the 1970s, as Serbian labor migrants moved into Slavonia in search of work. From 1945 until the late 1960s, there was no evidence of Serbian autonomism in Croatia,[147] but under the impact of the so-called Croatian mass movement of 1967–71,[148] Serbs of Dalmatia, Slavonia, and the Krajina began to circulate such ideas once again. The quashing of the mass movement and the purge of party liberals across four republics (Croatia, Serbia, Slovenia, and Macedonia) ended any further discussion of sensitive matters. The problems were to resurface with greater force not quite twenty years later.

Without wanting by any means to saddle the authors of the ill-famed Memorandum with exclusive guilt for stoking the fires of nationalism that would engulf first Serbia and then all of Yugoslavia, I think that one can usefully date the distillation of Serbian resentments against perceived injustices into a coherent ideological program to 1986. It was in that year that Dobrica Ćosić, Kosta Mihailović, and other unnamed scholars penned the Memorandum subsequently issued in the name of the Serbian Academy of Sciences and Art. In one of the more inflammatory passages, the authors of the Memorandum charged:

> Except for the period of the existence of the NDH, Serbs in Croatia were never so endangered as they are today. The solution of their national position imposes itself as a first priority political question. Unless a solution is found, the conse-

quences can be damaging in many ways, not only for the situation in Croatia but for all of Yugoslavia.[149]

The Memorandum thus spread fears concerning the fate of Serbs in Croatia four years before Franjo Tudjman was elected president of Croatia; indeed, the fears and consequent hatreds crystallized by the Memorandum evoked a backlash among Croats, producing a surprise upset victory for Tudjman in spring 1990. Ironically, then, Tudjman may well owe his political success to the Serbian Academy.

Furthermore, Serbian autonomism resurfaced well before Tudjman's election.[150] Specifically, in the summer of 1989, while Croatia's communists were still in power, Jovan Opačić (a clerk) and other local Serbs tried to set up an autonomous Serbian cultural society, the Zora Society. The Croatian communist authorities banned the society, and thereupon the Serbian Writers' Association in Belgrade took up the defense of Opačić and also raised a claim to political autonomy for Croatia's Serbs. The Croatian communist authorities assailed the call for autonomy, warning that such a measure would destabilize the republic.

From the very first, Tudjman inflamed the Serbs. On 24 February 1990, for example, then-candidate Tudjman addressed a party congress of his Croatian Democratic Community (Hrvatska Demokratska Zajednica, or HDZ). In the course of his speech, Tudjman remarked, "Thank God my wife is not a Jew or a Serb."[151] That same month—indeed, only days earlier—Jovan Rašković, a psychiatrist working in Šibenik, and Opačić combined their energies to construct a political party for Croatia's Serbs. The Serbian Democratic Party came to life on 17 February. Addressing a rally of ten thousand people in Petrinja in June, Rašković unfurled the autonomist banner. "The Serbs do not want a second state in Croatia," he told his listeners in Petrinja, "but they demand autonomy. . . . The Serbian people in Croatia should be enabled to speak their language, to write their script, to have their [own] schools, to have their education programs, their publishing houses, their newspapers."[152] The demand was political in nature, because Rašković and those Serbs flocking to his banner expected the state—that is, the government in Zagreb—to pay for the parallel school system, the additional publishing houses, and the additional newspaper out of tax revenues. By then, moreover, Rašković had rejected Tudjman's offers of high-level posts in the government. Following the same line as the Albanians in Kosovo, Rašković demanded, in conversations in May 1990 with President-elect Tudjman, that the Serbs be defined in the constitution as a constituent nation of Croatia and that their 11.6 percent representation in the Croatian population not be described as a "minority."[153]

Tudjman and the HDZ had four alternatives: (1) to accommodate the demand registered by the Serbian Democratic Party of Croatia and to draft a constitution defining the Republic of Croatia as a national state of two constituent nations, Croats and Serbs; (2) to make the demand irrelevant by drawing up a constitution for a citizens' state, so that there would not be any reference to any constituent nations whatsoever; (3) to postpone the drafting of the constitution, while negotiations with the Serbian Democratic Party and Serbian political activists not affiliated with this party could continue; and (4) to push through a constitution for a "national state," defining the Republic of Croatia as the national state of one constituent nation, the Croats. While any visitor to Yugoslavia in 1989 or 1990 would have been aware of the heavy doses of hate propaganda being churned out by Milošević and his minions, a propaganda barrage that was rapidly changing the way Serbs of Croatia thought about their neighbors, there was at least a chance that had Tudjman adopted any of the first three alternatives, the crisis might have been averted. The challenge, in essence, was for Tudjman to take the high road, showing up Milošević for what he was. Instead, Tudjman chose the fourth option, which was clearly the most dangerous. In June, just one month after the Tudjman-Rašković meeting, the HDZ-controlled Sabor passed a draft constitution of an overtly Croatian nationalist cast.[154] Two months later, in August 1990, Croatian Serbs organized a referendum among local Serbs on Serbian autonomy within Croatia. Conducted 9 August–2 September 1990, in defiance of a proscription by the Tudjman government, the referendum provided the justification for a declaration of autonomy, which followed on 1 October 1990. This declaration sparked the breakdown of civil order in Croatia. Moreover, by that time, Rašković had become a political irrelevance, while Milan Babić, a young dentist with an office in Knin, had established himself as the drillmaster of the SDP. Babić's concept was to prepare for an insurrection, in order to extract the Serb-inhabited areas from Croatia altogether. As Silber and Little note, "By no means all the Serb-populated areas backed Babić's rebellion. Many were interested in dialogue with Zagreb, and were far from hostile to the new government. In these areas, Babić used force to impose his authority."[155]

By the spring of 1991, the Krajina Serbs, led by Milan Babić and Milan Martić, were in more or less open rebellion. The rebellion spread to western Slavonia, where activists loyal to Babić proclaimed the creation of a Serbian Autonomous Region and announced that they would not accept instructions from the Croatian Ministry of the Interior, only from its ad hoc counterpart in the self-declared Serbian Autonomous Region of Krajina. The Belgrade daily *Večernje novosti* published an inflammatory article at this time, reporting on the front page that Croats had killed a Serb Orthodox priest and running, on page 3, a statement from the selfsame priest concerning the incident in which he had supposedly been killed.[156] With the outbreak of war in June and July of that year, secessionist-minded Serbs in the Krajina and Slavonia wrested large swaths of territory from Zagreb's control and announced their intention to associate themselves with the rump Yugoslav state controlled by Slobodan Milošević.

But not all of Croatia's Serbs took this path. Some Serbs chose to cooperate actively with the Tudjman government, organizing the loyalist Serb People's Party. Formed in 1992, this party received less than thirty thousand votes in the elections of 1992, or 1.06 percent of the total vote.[157] Other Serbs, led by Milorad Pupovac, attempted to strike a third path, independent of the influence of both Babić and Tudjman, and prepared to work within the framework of the Republic of Croatia, but insisting on respect for the human rights of Serbs. Pupovac was the prime mover behind the organization of the Serbian Democratic Forum and later, in early 1995, set up the Serbian Independent Party. Pupovac has proposed that Croatia look to Finland and its guarantees to indigenous Swedes as a model for constructing a system of guarantees for Serbs.[158]

The European Union tried, rather unsuccessfully, to mediate between Tudjman and Babić, more or less ignoring Pupovac, and drew up a so-called constitutional law in December 1991 that proposed that communities comprising 8 percent or more of the Croatian population (only Serbs would benefit from this formulation) be given special rights of cultural and territorial autonomy. Had the law been put into effect, it would have allowed for different systems of rights within the Serbian Autonomous Regions and the rest of Croatia, so that Serbs would enjoy protection within the autonomous regions that they would not enjoy elsewhere in Croatia. But Žarko Puhovski, a professor of philosophy at the University of Zagreb who has been outspokenly critical of the Tudjman government, has criticized this approach. As Puhovski noted in a 1995 interview:

> The main error—in both the Constitutional Law and the European approach to Croatia and Bosnia and Herzegovina—is the idea that the Serbs must be protected in Knin and Croats in Zagreb. The real problem is how to protect the Croats in Knin and the Serbs in Zagreb.[159]

Indeed, the Serbs appeared to require such protection. During 1992, some 7,489 homes and other buildings belonging to Serbs living within the Republic of Croatia (i.e., within the areas still under the control of Zagreb) were damaged or destroyed by explosives or acts of arson. An additional 220 Serbian homes were destroyed between January and March 1993.[160] These acts of destruction were not connected with battle action.

Croatia's Serbs also came under religious pressures. Soon after winning the 1990 elections, President Tudjman introduced technically voluntary Catholic religious instruction in state schools. By the 1992–93 school year, religious instruction had assumed a regular and stable place in the elementary- and middle-school systems in Croatia. The difficulty, where Serbian families were concerned, is that peer pressure and pressure from teachers combined to make it extremely difficult for Serbian children to decline to enroll in Catholic religious instruction. As P. B., a thirty-six-year-old Serbian engineeer who eventually fled Croatia, put it:

> My daughter enrolled in the first grade. She had to say whether she was going to take religion or not. How can you say that you do not want to, when I had seen how a Croatian family in Velika Gorica had suffered, people who were simply atheists, but they had to move because their children were mistreated by other children? And then, what could we do but say: She will take religion! . . . Then they adopted rules to the effect that children must attend weekly masses. This is monitored by the religion teacher. They took special satisfaction in putting the Serbian children in the choir to sing in the service on the Catholic Christmas Eve.[161]

Teachers in Zagreb and Osijek were reported to have said to their classes that children who refused to attend Catholic religion classes would be considered "Chetniks."[162] This policy induced many otherwise loyal or apolitical Croatian Serbs, clergy and believers alike, to take flight. By 1993, there was not a single Orthodox priest remaining in Split, Šibenik, or Zadar.[163]

Nationalism, it appears, fueled both Croatian separatism and Serbian autonomism/separatism and, in the process, led to the perpetration of injustices on both sides. The Croatian Serbs, enjoying nominal support from Milošević and the sanction of the presence of a UN protective force, remained in control of about 30 percent of the territory of the Republic of Croatia until 1995, when, in a series of campaigns, the Zagreb government reasserted its control of all of Croatia except eastern Slavonia, in the process setting hundreds of thousands of Serbs to flight. According to Helsinki Watch, about two hundred thousand Serbs fled from western Slavonia and the Krajina during the 1995 military offensives.[164] As a result, of the roughly six hundred thousand Serbs who lived in Croatia as of 1991, less than one hundred thousand remain today.[165]

Post-Dayton Bosnia

Peace in our time—that is, at least, the promise made in Dayton through the signing of the tripartite peace accords on 22 November 1995. The West was egregiously ill equipped to broker a peace for Bosnia, however, both because so many of its diplomats and politicians were making policy recommendations on the basis of pitiful extremes of ignorance[166] and because the West's sundry plans for Bosnia were, from the very beginning, drawn up on the presumption of autonomist thinking.[167]

Accordingly, the Dayton peace accord incorporated some very damaging principles, alongside entirely logical and healthy principles. On the positive side, the Dayton peace accord provided for:

- the termination of ethnic cleansing;

- the right of displaced persons to return to their homes;

- an agreement on all sides to desist from further violence;

- the holding of free elections as soon as possible;

- the free movement of all persons, without constraint or restraint;

- the arrest of accused war criminals;

- the emplacement of Implementation Force (IFOR) troops entrusted with the task of protecting vulnerable civilians and carrying out arrests of war criminals; and

- the emplacement of an international police task force (IPTF) that would be enabled to undertake to identify the dead.

But all these provisions have been either obstructed or subverted. Even as the Dayton accord was being negotiated under conditions of ceasefire, ethnic cleansing continued in parts of Bosnia held by Radovan Karadžić's forces.[168] Bosnian Serb police have charged unauthorized tolls (payable in Deutschmarks) to cross their lines, and both Serbian and Croatian forces have obstructed free movement. Karadžić's forces have, further, forcibly resettled both Serbian and non-Serbian communities since the Dayton peace accord. IFOR has found itself unable to perform either of its two chief tasks and has had to be content with defending itself, and as for the identification of the dead, the Bosnian Serb forces loyal to Karadžić and Krajišnik tampered with mass graves, making identification more difficult. As Helsinki Watch reported in June 1996:

> The parties to the conflict have refused to comply with critical components of the accord. They have refused to allow people to return to their homes, have prevented free movement throughout Bosnia, and have convinced their own people to abandon their life-long homes, telling them it is not possible to coexist with

people of different ethnicity. Most recently, in late May [1996] Bosniaks around the town of Teslic, in central Bosnia, were forced to flee their homes following a campaign of bombings, beatings, stone-throwing and threats by Bosnian Serb displace[d] persons. Local Republika Srpska police refused to offer protection or to stop the violence and expulsions. Political leaders have refused to cooperate with the International Criminal Tribunal for the Former Yugoslavia, . . . defying their obligation under the Dayton accord to arrest and turn over persons indicted for war crimes. The most important figures indicted, Radovan Karadžić and Gen. Ratko Mladić, who masterminded the slaughter of thousands of innocent civilians, remain in control of both political and military forces. Freedoms that are necessary to exercise political choice—such as freedom of assembly, association and the press—are systematically restricted.[169]

Indeed, as of June 1996, of the three parties to the accord, only the Bosnian government of Alija Izetbegović had turned over indicted persons to the tribunal.[170] The violations of accord provisions continue at this writing. Indeed, during November 1996, Bosnian Serb forces loyal to Karadžić and Krajišnik were reported to have burned or blown up Muslim homes in Prijedor and Lješkovica, while Bosnian Croat forces were said to have burned some sixt Serb-owned homes in Drvar.[171]

But as important as noncompliance with the provisions of the accord has been, equally important have been certain negative features of the accord, specifically:

- its explicit endorsement of the principle of autonomism, and the implicit endorsement of the de facto partition of Bosnia;

- the failure to proscribe hate speech or to take any measures designed to foster tolerance and mutual respect in the region;

- the failure to provide any guarantees or protections for genuinely free media, in the face of Helsinki Watch's recommendations that joint media be established, to be operated by nonnationalist moderates; and

- the failure to exclude nationalist parties from competing in the electoral contest or to protect nonnationalist parties and media from the nationalists.

Instead, nationalists were allowed to maintain their stranglehold in the Serbian and Croatian sectors of Bosnia. In Republika Srpska, Bosnian Serb authorities have intimidated independent media. In Banja Luka, for example, journalists working for "independent Serb media received death threats following publication of information supportive of Rajko Kašagić," a Karadžić foe, while Radio Big, a popular Banja Luka radio station that maintained a degree of distance from Karadžić's line, was taken off the air on 20 May 1996.[172] One might say that the "ethnic cleansing" visited upon non-Serbs has been mirrored in a kind of "political cleansing" unleashed by Karadžić's people on fellow Serbs. The sponsors of Dayton never asked themselves, however, if permitting an authoritarian party such as Karadžić's to squeeze out other Serb parties or, for that matter, even to compete in the elections might not prove to be subversive of any project of producing democracy and moderation in the region or of protecting human rights.

As Helsinki Watch reports, "print, television, and radio are also strictly controlled in Croat-controlled areas of Bosnia and Hercegovina such as Mostar." Indeed, continues Helsinki Watch, "citizens in Bosniak-, Serb-, and Croat-controlled areas are largely dependent upon the government-dominated media, which continues to propagate ethnic hatred and the ideal of ethnically pure states."[173] Such a situation is conducive neither to stability nor to democracy. On the contrary, the most optimistic projection as to the eventual results of the Dayton peace accord would forecast the consolidation of authoritarian regimes operating shattered economies.[174] There is yet another dangerous trend emerging, that is, the rapid growth of a well-organized criminal underground, using payola to corrupt police and buy up state-owned enterprises that are for sale.[175]

Meanwhile, with the election of Serb nationalist Momčilo Krajišnik and Croat nationalist Krešimir Zubak to serve alongside Alija Izetbegović on Bosnia's three-member collective presidency, the prospects for the triumph of political moderation remain bleak. In token of the bleakness of prospects for moderation or stability, all sides are thought to be hiding and importing weaponry.[176]

The failure to take any measures to remove the nationalists from power in the Serb and Croat sectors of Bosnia is particularly troubling and suggests a pervasive nonchalance on the part of Western diplomats with regard to the future of Serbs, Croats, and Muslims alike, all of whom will suffer from the continued political hegemony of nationalists in the region. But in approaching the Bosnian war, Western diplomats have figured neither as upholders of Universal Reason (moral universalists) nor as consequentialists concerned with outcomes (moral hedonists), but as advocates of conventionalism in morals (which, as I have explained, manifests itself as moral relativism). Moral universalism would have been the surest guide, but even moral hedonism could have produced results more promising than those we find in Bosnia today.

Renata Salecl has drawn attention to the pernicious and erosive nature of the moral and cultural relativism underlying the Western approach to Bosnia and "peace" in Bosnia. As she warned in a 1996 publication:

We are now witnessing the emergence of a cultural relativism that forbids any intrusion into other cultures and confines the notions and applications of universal values to Western civilization. These relativists seem to reason as follows: "We admit that our culture was imperialist in the past, but we now reject this past and embrace cultural differences; we therefore urge that our so-called 'universal' values not be imposed on others." If one wanted to be truly consistent in defending cultural relativism, then one would also have to claim that we are not in a position to judge or actively oppose totalitarian regimes (fascism, Stalinism, Islamic fundamentalism and so on), since they all emerged in historically different circumstances incompatible with our own.[177]

Conclusion

In postcommunist Central and Eastern Europe, appeals for and against secession and autonomy, on the basis of one or the other nation's (or Church's) alleged rights of self-determination (or monopoly on truth) are widespread. Both separatism and autonomism, as long as they are based on the spurious foundation furnished by supposed rights of *national* self-determination, suffer from the lack of any logical basis on which to set a limit to what could easily be justified as an endless parade of new separations and autonomies. Indeed, if every group of people that so wishes may declare itself a separate nation, what is to stop every family that does not want to pay taxes or recognize the local police magistrates from declaring itself a separate nation? An appeal to practicality or possibility misses the point, which is that the doctrine of national self-determination is supposed to furnish a *moral* justification for separatism and/or autonomism and cannot do so, and, in fact, it must ultimately rely on the old saw "Might makes right." But hegemonism, the supposed right of dominant nations and Churches to impose their cultures on minorities living within the same societies as they—which also bases itself on the doctrine of collective rights, if for opposite ends—likewise finds itself adrift at sea, without a moral anchor to moor it to a fixed (and logically consistent) position.

No one to date has been able to demonstrate why one should accept the notion of a right of national self-determination, indeed why people of the same stock should necessarily live together (as Ćosić, Milošević, and Karadžić have repeatedly insisted). On the contrary, insofar as the political expressions of this supposed right have shown themselves to be associated with moral relativism and moral nihilism (as argued above), they would appear to be challenged by any theory based on Universal Reason and natural rights. Few observers have seemed to notice that intolerance and moral relativism go hand-in-hand (and this includes that species of religiously derived moral relativism that renders all morality relative to God's command). On the other hand, moral universalism and tolerance imply each other, so that one may suggest, further, that tolerance—a prerequisite for the maintenance of a liberal democratic society[178]—can only be built on the firm foundation of the secular concept of Universal Reason.

And yet, there are clearly occasions when a people may be entitled to separate from an existing government or to seek autonomy. These occasions are to be sought in cases where the existing government acts systematically in contravention of Universal Reason. Both Locke and Hegel recognized the right that people (whether the entire society or any portion of it) enjoy to resist and overthrow tyranny; the same right justifies separation in instances where tyranny cannot be overthrown. That there is a subjective character in identifying a government as "tyranny" has been pointed out by Hobbes and Kant, who drew from this fact the conclusion that there is no right to revolt.[179] One may, however, justify embracing Locke and Hegel against Hobbes and Kant on the argument that insofar as a society may be construed as a moral-ethical community and insofar as the state is the legal embodiment and enforcer of the communally comprehended moral code,[180] the state owes its legitimacy to its conformity to the moral code that it is appointed to uphold and, upon failing to uphold that code, loses its legitimacy. This corresponds with the deep-seated longing of people for justice; or, as Montesquieu once put it, "In all countries and governments, people wish for morality."[181] On this argument, the disassociation of Slovenia, Croatia, Macedonia, and Bosnia-Herzegovina was ultimately morally justified, not on the basis of some illusory notion of national self-determination, but because of the threats to which they were exposed as a result of the rising political power of Slobodan Milošević and the rising tide of Serbian xenophobia. Tyranny—which may be defined as any government that undertakes policies that are systematically subversive of Universal Reason—may, indeed must, always be opposed; but opposition to tyranny does not require that there be any difference of nationality or religion to be operative.

More generally, societies experience a loss when they become more homogeneous. This point was stressed in *The Federalist Papers* by James Madison and also inspires the writings of Hannah Arendt. Lord Acton (1834–1902), the famous British historian, made the same point in 1862, observing:

> The presence of different nations under the same sovereignty is similar in its effects to the independence of the Church in the State. It provides against the servility which flourishes under the shadow of a single authority, by balancing interests, multiplying associations, and giving to the subject the restraint and support of a combined opinion. . . . The co-existence of several nations under the same State is the test, as well as the best security of its freedom. It is also one of the chief instruments of civilisation; and, as such, it . . . indicates a state of

greater advancement than the national unity which is the ideal of modern liberalism [and, for that matter, ethnarchy].

If we take the establishment of liberty for the realisation of moral duties to be the end of civil society, we must conclude that those states are substantially the most perfect which . . . include various distinct nationalities without oppressing them. Those in which no mixture of races has occurred are imperfect; and those in which its effects have disappeared are decrepit. A state which is incompetent to satisfy different races [and orientations with regard to religion] condemns itself; a State which labours to neutralise, to absorb or to expel them, destroys its own vitality; a State which does not include them is destitute of the chief basis of self-government.[182]

4

Theocratic Impulses in Poland

In the 1980s, the Polish Catholic Church was closely associated with the democratic movement and played a role that was broadly supportive of the nascent repluralization of Polish society.[1] Pope John Paul II lent his considerable authority to demands for the relegalization of Solidarity, while Father Jerzy Popiełuszko achieved martyr status when, after he had established a tradition of delivering fiery weekly sermons on behalf of workers' rights, he was brutally murdered in October 1984. Whatever the Church's claims to infallible truth, it had bound itself unambiguously to those forces working to dismantle the communist ideological and organizational monopoly.

After the installation of noncommunist Tadeusz Mazowiecki as prime minister in August 1989, however, and the attendant collapse of communist structures of control, the Church reversed itself. Instead of remaining opposed to ideological monopoly and supportive (at least ostensibly) of ideological pluralism, the Church began to demand the fulfillment of certain desiderata that, taken in sum, revealed an unmistakable theocratic impulse. Particularly telling with respect to questions of ideological monopoly was the Church's insistence that the Sejm (the lower house of the Polish bicameral parliament) pass a law barring radio and television broadcasts from including material insulting to or incompatible with "Christian values."

The new era began on 17 May 1989 with the passage of a law granting the Catholic Church the status of a juridical person and officially sanctioning the Church's sundry educational, cultural, and charitable activities. The law also stipulated that the Church enjoys the right to construct places of worship, hospitals, radio stations, and other facilities it deems necessary.[2] But the Church's ambitions extended far beyond obtaining mere legal guarantees for its work. What it wanted was to exert a decisive influence on state and society in any spheres it deemed important to its creed and mission. As Jan Łopuszański, chair of the Christian-National Union Supreme Council, put it in 1992, "The

Church has a right and even a duty to assess in terms of ethical norms any political, social, or economic measures that are proposed."[3]

That the Church took for granted the irreproachability of its aspirations was made clear in its demand in 1989 that Catholicism be declared the official state religion of Poland. The Church was forced to back down on this demand, but in other spheres the Church succeeded in marginalizing its opponents, and by the end of 1993, it could tally up major victories in three controversial areas: abortion, religious education, and broadcasting. A concordat had been signed on behalf of the prime minister and was awaiting parliamentary ratification. And Polish clergy had come to enjoy extensive access to the airwaves as well as to play a highly visible role in public life, including consecrating all official ceremonies.

But these gains were obtained at the expense of the Church's credibility. Public opinion surveys showed that the Church's approval rating declined steadily from a high of 87 percent in 1989 to 70 percent in 1991, 40 percent in 1993, and 31 percent in February 1995.[4] As early as 1991, some Poles were scrawling the words "Ayatollah Glemp" on public walls in Kraków, contemptuously comparing the archbishop of Warsaw with Iran's Ayatollah Khomeini. As the London *Times* reported, "The expansion of Church power can be sensed everywhere."[5]

The Abortion Controversy

When I speak of theocracy, I mean the successful manipulation of state mechanisms to impose the rules and religious values of one faith on all persons living in a given country, including members of other faiths. The Catholic Church's successful campaign to obtain the criminalization of abortion in Poland is a quintessential example of a theocratic impulse, insofar as the Church ignored both other religious organizations and the perspectives of nonbelievers in pursuing its objectives. More than that, it has ignored its own flock, turning a blind eye to repeated opinion polls showing overwhelming opposition among Polish Catholics themselves to the ban on abortion. A November 1990 poll revealed that only 13 percent of Poles favored an absolute ban with penalties;[6] a subsequent poll, conducted in April 1992, found that more than 80 percent of Poles favored abortion in cases where the continuation of pregnancy endangered a woman's health or where the pregnancy itself was the result of rape.[7] As the Sejm formulated a draft bill designed to curtail access to abortion, opinion polls reported that only 37 percent of respondents favored the measure, with 51 percent opposed.[8]

Abortion during the first three months of pregnancy had been legalized in

1956, albeit in the face of immediate criticism and obstruction on the part of clerical bodies. But with the Round Table discussions between the regime and the opposition in the winter of 1988–89, the Church saw its opportunity and contacted sympathetic deputies in the Sejm to press for the adoption of new, more restrictive legislation. At the same time, the Church applied pressure directly on the medical establishment. Even before the end of 1989, the Kraków Medical Academy ruled that its members were not to perform abortions.[9] Subsequently, in December 1991, the Supreme Council of Physicians at a national convention voted 449 to 75 to adopt a new medical code that, among other things, threatened to revoke the professional licenses of physicians performing abortions except in cases of risk to the woman's life or rape.[10] In the meantime, the Ministry of Health canceled state subsidies for contraceptives and introduced new procedures requiring a woman seeking an abortion to obtain approval from three specialists, to be consulted individually.

In opposition, the Warsaw Committee for an Abortion Referendum, headed by Sejm deputy Zbigniew Bujak and university professor Jan Haftek, gathered signatures to demand that the issue be referred to a public referendum. An April 1991 poll found that 75 percent of Poles favored a referendum.[11] By the end of November 1992, the committee had collected more than three hundred thousand signatures.[12] But the episcopate squelched the initiative, arguing that there are some "laws which no man has established and no man can change. The very foundation of all rights native to man is the inalienable right of life from the moment of conception. The source of this right is GOD, the GIVER OF ALL LIFE. This right must not be the subject of any referendum."[13] To combat the initiative, the episcopate organized a letter-writing campaign, deluging Sejm deputies with letters from opponents of abortion. The Club of Catholic Intelligentsia (KIK), headquartered in Warsaw, also entered the fray, protesting the proposed referendum.[14] The campaign had its intended effect: the legislature ignored pleas for a referendum and proceeded with formulating a legal ban on abortion.

As debate mounted, the abortion controversy came to eclipse all other issues, whether relating to privatization or the exclusion of ex-communists from positions of responsibility or the role of the media or even redrafting the constitution. It also became clear that there were, in fact, two intertwined aspects to this controversy: first, whether the state should legislate for all citizens on the basis of the teachings of one particular faith; and second, whether an eventual ban should be all-inclusive and ironclad (as Cardinal Glemp preferred). In the course of 1992, it became obvious that exceptions had to be allowed in cases of rape or incest—albeit in the face of unremitting opposition from the Catholic hierarchy[15]—and in cases where the pregnancy endangered the woman's life or where the fetus had been irreparably damaged.

These revisions were incorporated into the draft bill passed by the Sejm on 7 January 1993.[16] The Senate lent its approval later that month, and on 15 February, Polish president Lech Wałęsa signed the bill into law.[17]

In the twelve months following the passage of that law, the number of illegal abortions skyrocketed, abortion tourism (arranging for middle-class Polish women to obtain abortions abroad) became a high-growth industry, and deaths from infanticide mushroomed. Between 1992 and 1993, the number of miscarriages rose by 1,225 to 53,057 (the first increase in miscarriages in many years), while some 153 newborn infants were simply abandoned in hospitals in the course of 1993.[18] Meanwhile, opinion poll data showed that more than half of Poles felt that financial difficulties should be considered a legitimate basis for authorizing an abortion.

By spring 1994, opponents of legal restriction had prepared a series of amendments to the 1993 law. These amendments proposed to allow abortion in cases of economic or personal hardship. Parliamentary deputy Barbara Labuda, one of the bill's cosponsors, said that the 1993 law had "caused a lot of harm, suffering, and human tragedy"[19] and that it had "stimulated criminality and demoralized women."[20] Archbishop Kazimierz Majdański of the Warsaw Academy of Catholic Theology, in turn, sounded the Church's alarum, asserting that the contemporary family was "threatened by the propaganda of hedonism, permissiveness, [and] pornography, as well as by a fascination with material success and birth control programs."[21]

In spite of protests from Catholic lay activists and homilies from the pulpit, the Sejm voted 241 to 107, with 32 abstentions, in June 1994 to adopt the amendments. Wałęsa predictably vetoed the measure, but there was still a chance that the bill's advocates might muster a two-thirds majority in the Sejm to override Wałęsa's veto. In that event, Wałęsa, as president, would have been required to sign the bill into law within seven days. Yet so firmly opposed to this measure was Wałęsa that he announced that he would resign his office rather than sign the bill. *Rzeczpospolita* reported that in that event, Wałęsa risked being summoned before the state tribunal.[22] But despite the strong backing of women's pressure groups, the measure could win only 232 votes on the second tally, with 157 votes against and 22 abstentions, and the measure failed.[23]

Six months later, Pope John Paul II took up the theme of abortion in his eleventh encyclical, *Evangelium Vitae* (The Gospel of Life). In a key passage in this encyclical, the pope warned: "I declare that direct abortion, that is abortion willed as an end or as a means, always constitutes a grave moral disorder, since it is the deliberate killing of an innocent human being."[24]

For the Catholic Church, gender is fundamentally determinative of social role. Directly criticizing the career choices of professional women, Cardinal

Glemp used the occasion of a sermon at Częstochowa's Jasna Góra shrine in May 1995 to hold up two paths for Polish women—maternity and virginity—and to describe "the currently promoted model of a woman 'who uses the world and is used' [as] below feminine dignity."[25]

Christian Values in Schools and Broadcasting

Although the abortion controversy has been the most salient issue affecting the Catholic Church's relation to society at large, disputes quickly arose likewise over the Church's proposal to include Catholic religious instruction in the curricula of state schools. As early as autumn 1989, the Church mounted pressure on the Ministry of Education to permit religious classes in state schools. The ministry eventually agreed, in spite of vociferous opposition from Poland's small Orthodox and Protestant communities,[26] to introduce nominally voluntary Catholic religious instruction in state schools. Janusz Eksner, spokesperson for the attorney general, justified the move by asserting that "only by accepting universal religious values can a person 'be of true value to society and the nation.'"[27] The ombudsman protested that it was unconstitutional for the ministry to adopt this measure without consulting the Sejm, but the Constitutional Court decided in favor of the ministry. Meanwhile, warnings that peer pressure and pressure from teachers would quickly render any such nominally "voluntary" religious instruction mandatory were being borne out. In due course, crucifixes were also affixed to the walls of state schools where portraits of Marx and Lenin had once hung. From the beginning, the Catholic Church enjoyed complete control over the appointment of religion teachers, the selection of religion textbooks, and the curriculum of religion classes. In addition, soon after the collapse of the communist order, the state took the Catholic University of Lublin under its financial wing. Then, in May 1996, the Government-Episcopate Joint Commission agreed that, effective autumn 1996, priests teaching religion at state schools would be paid by the state, even though they are selected by the Church, and would enjoy the same rights and privileges as other teachers. The salaries of Roman Catholic priests teaching religion were expected to cost the state treasury around PLN 300 million per school year.[28]

At the same time, the Church succeeded in expunging sex education from school curricula, in the process suppressing altogether a two-hundred-page textbook entitled *Preparation for Family Life,* which included a few line drawings indicating what couples do in bed.[29] One is reminded of the claim made in an educational directive issued by the Polish communist government at the height of Stalinism. "The Great October Revolution," the directive claimed, "has liquidated all reasons for masturbation."[30]

The Church also had its way with broadcast media. Specifically, on 29 December 1992, the Polish parliament voted 198 to 172, with 12 abstentions, to adopt a new law requiring radio and television broadcasts to respect "Christian values."[31] The relevant clause of the law on broadcasting stipulated: "Broadcasts should respect the religious feelings of audiences, and, in particular, they should respect the Christian system of values."[32] It seemed self-evident that only recognized authorities from the Church could determine just what were "Christian values." This led directly to the proposal that a commission representing the episcopate be empowered to determine where public broadcasts were inconsistent with the Church's values.[33] The regulatory council established to adjudicate claims and disputes relating to this law consisted of eight members; two of the members appointed to this council had close ties to the Church, while a third member had served previously as a senator representing the Polish Peasant Party, a party known for its support of many Church desiderata.[34] That this bill was tantamount to the imposition of a new form of censorship was duly noted by critics of the new theocracy. *Trybuna Ludu,* for example, called the bill's adoption the "triumphant return of censorship."[35]

The Church not only succeeded in legislating its values in hospitals, schools, and broadcast media; it also became far more visible than heretofore, with bishops blessing banks and supermarkets, chaplains garnering high military awards, and priests appearing regularly on television.[36] Within this context, it came as a bit of a surprise when, in May 1995, the pope complained that Polish Catholics were the victims of "intolerance and discrimination."[37] Even more surprising, perhaps, was Father Czesław Bartnik's well-publicized charge, two months later, that "today the Church's spiritual existence is more endangered in our country than it was in the times of open Marxism. Political atheism supported by pseudo-liberalism, Western and Eastern amorality and hatred toward the Catholic Church—all of this wants to dominate everything, destroying all that is ours."[38] The weekly newspaper *Warsaw Voice* expressed amazement that anyone could reach such a conclusion about Wałęsa's Poland.

Quest for a Concordat

Even before Mazowiecki assumed the prime ministership, the Holy See aspired to sign a concordat with Poland's government. A joint governmental-ecclesiastical commission set to work in Warsaw and produced a draft concordat in 1988 that was thereupon sent to Rome for approval. The Holy See rejected the draft, however, and more than three years later returned with a new draft, prepared by the Curia.[39] On 28 July 1993—two years after the Curia first submitted its draft—the foreign minister of Poland and the papal nuncio signed a mutually agreeable text. But the signing came on the heels of a parliamentary vote of no confidence in Prime Minister Hanna Suchocka, with the result that parliamentary ratification was postponed until after the September 1993 elections.

The elections of September 1993 brought victory to a coalition of the Alliance of the Democratic Left (SLD) and the Polish Peasant Party (PSL). The new coalition government duly appointed a committee of experts to review the draft concordat in order to verify its compatibility with Polish laws. The committee in turn reported that the concordat was inconsistent with sixteen existing laws (including the Law on Guarantees of Liberty of Conscience and Faith and the Marital Status Law), two codices (the *Code of Family and Guardianship* and the *Code of Civil Procedure*), and many decrees, including the civil and family codes, the law on freedom of conscience and belief, and the law governing Church-state relations.[40] The draft concordat exempted Catholic clergy from taxes, stripped the government of any say regarding textbooks to be used in religion classes in state schools or the teachers of those classes, enabled Catholic parish cemeteries to deny burial to non-Catholics even where no municipal cemetery is locally available (in contravention of Polish law), and provided that Roman Catholic priests would enjoy privileged access to care facilities operated by other Churches.[41]

Immediately after the 1993 elections, representatives of the government contacted the episcopate to ascertain whether the Church might be willing to renegotiate certain points. Initially, the episcopate gave some encouraging signals, but it subsequently stiffened its position.[42] The Holy See now insisted that the draft concordat needed no further refinement and could be ratified as it was. Deputy Prime Minister Aleksander Łuczak took the Vatican's point of view in discussions within the Polish government.[43] So did the Ministry of Foreign Affairs, which argued that postponement of ratification could hurt Poland's international credibility.

In spite of the Church's impatience to sign a concordat, the Sejm voted on 1 July 1994 to delay ratification until after passage of a new constitution. Some Church officials took umbrage at this further delay, calling it a "frontal attack on the Church."[44] A year later, still with no concordat in sight, Bishop Alojzy Orszulik of Łowicz claimed that the concordat had become "a subject of political games and an electoral bait in the hands of the postcommunists" and called the continuing delay "shameful."[45] In September 1995, an extraordinary commission appointed by the Sejm completed its work and filed a report indicating that the draft concordat was not incompatible with Poland's provisional "short constitution" but confirming its incompatibility with various laws, decrees, and codices (as specified above). The commission, dominated by clerically inclined deputies, recommended that the laws, codices, and decrees in question be amended to bring them into harmony with the draft concordat. The Sejm, however, rejected the commission's recommendation.[46]

Slightly less than half of Poles considered it necessary to sign the concordat;[47] this division of opinion was reflected even within the ruling coalition, where the peasant party (PSL) began to protest, on the eve of the November 1995 elections, that it did not agree with its SLD coalition partner and, on the contrary, favored a "quick ratification" of the concordat.[48] Curiously, as if fearing that the election might prove a setback, Wałęsa met with legal experts on 11 October to determine whether it might be possible for him to dispense with parliamentary ratification and simply sign the concordat on his own authority. Following the experts' advice, Wałęsa submitted a special bill to the parliament on 18 October asking the Sejm to empower him to sign the document without further involvement on the part of the parliament. The Sejm declined to accommodate Wałęsa's wishes.[49]

After the November 1995 presidential elections, President-elect Alexander Kwaśniewski made overtures to the Catholic Church, suggesting further bilateral talks with the Holy See to iron out some of the problems associated with the draft concordat. However, Bishop Tadeusz Pieronek, secretary of the Episcopal Conference of Poland, declared that the Church was not interested, "because, in his opinion, the Episcopate had already devoted too much time to the issue and had not been treated seriously."[50] In spite of this hostile outburst, Primate Glemp agreed to meet with President Kwaśniewski and parliamentary president Zych, together with Archbishop Józef Kowalczyk, the papal nuncio, in March 1996.[51] But although the Church has attempted to obtain the concordat quickly and to compel the government to adapt the constitution to a preexisting concordat, the government has repeatedly indicated that it wishes to pass the new constitution first, only then taking action on the concordat, which, of course, would have to be brought into broad compatibility with the constitution.[52] As 1996 drew to a close, there was still no concordat in sight.[53]

If the concordat has suffered repeated delays, so, too, has the constitution. And here, if anything, the lines of battle have been even more sharply drawn. In a word, the episcopate rejects the notion of a secular state. Instead, according to Bishop Tadeusz Pieronek, "The constitution, if it is to be for man and not against him, should not only guarantee ties between God and man but should also promote them and provide protection for them." Writing in *Gazeta Wyborcza,* Pieronek continued, "The constitution should also explicitly prohibit everything that is an obstacle to or destroys man's links to God, as well as man's links to other men, particularly in the natural form of interactions."[54]

What that has meant in practice is that the Church has demanded (1) that there be a preamble with overt religious content (beginning with the words, "In the name of God"), (2) that the constitution include a clause guaranteeing the protection of human life "from the moment of conception until natural death," and (3) that the constitution enshrine the principle that religious instruction be included in the curricula of state schools.[55]

In February 1995, representatives of the small Orthodox, Seventh-Day Adventist, Pentecostal, and Assemblies of God Churches let it be known that they favored inclusion in the constitution of a clause affirming the separation of Church from state; however, the Polish (Catholic) episcopate immediately repudiated this initiative.[56] Speaking on this subject somewhat later on behalf of the episcopate, Bishop Pieronek asked, "Do you expect 95 percent of the nation . . . to keep quiet because 5 percent want to have their constitution? Don't we have rights? We are guided by the concern for our common good. If we say that the Church is the community of the faithful, then it totals 95 percent of the nation."[57] After some initial agonizing, SLD leaders agreed in late March to drop any reference to Church-state separation but proposed, instead, to include a clause about the state's being "neutral regarding world view."[58] This too offended the Church. Still searching for a formulation that might appease the Church without conceding too much, the parliament returned in early April with a proposal to describe the state as "impartial." This phrasing was accepted by the Catholic hierarchy.[59]

On 12 April 1995, the Polish parliament issued a draft constitution. This draft was published in the Polish daily newspaper *Trybuna* in early May. The key articles where religion is concerned are articles 16 and 38. Article 16 contains five clauses. The key clauses are as follows:

> Article 16.1. Churches and denominational unions receive equal treatment.
>
> 16.2. The government of the Republic of Poland remains impartial on matters concerning religious, personal, and philosophical beliefs, upon safeguarding the freedom of their expression in public life. . . .
>
> 16.4. The relations between the state and the Roman Catholic Church are defined by the international agreement concluded with the Apostolic See and by law.[60]

Article 38 affirms the principle of freedom of conscience and religion, declaring, "No one may be forced to participate in religious practices."[61] The same article provides for the availability of religious instruction, though it makes no explicit assurance that such instruction will be offered at *state* schools.

Poland's Catholic bishops were, in any event, angered by the draft constitution. "A draft like the one which exists today is unacceptable," said Archbishop Józef Michalik, head of the episcopate's committee to review the constitution. "It is a nihilistic draft which contains a coded struggle against everything moral."[62]

By late spring 1996, the government was thinking in terms of letting the Church have its way with the preamble in order to obtain the episcopate's approval of the remaining articles as drafted.[63] But this compromise left everyone dissatisfied. Thus, as of November 1996, Church and parliament remained deadlocked, with no constitution in sight.

The Kwaśniewski Presidency

The presidential elections of November 1995 offered the Church an opportunity to come to terms with the secular state and to distance itself from direct politicking. The Polish Church failed the test, however. As early as August 1995, the Polish bishops issued a letter to the faithful calling on them to vote against former communists and to choose candidates "who will defend ethical and evangelical values" (meaning the Church's preferred candidate, Hanna Gronkiewicz-Waltz, chief of the Central Bank). Even before the first round of voting (on 5 November) narrowed the field to two candidates—incumbent President Wałęsa and SLD challenger Aleksander Kwaśniewski, the Church realized that Gronkiewicz-Waltz had virtually no support and switched its support to Wałęsa.[64] Archbishop Glemp called SLD candidate Kwaśniewski a "neo-pagan,"[65] while Archbishop Ignacy Tokarczuk described left-wing politicians' behavior as "hysterical and traumatic, the result of an anti-religious and anti-God complex going back to the seeds of Marx and Lenin."[66] Kwaśniewski, on the other hand, struck a moderate pose, promised to support passage of the concordat (albeit in renegotiated form), and pledged to work with Church authorities in the spirit of cooperation.[67] The Church remained unmoved, however, and many parish priests used the pulpit to warn against voting for Kwaśniewski or said prayers in church for Wałęsa's victory.[68]

But opinion polls suggested that there was a danger that the Church's tactics might backfire. In a poll conducted in October 1995, some 74 percent of respondents said that the Church's involvement in the election was inappropriate,[69] while another survey found that less than 25 percent of Poles expressed "strong attachment" to Catholic traditions.[70] In due course, Kwaśniewski garnered 51.7 percent of the vote, defeating Wałęsa in a runoff election. Marcin Król, a Catholic intellectual and editor of the monthly magazine *Res Publica Nowa,* drew the inevitable conclusion: "There was a big percentage of voters who voted for Kwaśniewski because of the negative feelings they had about Wałęsa," he explained, "and the Church's approval of Wałęsa added to that."[71] Cardinal Glemp drew a somewhat different conclusion, noting that "it is a fact that a part of the baptized people identifying as Church members voted for a nonbeliever."[72] Overall, Glemp attributed Wałęsa's defeat to "the moral sickness of society."[73] Thus, far from considering the secularization of politics to be one of a number of legitimate alternatives, the Polish primate equated secular politics with "moral sickness." And if secular politics is tantamount to sickness, then only theocracy may be viewed as morally "healthy."

In the wake of his election, as already noted, Kwaśniewski repeatedly signaled his receptiveness to a compromise on the concordat, underlining the importance of further meetings between representatives of Church and government.[74] One of the difficulties in attempting to bridge the gap between secular and ecclesiastical authorities has been the enormous differences in their understandings of what the concordat signifies. Thus, for example, ignoring complaints by non-Catholics that the concordat would give the Catholic Church "special privileges" over other religious organizations,[75] Archbishop Kowalczyk called the concordat "a gift from the Holy Father, John Paul II, to Poland."[76]

Meanwhile, leaders of other religious organizations made their concerns known. Orthodox Bishop Jeremiasz, for example, complained at a meeting of the Polish Ecumenical Council in April 1996 about Catholic priests allegedly forcing non-Catholics entering into mixed marriages to convert to Catholicism. He also lamented the alleged difficulties experienced by non-Catholic parents in obtaining baptism certificates that would show their children as having any faith other than Roman Catholic.[77] Konrad Raiser, secretary-general of the World Council of Churches, who had come to Poland to attend the same meeting addressed by Bishop Jeremiasz, took advantage of his visit to meet with President Kwaśniewski, expressing concerns about the rights of religious minorities in Poland.[78]

Meanwhile, Poland's left-dominated parliament set to work in March 1996 on a bill to liberalize the law on abortion.[79] A subcommittee was appointed by the Sejm to prepare amendments to the law. By early June, the subcommittee was nearing the end of its work, amid volleys from senior clerics against "libertarian-socialist parliamentarians" and "anti-Catholics."[80] In spite of sundry pressures brought to bear by the Church hierarchy and various antiabortion groups, on 30 August the Sejm voted 208 to 61, with 15 abstentions and 120 deputies absent, to approve the amendments liberalizing the law.[81] Among other things, the amendments provided that a woman could obtain an abortion through the twelfth week of pregnancy in cases of emotional or financial hardship, restored state subsidies for contraceptives, and authorized the introduction of sex education in state schools. Pope John Paul II, Primate Glemp, and other senior clerics immediately denounced the legislative act. But the measure had to be approved by the Senate, the upper house of the parliament, before becoming law. As the date for the Senate's vote drew near, Polish bishops issued warnings, threatening to excommunicate legislators who supported the amendments.[82] Some critics reacted strongly to such threats. Sociology professor Mikołaj Kozakiewicz, for example, wrote in the 2 October issue of *Przegląd Tygodniowy* that "when it wants to imprison, excommunicate and demote the deputies who think differently, the Church violates the principles of the democratic state."[83] The Senate met on 4 October 1996, and, ignoring the recommendation of its own health committee, voted against the measure by a vote of 52 to 40.[84] With that, the measure was returned to the Sejm for a second vote, allowing the Sejm to overrule the Senate if a majority of votes could be obtained.

Polls taken on the eve of the Sejm's second vote showed that some 59 percent of the electorate favored the proposed amendments to liberalize the abortion law; Catholic women's groups were said to be strongly in favor of the measure.[85] The vote was originally scheduled for 23 October, and on that day, between thirty-five thousand and fifty thousand antiabortion activists from all over Poland staged a mass rally in Warsaw in order to exert pressure on the legislators. The legislators decided to postpone the vote by a day but on 24 October voted 228 to 195, with 16 abstentions, to approve the measure.[86]

In the wake of the vote, pro-choice activists began receiving anonymous abusive and threatening phone calls from antiabortion activists,[87] while many physicians, perhaps fearing that they might be subjected to abuse or violence at the hands of "those who honor Mary and follow Christ,"[88] announced that they would refuse to perform abortions, regardless of the law.[89]

In fact, opinion polls showed that only 33 percent of Poles actually opposed the liberalization of the abortion law.[90] In spite of that, Piotr Zak, Solidarity press spokesman, tried to suggest that the legislature and Kwaśniewski were obliged to observe the wishes of the minority. "It is a bad thing that President Kwaśniewski signed the law," Zak told PAP, "because it means that he had no intention to take into consideration the opinion of those Poles [the activists who represented the views of 33 percent of Poles] who had requested him not to sign it."[91] Translating this into the discourse of nationalism, one might say that just as the Bosnian Serbs claimed a right to veto the decision of the majority in Bosnia on the strength of their claim to be a "state-forming nation," so, too, the Catholic Church claimed a right to veto the decision of the majority in Poland, in some ways thinking of itself as a kind of "nation-forming Church." Bishop Pieronek put it this way: "This law is unethical . . . and therefore, in terms of conscience, it is not in force."[92] But Pieronek's appeal to conscience was spurious, for the Church does not recognize the right of women to have abortions if their consciences permit, only their right to fight against abortion.

Consistent with this orientation, antiabortion activists announced in late November that they would seek the president's "dismissal" on grounds that he had signed a measure approved twice by the Sejm.[93]

Meanwhile, on 11 November, Army Field Bishop Leszek Głódź stirred controversy during celebrations marking Independence Day by calling passage of the amendments an act of "aggression against Polish independence" and by questioning the right of the state authorities to issue orders to the military.[94]

Conclusion

The Catholic Church's legislative advances in Poland have been made against the expressed wishes of most Poles. I have already mentioned that some 80 percent of Poles favored a more liberal law on abortion than that supported by the Church. A December 1992 poll found that 45 percent of those surveyed opposed the law guaranteeing respect for "Christian values" in broadcast media, compared with only 32 percent favoring the measure.[95] A poll conducted by the CBOS Opinion Research Center in Warsaw in February 1996 found that 85.8 percent of respondents opposed "the direct involvement of the Church in public life," with 66.7 percent criticizing public expressions of faith by civil servants.[96] Only where religious instruction in state schools is concerned has the Catholic Church found majority support for its objectives. Here some 79 percent of Poles said in survey data released in February 1996 that they "did not object" to this practice.[97]

Yet the Polish Church—or at least the politically predominant conservative wing in its leadership—has shown little interest in such survey data.[98] On the contrary, such data are at best irrelevant, in the eyes of Church conservatives, since the Catholic Church has traditionally construed its values and doctrines as having absolute validity. But liberal democracy entails a basic tolerance, a willingness to concede that, if a particular issue is persistently controversial and defies all efforts to achieve consensus, then perhaps the only appropriate remedy is to allow that there may be different points of view. But the senior clerics of Poland's Roman Catholic Church have experienced difficulty accepting this principle. For them, matters relating to sexuality (divorce, sex education, abortion) are black and white, and no other points of view can be accepted. As Pieronek put it, "The Church has to say that abortion is [a] crime because this is what it is. The Church has the duty to tell what is evil and what is good. . . . If anybody interprets this as political action, then let me make this clear that in this sense the Church will always involve itself in politics."[99] And yet, there are generational differences within the Church. The older generation, whose leading figures control the Church, is conservative in outlook and can be expected to uphold the Vatican's traditional agenda without compromise. But among the lower clergy, especially younger clergy, other views can be found, views which are more liberal, more tolerant, more open-minded.[100] It is at least conceivable that as the current generation gives way to the next, the Polish Church, if not the Roman Catholic Church worldwide, may adapt in some ways. Recent Vatican concessions concerning Jan Hus, Galileo, and evolution may be hints of more significant concessions yet to come. But that is for the future. For the time being, it is clear that there are unmistakable theocratic impulses at work within the Polish Church, that these theocratic impulses have already achieved some success, having an impact both on the institutions and on the political agenda, and that these impulses risk alienating sectors of the Church and in the long run perhaps eroding the very strength of the Polish Church. Attendance at mass stood at nearly 60 percent in 1989 but had fallen to about 35 percent by November 1996.[101] And as public opinion polls recorded steadily lower credibility ratings for the Church, observers began to talk in terms of the Church's declining influence in Polish society and life. Indeed, a 1996 poll found that more than 70 percent of Poles opposed any preaching of politics from the pulpit.[102]

The Church still speaks of universal values, but from time to time there are telltale signs that the Polish hierarchy may find itself at odds with the premises and principles of liberal democracy. During the 1995 elections, for example, one unidentified bishop appealed to a species of the doctrine of collective rights in offering this advice: "Let Catholics vote for a Catholic, Jews for a Jew, communists for a communist."[103] And the Catholic Church in Poland has become an angry Church as of late. As Agnieszka Wolk-Laniewska put it in a September 1996 article: "The Catholic Church in Poland has begun to use the language of hatred and anger. Instead of education, it resorts to threats. Instead of persuasion, it applies blackmail. Compassion, tolerance and the spirit of ecumenism are not to be found in the official position of the Church."[104] One may even speak of a certain tension between traditional Catholic morality and the political culture of liberal democracy. More particularly, the Catholic Church, in its conviction that it is the living embodiment of God's will on earth, remains convinced that on all matters that it defines as questions of public morality or ethics, its own word must be taken as final. Or, as Cardinal Ratzinger once put it, expressing the viewpoint of Church conservatives, you cannot vote about truth.[105]

5

The Struggle for Collective Rights in Slovakia

On 9 June 1992 came the shattering announcement by newly elected Prime Minister Václav Klaus of the Czech Republic that the Czechoslovak federation was no more. An interim (but trimmed) federal government was to be set up to preside over the hasty dismantlement of the seventy-four-year-old state. On 30 September the Czechoslovak Republic was split in two. And by January 1993, the finances of the state were completely divided.[1]

At first sight, Slovak independence seems to accord well with vaguely defined notions of rights of national self-determination. But most observers predicted that the split would be economically—and perhaps also politically—deleterious for Slovakia. Slovak industry is more narrowly based than Czech industry, being concentrated heavily in armaments production developed for the now-lost Soviet market and semifinished steel marketed largely to Czech factories. In political terms, the sudden wave of Slovak nationalism immediately showed signs of provoking fear and restiveness among the six hundred thousand ethnic Hungarians living in southern Slovakia alongside smaller numbers of Ukrainians, Roma (Gypsies), and other groups.

If the Slovak case is riddled with complications, it is also colored with irony, above all because it is not, in fact, a case of national self-determination at all (as it would appear superficially) but of nationalist manipulation and politicking. Even at the very time that leaders of the Czech and Slovak republics agreed on the disintegration of their state, a reliable opinion poll found that 11 percent of Slovaks preferred a unitary state with the Czechs, 32 percent preferred a federation, and 31 percent spoke in favor of a confederation. Only 18 percent of Slovaks advocated splitting Czechoslovakia into two states.[2] These figures held relatively steady over successive months. A June 1991 poll found that 79 percent of Slovaks surveyed wanted to retain some form of political union with the Czechs and that 34 percent of Slovak respondents even considered Czechs and Slovaks to be members of the same nationality.[3] How, therefore, to account for the reemergence of the question of Slovak independence, the surrounding controversies, and the strategies adopted by advocates of independence? And how, further, to account for the very different political paths taken by the Czech and Slovak successor states?

The resurgence of Slovak national consciousness after 1989 ought not to have come as a surprise. In a 1976 work, Austrian sociologist E. K. Francis provided the theoretical groundwork for understanding the causal linkage between decolonization (emancipation from Soviet control, in this context) and the activation or reactivation of latent ethnic frictions. As Francis put it, "Regional differences or shifts in the distribution of political power and/or economic prosperity in a former exploitation colony are likely to activate latent conflicts between ethnic units; at the same time, economic and political problems are likely to be expressed in ethnic terms."[4] Harder to anticipate was that Slovak nationalism would be exploited by a populist politician whose policies would soon prove unfavorable for democracy.

In this chapter, I shall trace the fissiparous forces that led to the breakup of Czechoslovakia in 1992; describe the 1990 controversy in Slovakia concerning a language bill; show how Slovak prime minister Vladimír Mečiar has not only held onto power but also used his power to erode democratic freedoms; and explore in some depth two key controversies that have plagued Slovakia since 1992: the status of the Hungarian minority and the independence of the Slovak press. Slovakia, as we shall see, has found its path to pluralism strewn with thorns and has slipped, in fits and starts, in the direction of authoritarian-nationalist rule.

From Communism to Nationalism

The reemergence of the Slovak national question in summer 1990 took Europe, and the Czech politicians in particular, by surprise. Except for its brief incarnation as a nominally independent republic under Nazi auspices between 1939 and 1945, Slovakia had never known independence and had rarely been able to make its voice heard. Ruled by Hungarians in the nineteenth century, the Slovaks came under rule from Prague in 1918. The Czech politicians of that day viewed Slovaks as fellow members of a single nationality, the Czechoslovak nation. But there were fewer Slovaks, particularly educated ones, than Czechs, and the Slovak economy was far less industrialized and hence far less prosperous than the Czech economy. For these and other reasons, it was Czech politics that set the agenda for most policy in the interwar era.

The communists had promised equality to Czechs and Slovaks, signing agreements at Košice in 1945 guaranteeing the preservation of Slovak autonomy. But before the communists came to power, they repudiated these pledges; upon coming to power, they thus failed to honor the promises made in Košice. Slovak citizens accommodated themselves to what they came to call "Pragocentric" rule. Emblematic of this situation was the fact that in 1949, only about 10 percent of the members of the communist party were from Slovakia, even though Slovakia accounted for 28 percent of the total population. At the Tenth Congress of the Czechoslovak Communist Party in 1954, 10.2 percent of the delegates were Slovaks; and even in 1958, ten years after the revolution, Slovaks accounted for only 14 percent of the party membership.[5] The 1968 "Prague Spring" ignited a brief push for state federalization and substantive autonomy for Slovakia, accompanied by stirrings among the Hungarians of southern Slovakia, who demanded the restoration of the original (Magyar) names of their towns.[6] The Slovaks obtained the federalization, but without much substantive autonomy, and ultimately took small satisfaction in the fact that Moscow's henchman in Prague between 1969 and 1988, Gustáv Husák, was a Slovak. But from 1969 until recently, nothing was heard from Slovakia. The 1970s and 1980s were so calm that many observers assumed that the Slovak national question had simply disappeared. Others were skeptical about this proposition.[7]

The suddenness of the issue's reemergence makes it obvious that its timing was linked to the collapse of the communist system. But there are three more proximate causes that stimulated the Slovak national revival: the democratization of Czechoslovakia from 1989 through 1992 and the sheer possibility of pressing for greater self-rule; persistent economic problems that were in any event more serious in Slovakia than in the Czech lands; and the sudden registration and activity, in conditions of pluralist democracy, of a string of minority associations, especially those representing the six-hundred-thousand-member Hungarian minority living in Slovakia.[8] Representatives of the Hungarian minority set up three ethnic organizations in Czechoslovakia as early as November 1989: the Forum of Hungarians in Czechoslovakia, the Independent Hungarian Initiative, and the Hungarian Students' Federation. The Association of Hungarian Writers was set up the following month, followed by the Federation of Hungarian Teachers and the Hungarian Journalists' Association. The latter three are special interest lobby groups. In addition, the Cultural Association of Hungarian Working People in Czechoslovakia (CSEMADOK), which had been set up by the communists in 1949, survived the collapse of the communist political order and sought to adapt itself to the changed circumstances, becoming in the process an outspoken advocate of minority rights.[9]

Despite initial moves toward the creation of democratic institutions and the privatization of the economy, there were danger signs in 1991, including the rise of extremist right-wing parties and the increasing frequency of political name-calling being passed off as serious political discourse. In May 1991, for example, Stanislaw Dudáš of the Slovak National Unity Party called Czechoslovak president Václav Havel "the second [most] negative character of the twentieth century right after V. I. Lenin."[10] Three months later, Miroslav Sládek, chair of the Association for the Republic–Republican Party of Czechoslovakia, told one hundred to two hundred demonstrators that Havel was "a murderer, an alcoholic, a drug addict, a thief, a blackguard, and a rogue" and expressed his hope that Havel would soon be imprisoned once more. Sládek followed this up with a comment directed at Czechoslovakia's politicians and journalists generally: "They are all lying swine."[11] The political climate became so polarized in March 1991 that Pavel Rehetský, the deputy prime minister of Czechoslovakia, warned that the country's "democratic institutions [were] being undermined in much the same way that Germany's were during the Weimar Republic."[12]

The First Hints of Trouble

In late June 1990, shortly after the first free elections in Czechoslovakia in more than forty years, President Havel addressed the members of the newly elected federal parliament, highlighting what he expected to be the chief tasks of his administration. These tasks were, in his words, "to build a modern, democratic state in which freedom of the press and of assembly underpin an atmosphere of pluralism," to press on with economic transformation without provoking "social convulsions," to nurture culture and the schools, and to strengthen the autonomy of the republican governments in Prague and Bratislava.[13] But despite his acknowledgment of the need to deepen the autonomy of the two constituent republics, there had actually been little to suggest future trouble.

Probably the first hint of the new nationalism came in the form of the unexpected eruption of a series of anti-Hungarian demonstrations in several ethnically mixed localities in southern Slovakia in February, March, and April 1990. Among the towns affected were Nová Zámky, Trnava, Filákovo, and Bratislava itself.[14] But it was not until the outbreak of the so-called hyphen debate in March 1990 that foreign observers took note of the change in political climate.[15]

The "hyphen debate" arose from the need to rename what had been the Czechoslovak Socialist Republic. Clearly, the middle term was to be dropped. But from there, Czechs and Slovaks disagreed. The Czechs preferred the designation "Czechoslovak Federative Republic." The Slovaks, however, wanted to hyphenate the name in order to stress that Slovaks are a people in their own right and suggested the designation "Czecho-Slovak Republic." Since the two sides could not agree, the initial compromise, adopted on 29 March 1990, was to allow each side to use a different variation of the common name: "Czechoslovak Federative Republic" for the Czechs and "Czecho-slovak Federative Republic" (albeit with a small "s") for the Slovaks.[16] But three weeks later, the parliament changed the name again, agreeing to the name "Czech and Slovak Federative Republic" after thousands of Slovaks demonstrated against the initial compromise.[17]

Clearly, this was only the symbolic dimension of a much deeper concern. The overthrow of communism had reopened the fundamental questions of state, among them the form and depth of political devolution to the constituent republics. Soon after the 1989 "Velvet Revolution," Slovak authorities proposed that the system be organized on a strict federal basis. Czech politicians countered by suggesting a more modest degree of administrative decentralization.[18] Moravian and Silesian politicians then entered the debate, calling for reorganization of the state as a tripartite federation consisting of Bohemia, Moravia-Silesia, and Slovakia. The Slovaks feared that Moravian Czechs would automatically side with the Bohemian Czechs in any vital political debate (not only because of shared national heritage but also because of shared economic interests) and vetoed the proposal.[19] President Havel supported various alternatives as he tried to respond to shifting winds and changing political circumstances. In February 1991, for example, Havel offered tentative support for the idea of creating a Moravian-Silesian republic, alongside Bohemia and Slovakia. But when the Slovak leadership remained adamantly opposed, Havel dropped the idea.[20]

The Czech authorities then suggested the abolition of the federal system altogether and the reorganization of the state into three parts, with Slovakia to be divided in two. The rationale for an east-west division of Slovakia was not made clear, but in any case Slovakia's prime minister, Vladimír Mečiar, rebuffed this plan immediately. "Regarding this proposal," Mečiar recalled later, "I naturally said that this idea would perish as its authors would perish."[21]

By this point, large-scale demonstrations against alleged Czech domination of Slovakia were taking place more and more frequently. The first party to advocate complete independence for Slovakia was the Movement for Independent Slovakia, headed by Vojtech Vitkovský. Founded on 23 July 1990, the organization was thus established only after the first parliamentary elections.[22] The Slovak National Party, headed by Víťazoslav Moric, did not run on a separatist platform in the June 1990 elections, but it subsequently became the first party with parliamentary representation to advocate Slovak secession.

A year later, there were at least three more nationalist-oriented parties in Slovakia favoring secession: the Slovak People's Party, the Party of Christian Democracy, and the Party of National Prosperity. These three parties, together with the Slovak National Party, agreed to write a draft constitution modeled on that of the Nazi-sponsored quisling Slovak state of 1939–45.[23] In July 1991, a sixth secessionist party announced itself: the National Slovak Unification Party, claiming five thousand members.[24] In the meantime, a pro-independence periodical called *Nový Slovák* started publication. Its first issue reprinted in full Monsignor Jozef Tiso's speech in his own defense at his 1946 collaboration trial; Father Tiso, the wartime president of Slovakia, had received a death sentence at that trial.[25]

Unionist sentiment remained stronger than secessionist sentiment among Slovaks, however. When, for example, Slovak separatists took over the August 1990 celebration of interwar Slovak autonomist Father Andrej Hlinka, the Public Against Violence (PAV, the Slovak sister organization of the Czech Civic Forum, and then Slovakia's strongest party) issued a statement condemning the separatists.[26] Slovak prime minister Mečiar himself repeatedly affirmed his commitment to working within the framework of a political union between Czechs and Slovaks, cautioning only that the existing model was "not functional."[27] As he argued in August 1990, "We reject the accusation of trying to destroy the Czechoslovak federation. If we want to destroy something, it is centralism and bureaucracy. We want to change the federation to a better and more effective model."[28]

The nationalists then took their grievances to the streets, resulting in a rash of prosecessionist demonstrations, most notably in Bratislava. But these demonstrations were often small. A November protest, for example, attracted just three hundred participants, whose main activity was to shout various anti-Czech slogans.[29] Probably more representative of general Slovak sentiment was the Society of Normal Slovaks, set up in mid-November 1990. Forswearing any interest in political office, the society declared, on its founding, that its purpose was to provide "a counterbalance to intolerance."[30]

Escalation

As of November 1990, only 16 percent of Slovaks and 12 percent of Czechs favored dividing the country in two.[31] As already noted, the figure was scarcely much greater even in June 1992. But such figures miss the point. Such polls were taken among a cross section of the population, and inevitably many of those surveyed were politically inactive or even politically uninformed. One would have obtained a much more indicative reading from a poll among politically active Slovaks or among Slovak politicians and political figures. Such data would have revealed a much higher level of commitment to secessionism than was apparent from the more general data. Be that as it may, a number of factors contributed to a sharpening of the controversy.

First, once the initial postrevolutionary glow had worn off, public trust in the leading political figures, as well as in the dominant political parties, began to erode. More precisely, the approval rating of the (Czech) Civic Forum and its Slovak counterpart, the Public Against Violence, slid from 60 percent in February 1990 to 38 percent by October of that year.[32] Although this was not dangerous in and of itself, declining Slovak trust in Prague, Havel, and the Civic Forum satisfied a basic precondition for escalation (48 percent of Slovaks in July 1991 said they did not trust Havel).[33]

Second, Slovaks started to complain that the economic crunch was more serious in Slovakia than in the Czech lands, that unemployment in Slovakia (5.38 percent on 31 May 1991) was more than twice as high as that in the Czech Republic (2.02 percent), that the economic reform advocated by Prague, while helpful for the industrially more diverse Czech lands, was harming the Slovak economy, and that the federal cabinet's decision (later temporarily reversed) to cut back arms production would have cost seventy thousand Slovaks their jobs.[34] Slovaks complained that a currency devaluation in January 1991 was particularly harmful to Slovak enterprises. That same month, the Christian Democratic Movement of Slovakia demanded that the Slovak Republic obtain full responsibility for, and control of, taxation, customs duties, price policy, foreign economic relations, and banking within its territory.[35]

Third, Slovaks suddenly gave expression to Hungarophobic feelings. Slovaks living along the southern border with Hungary talked of feeling "threatened" by local Hungarians and said they feared efforts to Hungarianize them.[36] The leading Bratislava daily, *Pravda,* itself gave vent to these fears with a signed commentary that claimed that in Hungarian eyes, "We are again merely the upper part of pre-Trianon 'greater' Hungary."[37] Slovaks started to talk of the need to pass a language law declaring Slovak the official language of Slovakia and restricting the official use of other languages, including Hungarian and Czech.[38] As early as November 1990, Miroslav Purkrábek, adviser to the Czechoslovak deputy defense minister, called for the establishment of a Slovak army. This statement echoed a demand put forth two weeks earlier by the right-radical Slovak National Party.[39] Not surprisingly, Slovakia's minorities themselves felt threatened by the new mood. For example, Emil Ščuka, chair of the Romany Civic Initiative Movement, told *Mlada Fronta Dnes,* "We are a part of the joint Czech and Slovak Federation. We know well the consequences of the Slovak state. Jozef Tiso's visiting card was, for us, labor camps, annihilation of villages, and thousands of people tortured to death in concentration camps."[40]

And fourth, Slovaks suddenly found that with the closure of the censorship bureaus of communism, newspapers happily reported the high proportions of Slovaks who felt that the Czechs received preferential treatment (60 percent of Slovaks in July 1991)[41] and the open questions about what benefits there were for Slovaks in remaining in a common state with the Czechs.[42]

In early November 1990, Czechoslovak prime minister Marián Čalfa, Czech prime minister Petr Pithart, and Slovak prime minister Vladimír Mečiar held a series of meetings to try to hammer out a power-sharing scheme that would be satisfactory to all parties. On 13 November, Prime Minister Čalfa announced that the three had agreed on "a complete draft of amendments to the constitutional law [of] the Czechoslovak Federation in the part concerning the division of powers between the Federation and the republics."[43] The agreement allowed autonomy in many sectors for the two halves of the country, but left foreign affairs, foreign trade, the central bank, taxation, and price policy under federal control. But Slovak prime minister Mečiar said he was "disillusioned" by the compromise.[44] "The meeting produced nothing new," Mečiar commented after the talks ended. "This is the greatest tragedy."[45] A month later, as the shortcomings of the agreement became fully apparent, President Havel pleaded for unity, telling deputies, "The situation is grave. This is the toughest test that our young democracy has had to face thus far."[46] Subsequently, the Slovak National Council (SNC) prepared a draft declaration of the sovereignty of the Slovak republic.[47] Havel's reaction to this draft declaration was forceful and immediate. Addressing the nation in a public address at Bratislava Castle, Havel said that he feared that the adoption of the draft declaration would lead to the "disintegration of our entire legal order as well as the entire network of international and legal commitments that define and guarantee our common statehood. This would be the beginning of a chaotic disintegration of our state."[48] In the context of the increasing frequency of nationalistically inspired demonstrations, the reference to "chaos" was resonant.

Searching for a way out of the impasse, Havel on 13 March submitted to the public his own draft for a new federal constitution. The draft was based on the existing system, recognizing the Czech and Slovak republics as the exclusive subjects of political sovereignty. Havel's draft was immediately rejected in Moravia and Silesia, even before the Slovaks could get to it; in fact, representatives of twenty-five political parties and movements in Moravia and Silesia issued a statement, just days later, repudiating Havel's draft.[49]

As already mentioned, Havel had chosen 13 March as the day on which he would unveil his proposed constitutional draft, and he had decided to come to

Bratislava to do so as a gesture of good will toward the Slovaks. By coincidence, 14 March was the fifty-second anniversary of the founding of the quisling Slovak state, and some five thousand Slovaks gathered in downtown Bratislava to celebrate the anniversary and to listen to a tape of Tiso reading the declaration of Slovak independence on 14 March 1939. As if drawn there by fate, Havel unexpectedly turned up at the rally, surrounded by an entourage of supporters and bodyguards. Angry demonstrators spied Havel and turned on him, shouting "Judas! Judas!" "Down with Havel!" and "Away from Prague!" Scuffles broke out between Slovak nationalists and Havel's supporters. Havel was forced to run to his car but escaped unscathed, although not without watching angry demonstrators kick and spit on his car. The independent Slovak daily *Národna obrodá* called Havel's appearance at the protest "one of the greatest mistakes of his administration," while *Slovenský Denník,* the Christian-Democratic paper of Slovakia, wondered who stood to profit "from this vulgar manifestation of hatred vis-à-vis the highest state official."[50]

Controversy over the Language Bill

The Slovak language bill, debated and passed during Mečiar's tenure as prime minister, was without question the most controversial piece of legislation to be enacted in postcommunist Slovakia between 1990 and 1991.

Although there had been some inchoate grumbling about inadequate protection for Slovak speakers in predominantly Hungarian villages and towns over the months, the question was given focus by the demand, issued collectively by ten Slovak political parties in mid-August 1990, that the Slovak National Council pass a law declaring Slovak the official state language in Slovak territory.[51] Matica Slovenská, the Slovak Heritage Society, drafted a language bill that it pressed the Slovak National Council to adopt; in that draft, only Slovak would have been allowed in official and public dealings and communications in Slovakia, even in purely Hungarian villages. An overwhelming majority of Slovaks in ethnically mixed areas (78 percent in southern Slovakia) favored the designation of Slovak as the official language of the republic. But most Hungarians opposed it, fearing that discrimination and the curtailment of their basic rights would result from the measure.[52]

Aside from the draft submitted by Matica Slovenská, there were two other drafts before the Slovak National Council: one drafted by the Hungarian coalition party Coexistence (the details of which are not known) and the other prepared by the ruling coalition (the Public Against Violence, the Christian Democratic Movement, and the Slovak Democratic Party). A revised and toughened version of the coalition draft was eventually passed on 25 October

1990. In its final incarnation, the bill allowed members of a non-Slovak minority to use their language in official dealings, provided that the group comprised at least 20 percent of the local population. On the other hand, the law also banned the use of any non-Slovak names for any towns, villages, streets, squares, or geographical features in the territory of Slovakia.[53]

Despite the general toughness of the bill, Slovakia was immediately hit by a number of protests, demonstrations, and hunger strikes by Slovaks who resented the loophole left for the continued use of Hungarian and other minority languages. The aforementioned Vít'azoslav Moric, then chair of the Slovak National Council, condemned the bill, demanded that SNC deputies resign in order to set the stage for new elections, and called for protest actions, including acts of civil disobedience, until a new, more nationalist parliament that would pass a tougher law could be elected.[54] Moreover, within two weeks of the bill's passage, those Slovak organizations that preferred the tougher draft submitted by Matica Slovenská formed the National Salvation Front to work for "appropriate" amendments to the law. The same concern prompted the founding of the Authentic Party in Slovakia on 10 November.[55]

The Bratislava newspaper *Verejnost'* fanned the flames of Hungarophobia in Slovakia,[56] while Matica Slovenská, emboldened by the provisions of the new law, took aim at "unlawful" bilingual signs in predominantly (or in some cases, purely) Hungarian villages. As Matica Slovenská noted, with obvious satisfaction, "According to the law, these names are to be denoted in the Slovak language [only]."[57]

The Rise and Fall of Mečiar

Prime Minister Mečiar of Slovakia had been striking a careful balance. On the one hand, he had repeatedly avowed his commitment to the federation and had eschewed any endorsement of separatism. On the other hand, he had stressed nationalist concerns and had won for himself the strong and enthusiastic approval of Slovakia's nationalist associations. Thus, many people thought that Mečiar was really a separatist, and his tactics were too convoluted to allow his protestations that he was not a separatist to be taken at face value.

Mečiar and his followers had argued for months that the Public Against Violence should adopt a more nationalist stance. By March, tensions between Mečiar's faction and his opponents had reached a fever pitch. Mečiar wanted to control the party apparatus in Slovakia. He had tried but failed on 23 February to wrest the chairmanship of the party from Fedor Gál, a political ally of Havel, and to assume the chairmanship himself. Failing in that, Mečiar and his followers decided to break with the PAV and to set up their own organization, which they called the Movement for a Democratic Slovakia. The new party announced itself on 5 March.[58] On 11 March 1991, Mečiar sent a letter to branches of the Public Against Violence claiming that the program he had been pursuing and that he and his movement intended to pursue was fully in consonance with the original program of PAV. This was a barefaced attempt to woo the local branches away from the PAV hierarchy.

Rumors began to circulate that Mečiar would soon be ousted as prime minister.[59] Leading PAV figures raised questions about implied improprieties during Mečiar's visit to the USSR on 13–15 March in connection with talks about the sale of tanks to the USSR and guarantees for Slovak-Ukrainian borders.[60] *Verejnost'* claimed that Mečiar was paving the way for dictatorship by sowing rampant confusion in people's minds.[61] Other critics accused him of "using files of the former communist secret police to blackmail his political opponents."[62] Events moved very quickly, and on 19 March Mečiar's opponents authorized two parliamentary commissions to investigate the activities of Slovakia's interior ministry since the communists' fall from power in November–December 1989. The investigations were obviously intended to legitimize Mečiar's removal from office. Aside from Mečiar's factional grouping, only the Democratic Left (the former communists) supported the embattled prime minister. Finally, on 23 April, Mečiar and seven other ministers were dismissed from their posts on orders from the presidium of the Slovak National Council.

Like a latter-day Anteas, Mečiar semed to grow even stronger in defeat. The day after his dismissal, for example, some one hundred thousand supporters congregated on the main square of Bratislava to demand early elections and his return to office.[63] A more persuasive measure of Mečiar's popularity was provided by opinion polls taken at the time of his removal: when he was removed from office, the Slovak government's approval rating among Slovaks plummeted from 69 percent to 22 percent.[64] Within a matter of months, Mečiar built his new organization into the strongest party in Slovakia. By July 1991, polls showed that Mečiar's Movement for a Democratic Slovakia commanded 39 percent of the electorate, far ahead of the second-place Christian Democratic Movement's 17 percent. The Slovak National Party placed third with 13 percent, and the Party of the Democratic Left held fourth place with 9 percent. What was left of the old Public Against Violence was in sixth place, with a meager 4 percent of the electorate.[65]

From his position of strength, Mečiar proposed in August that his party be co-opted into the government and that a "grand coalition" be created. The Christian Democratic Movement, whose relatively unloved Ján Čarnogurský had been handed the prime ministership after Mečiar's removal, rebuffed Mečiar.[66] Yet, though out of office, Mečiar easily remained Slovakia's most popular politician.[67]

Pressure for an Independent Slovakia

In March 1991, both Mečiar and his Christian Democratic successor, Ján Čarnogurský, were still eschewing separatism. Six months later, both men had gravitated toward the separatist camp. This move on their part necessarily contributed to making Slovak secession seem more practical than it had at first appeared. Regardless of the minority appeal of secession, the nationalists were clearly politically ascendant and the most vocal and best organized opinion group in Slovakia.

This growth of secessionist strength was a logical consequence of the breakdown of the tripartite talks in Lány on 10 May 1991. Organized on the initiative of President Havel, the Lány talks involved representatives from the Slovak, Czech, and federal governments and legislatures. All sides agreed that the new federal constitution should be preceded by a treaty between the Czech and Slovak Republics. But the Czech representatives refused to go along with a Slovak suggestion that the federal constitution be subject to ratification by the national councils of the two republics.[68]

Interviewed two months later by the French daily, *Libération,* Čarnogurský revealed that he had given up on Czechoslovakia in the time since Lany. Slovakia's independence, he told *Libération*'s reporter, was inevitable.[69] Mečiar's advocacy of independence was somewhat softened by his continued support for a confederative arrangement, but even he argued that "if Slovak statehood is to take its final shape, then it must be put into practice with all its attributes. We must not go halfway."[70] Mečiar still argued for a state treaty between the Slovak Republic and the Czech Republic and urged coordination in foreign policy (perhaps including a shared foreign policy apparatus), common currency, common defense, and common executive bodies to promote "respect [for] our common interests."[71] Meanwhile, the Slovak public was faced with Christian Democrat Jan Klepac's proposal to establish a "Slovak Home Guard"—a proposal also supported by the extreme nationalist Slovak National Party. *Lidové noviny* expressed concern that the only logical "enemy" against which a Slovak armed force might be needed was the Czechoslovak federal army[72]— which was, of course, the whole point.

Certain Czech politicians, Havel included, offered to call a referendum on the future of the country, but the leading Slovak nationalists consistently rebuffed them, realizing that recourse to a vote would, at least at that point, take the wind out of the sails of separatism. Finally, in mid-November 1991, after debating the question of a referendum for several hours, the Federal Assembly shelved the idea, having failed to muster the required three-fifths majority.[73] Slovak nationalists preferred to take politics to the streets, and Bratislava was repeatedly the scene of separatist demonstrations. Inevitably, the resultant polarization of Slovak public opinion also affected the Slovak parliament.[74]

Federalists continued to hope that the controversy could be defused through the adoption of a new federal constitution, though they were loath to go as far in a confederative direction as Mečiar indicated. On the contrary, Czech parliamentary president Burešová expressly ruled out the signing of a state treaty in the sense of international law, while Czech prime minister Pithart criticized the Slovak claim to the word "sovereignty."[75] Havel made various proposals for a constitutional revision, including the expansion of the powers of the president, the restructuring of the assembly as a bicameral legislature in which one house would consist of delegates from the two constituent republics, a new election law, and the redrawing of boundaries for the jurisdiction of the republics.[76] By contrast, Jozef Belcák, the Slovak minister of economics, outlined a solution more favorable to Slovak demands, envisaging a confederative arrangement.[77]

Havel set in motion a new round of constitutional talks in November 1991, but these broke down before the month was out, leading foreign observers to question whether Czech and Slovak politicians would be able to preserve their federation for long.[78] By the end of 1991, advocates of Slovak secession had come to include not merely the Slovak National Party and a scattering of smaller parties, but also Mečiar's Movement for a Democratic Slovakia and the Democratic Left chaired by Peter Weiss. The Democratic Party (of Slovakia) and the Democratic Citizens' Union (formerly the Public Against Violence) remained loyal to the federation. And the Christian Democrats still tried to steer a course between these two extremes, even though Čarnogurský had openly declared that independence was only a matter of time.[79]

The Czech-Slovak controversy, therefore, unfolded against a backdrop of rising nationalist discontent among Moravians, Silesians, Hungarians, Romany, and even the few ethnic Germans who remained in the country. The Czech-Slovak controversy thus served as a catalyst for the unfolding of a much more complex set of issues, which in turn contributed to a largely veiled complexity in the Czech-Slovak discord.

The Battle over the Constitution

In January 1992, President Havel submitted a proposal for a constitutional amendment to authorize him, as president, to call for a national referendum without obtaining parliamentary approval. The Slovak deputies in the parliament blocked the proposal.[80] This was a setback for Havel, but not the end of the story. A joint commission of the Czech National Council and the Slovak

National Council on 8 February submitted a draft constitution for the Czech and Slovak Republic to the parliament for consideration. Interestingly, Article 1.3 contained the following assurance:

> The two republics respect each other's sovereignty and the sovereignty of the common state. Each of the two republics can secede from the common state or divide it by way of consent. This can be done only on the basis of the direct expression of the will of the majority of its citizens in a general vote.[81]

But this clause had the same disadvantage, as far as the Slovak nationalists were concerned, as the employment of a presidentially authorized referendum: it would have allowed the citizens to scuttle the secessionist ship. The Slovak parliament objected to this, as well as to references to a unified economic market and the refusal of the drafters to describe the text as an accord between two sovereign republics. On 12 February, the Slovak parliament rejected the proposed text. Six days later, Slovak deputies in the federal parliament defeated three amendments designed to redefine the relations between the president and the parliament and to reform the structure of the federal parliament.[82]

As a result, the June 1992 elections were conducted on the basis of the pre-existing framework and parliamentary structure. The campaign was easily dominated by Vladimír Mečiar, whom opinion polls judged to be easily the most trusted politician in Slovakia, with an approval rating of 47 percent—far ahead of second-place Alexander Dubček (24 percent), let alone Havel (16 percent) or Slovakia's then–prime minister, Ján Čarnogurský, (13 percent).[83] Mečiar hammered home two central points: that the common state should be converted into a confederation, and that Slovakia's economy was being hurt by Prague's policy of rapid marketization.

For Czechoslovakia as a whole, the reforms undertaken by federal finance minister Václav Klaus seemed, by June, to be proving their worth, albeit at a cost. After an unprecedented 29 percent decline in industrial production between January 1990 and the end of 1991, output was once more on the rise, fueled, in part, by an encouragingly steady flow of foreign investment. Meanwhile, inflation was lowered from 58 percent in 1991 to an annual rate of around 10 percent by April 1992. Real wages and savings were once more on the upswing, and exports registered a strong recovery in the first half of 1992 after a 30 percent drop between 1989 and 1991.[84]

The difficulty was that the economic recovery was concentrated in the Czech lands, which were garnering the lion's share of foreign investments. In 1991, for instance, of the $640 million in foreign investments, only 13 percent went to Slovakia. Since 1989, less than 20 percent of foreign investment had gone to Slovakia.[85] And while unemployment among Czechs edged upward from 2 percent in May 1991 to 3 percent in June 1992, unemployment among Slovaks in the same period swelled alarmingly, from 5.4 percent to nearly 15 percent.

There were, of course, explanations for this differential. Slovak industry was much more oriented to the now-collapsed Soviet market than the more Western-oriented Czech economy. Moreover, the arms industry in Slovakia, a linchpin of that republic's economy, suffered seriously from the contraction of its arms market following the close of the Warsaw Pact. Hardest hit in Slovakia were single-industry towns like Martin in central Slovakia, where the more than ten thousand workers who were once employed to build Soviet tanks were thrown out of work virtually overnight.[86] Mečiar built his strength above all among disgruntled industrial workers in Slovakia, whether unemployed or underpaid.[87] Mečiar demanded that Slovakia be allowed to establish its own central bank and to regulate its own privatization programs, promising to slow down the pace of privatization.

The elections of 8 June 1992 produced no surprises. In the Czech Republic, Václav Klaus's Civic Democratic Party (and coalition) won just over 33 percent of the Czech vote for the federal parliament and about 30 percent of the vote for the Czech parliament. In the Slovak Republic, Mečiar's Movement for a Democratic Slovakia (HZDS) likewise garnered about a third of the Slovak vote for the federal parliament and about 37 percent of the vote for the Slovak parliament. These results left Klaus and Mečiar as the two strongest politicians in the country. Two weeks later, Mečiar was returned to the Slovak prime ministership, swearing to abolish the federal ("lustration") law forbidding former high-ranking communist officials and secret police agents from holding public office for five years.[88]

A Fast Divorce

Klaus and Mečiar immediately entered into discussions to find a common political formula. The differences in economic orientation alone proved insuperable, however, and at the end of the first day of talks, they had agreed only on the need to substantially cut back the apparatus of the federal government, reducing, in particular, the number of ministries and deputy premiers.[89] It was a telling sign of things to come.

In further discussions, Mečiar, in fact, urged confederalization, but Klaus rejected this, arguing that what the Slovaks wanted was "to build the future institutions of an independent republic with federal subsidies."[90] Klaus's position was all or nothing—a closed marriage or a divorce.[91] Finally, on 19 June, after ten days of discussions, the two men announced that they had reached an agreement to split the state.[92] The division of the state was expected to be especially expensive for Slovakia, which would have to find suitable facilities for new institutions of government in Bratislava.[93]

Havel's protests that the citizens should be given a chance to express their opinions via a referendum on so momentous a step were brushed aside. At the same time, the antifederal momentum kindled a new nationalism among Czechs, some of whom began circulating a petition in support of Czech independence. By 17 June they had already collected thirty thousand signatures.[94]

In Slovakia, there was now a new mood. The Mečiar government immediately backed away from efforts to wind down state control of the economy, declaring that although private shares would be allowed, the government would retain controlling shares in larger enterprises. The Mečiar government also declared its intention to curb newly won press freedoms, to renationalize Danubiaprint, the monopoly printer for newspapers, and to assert a monopoly control in television broadcasting.[95] There were also renewed calls to tighten limits on the use of the Hungarian language in Slovakia.

The Hungarian minority in southern Slovakia had supported the federation but feared now that Slovak nationalism would become intolerant. Representatives of the Hungarian minority requested autonomous status for the regions with a local Hungarian majority[96]—a call subsequently endorsed and promoted by the Hungarian government in Budapest.[97] Deputy Premier Rudolf Filkus, however, quickly rejected "as unjustified the . . . view that Hungarians in Slovakia have the right to autonomy."[98]

Mečiar's Political Resilience

Mečiar's second term as prime minister lasted until March 1994. During this term, he offended sensibilities with scarcely veiled expressions of anti-Semitism,[99] encroached on the independence of Slovak media, and displayed an overbearing manner toward his fellow ministers. In March 1994, Mečiar was ousted from power—as before, through a parliamentary coup. Behind the coup was President Michal Kováč, a long-standing critic of Mečiar's style. The coup brought Jozef Moravčík to the prime ministership, supported by a four-party coalition. The Moravčík government quickly restored Slovak credibility in the West, brought the state budget under control, and curbed the increase in unemployment.[100]

But Moravčík remained in office less than a year. Mečiar took the elections in October 1994 and returned to the prime ministership the following month for his third nonconsecutive term of office. Mečiar's first official act was to appoint trusted political allies to take charge of state radio and television and the state regulatory agency supervising the media. The new director of state radio soon curtailed news and feature programs that had included free discussions of current political issues. In the wake of subsequent fiscal measures discriminating against nonparty papers, more than one hundred thousand Slovak citizens signed a petition charging the government with violating freedom of speech.[101] In the months that followed, as Adam Lewin has pointed out, Bratislava

> purged the civil service and state media of those suspected of being insufficiently loyal [to Mečiar], cut the budget of judges not in good standing with the government, tried to expel the opposition from the parliament under alleged electoral fraud, and even cut funds to cities that dared to elect opposition governments, including Bratislava. Opposition leaders have [even] claimed they have been assaulted in the streets by thugs not interested in robbing them.[102]

By the end of 1995, the intelligence service, the interior ministry, and even the judiciary were outside the control of the parliament.[103]

An opinion poll conducted in November 1995 found that 51 percent of Slovaks believed that human rights were not adequately respected in their country, while 67 percent said they were dissatisfied with the state of progress toward democracy in Slovakia. (Only 27 percent of Slovaks said they were satisfied with Slovak democracy, on the other hand.)[104] A subsequent poll conducted three months later found that fully 46 percent of Slovaks disagreed with the domestic policies of Mečiar's HZDS, exceeding the 44 percent who expressed agreement with HZDS policies.[105]

Authoritarianism, Slovak Style

By 1996, NATO and European Union officials were talking of Slovakia as an embarrassment, a country that should not expect rapid admission into the ranks of their respective international organizations.[106] Slovakia was increasingly coming to be viewed as a pariah state, thanks entirely to Mečiar's political behavior and policies.

Given that the Czech and Slovak republics shared a common institutional and legislative infrastructure until the latter part of 1992, one is entitled to ask why that infrastructure proved adequate as a vehicle for democratization in the Czech Republic and inadequate in Slovakia. Although there are important differences between the Czech and Slovak regions in economic structure, confessional affiliation, level of urbanization, and historical memories, I believe that differences in political leadership suffice to account for most of the differences between these two republics in their respective post-communist transitions. To put it simply, where the Czech Republic has had Havel and Klaus to guide it in its initial years after decommunization, Slovakia has had Mečiar, a former boxer, former communist, and highly charismatic populist.

Characteristic of Mečiar's political style is his choice of coalition partners. Instead of looking to moderate political parties for support and legitimation (no doubt bearing in mind that moderate coalition partners had removed him from office on two previous occasions), Mečiar established his 1994 coalition government with the extreme-nationalist Slovak National Party (SNS, led by Ján Slota, mayor of Žilina)[107] and the neobolshevik Association of Workers of Slovakia (ZRS, led by Ján L'upták).[108] Mečiar has attracted controversy. After all, it is not every politician who is called "a lying, double-talking, power-crazy tyrant who is driving Slovakia down the road to ruin."[109] But it is also not every politician who, moments after being sworn in as prime minister, sets about railroading through a package of measures (thirteen in all) that the *New York Times* claimed "sent Slovakia reeling back to the bad old days."[110] In the course of the all-night session in which Mečiar accomplished this feat, the parliament canceled the privatization legislation worked out by the previous government, granted Mečiar the authority to remove the director of the National Property Fund, and approved the appointment of Ivan Lexa, an old crony of Mečiar's, to head the Slovak Information Service, the successor to the old secret police.

But of all Mečiar's moves, it was his policies vis-à-vis the media that, at least in the early months of his third term, excited the sharpest criticism. Concerns about the erosion of the independence of the press and broadcasting had been voiced before Mečiar's third term.[111] But with the dismissal of the general director of Slovak Television and Radio came politically motivated changes in station staffing and political interference in program composition.[112] Among the other changes were the firing of Slovak Radio director Vladimír Štefko, who was replaced by Ján Tužinský, a Mečiar loyalist, and "replacement of senior officials in most of the Parliament-elected bodies" monitoring broadcasting.[113] Tužinský promptly announced "that Slovak Radio was broadcasting too much news and that it needed to be transformed into an institution that would produce more cultural and educational programs and help to 'strengthen the nation's conscience.'"[114] These moves did not go unnoticed, and there were repeated demonstrations by eight thousand to ten thousand persons at a time in downtown Bratislava protesting the constriction of broadcast freedom in Slovakia.[115]

Mečiar's government used the power of the purse and its authority to make key appointments to establish its control of the broadcast media. The Mečiar government's modus operandi has been to snuff out investigative reporting, keep criticism and opposition viewpoints off the air, and limit news to the official line.[116] With state radio and television in its pocket, the Mečiar government has been content to turn a blind eye to the critical reportage of such opposition papers as *Smena* (and its successor, *Sme*) and *Národná obroda* that, in any event, reach only a small number of readers. At the same time, Mečiar saw to it that the unofficial organ of his HZDS, *Slovenská Republika,* enjoyed a privileged position in the contest to produce a supplement for the Ministry of Defense and thereby obtain a lucrative defense subsidy.[117] Perhaps it is not surprising, under the circumstances, that almost one out of every five Slovak citizens prefers to watch Czech television, according to a poll conducted in December 1995 and January 1996.[118]

Slovak president Michal Kováč, who had orchestrated Mečiar's removal in March 1994, remained his foe. Among other things, Kováč pushed for the establishment of an independent body to supervise state television. Mečiar fought back by cutting the president's office budget in half,[119] staging a symbolic no-confidence vote against Kováč in the parliament and conspiring to push Kováč out of office altogether,[120] and, failing that, trying to discredit the president in the eyes of the Slovak public.[121] Members of the Slovak Information Service at one point discussed the possible use of a fabricated file to implicate Kováč as an alleged collaborator with the communist-era secret police.[122] Then on 31 August 1995 came the kidnapping of the president's son, thirty-four-year-old Michal Kováč Jr. The younger Kováč was driven to Austria by his captors and delivered into the hands of the Austrian police. Wanted in Germany under an international warrant in connection with a $2 million fraud, he was eventually returned to Slovakia after an Austrian court ruled that his freedom of movement had been violated.[123] But as early as October, the case investigator implicated the Slovak Information Service in the kidnapping of the younger Kováč, who suggested that the entire affair had been designed to undermine his father's position.[124]

There have been protests from time to time. On 14 July 1995, for example, some two hundred artists and intellectuals signed a statement accusing the government of "conjur[ing] up an atmosphere of hatred and fear that is dangerously reminiscent of the 1940s, 1950s, and 1970s,"[125] specifically protesting the centralization of the management of state cultural institutions, the firing of state gallery directors, and the government's "lack of respect for the plurality of contemporary art."[126] In November of that year, some five hundred members of the Forum of the Slovak Intelligentsia issued a statement criticizing Mečiar for "polarizing and brutalizing" Slovak society and for "destroying the country's democratic institutions."[127] Referring to Mečiar's pugilist past, the statement claimed that the prime minister was turning Slovakia into a "boxing ring" in which the prime minister's opponents were being politically trounced.[128]

Mečiar scarcely calmed such fears when, in March 1996, he told a press conference that he anticipated the necessity of a "total revision" of Slovakia's constitution, settling in particular the question of whether the system would be parliamentary, presidential, or based on a chancellery.[129] That this question had ramifications for the struggle between Mečiar and Kováč was certainly clear to all present.

The Hungarians of Slovakia

During the years 1945–92, there was a close correlation between Slovak and Hungarian autonomism in southern Slovakia. In periods when power was centralized and Slovak autonomism muted or suppressed, the Hungarian population of southern Slovakia was quiescent. But whenever the relaxation of the reins allowed Slovaks to make a bid for greater autonomy from Prague (or, in 1992, for independence), Slovakia's Hungarians registered parallel demands vis-à-vis Bratislava. It was thus only to be expected that the new stridency in Slovak politics signaled by the adoption of the language bill of 1990 should inevitably elicit some reaction from ethnic Hungarians, who suddenly saw their language, culture, and civil rights imperiled. At first, as already discussed, ethnic Hungarian parties thought in terms of territorial autonomy for the area populated by ethnic Hungarians. By 1994, however, these parties had moved from demands for autonomy to demands for local control of education and to guarantees for the preservation of historical names of towns and streets.

Until 1991, the standards for respect of the rights of ethnic minorities had been set by Constitutional Law No. 144 of the ČSSR (adopted in 1968). On 9 January 1991, a new document, "The Charter of Fundamental Rights and Freedoms," was adopted by the Federal Assembly, but by then the centrifugal energies were already gaining momentum. In September 1992, on the eve of independence, the Slovak Assembly adopted a new constitution over the protests of the thirty deputies of ethnic Hungarian parties. The Hungarians objected to several sections of the constitution, most especially to a section entitled "Rights of National Minorities and Ethnic Groups," which, in their eyes, "suggested that the national minorities and ethnic groups constituted a potentially destabilizing and subversive element, and that the pursuit of their interests may run contrary to the fulfillment of the rights of other citizens not belonging to that particular community."[130]

In June 1993, the parliamentary deputies of the Hungarian Christian Democratic Movement (HCDM) and Együttélés (Political Movement for Democracy and the Rights of the National Minority) proposed a kind of bill of rights that would be appended to the section of the Slovak constitution dealing with national minorities. They pointed out that some 14.7 percent of citizens of Slovakia are non-Slovaks. In a key passage, their proposed draft stated:

> On the territories where the ratio of population belonging to a minority community exceeds 10 percent, the state shall ensure the possibility of the usage of their mother tongue in offices and courts of justice both in written and spoken form. Prints, forms, and bills shall be bilingual in those regions. The names of municipalities, streets, public institutions and public services shall be indicated in the language of the minority community, too.[131]

But the opposition Slovak parties failed to rally to the support of this measure, which therefore died on the table.

Meanwhile, Slovakia had gained admission to the Council of Europe on 3 June 1993, on the strength of the Mečiar government's promises to liberalize its minority policies. But the Mečiar government failed to deliver on its promises. Instead, as David Lucas explains,

> after a brief flirtation with compliance with the Council's standards on minority rights, as evidenced by the drafting of a relatively liberal law on the use of minority languages with names and surnames on 7 July, the Slovak government reverted to oppressive measures against the Hungarian minority in blatant and intentional disregard for Council of Europe standards. In early August, pursuant to a directive issued by Slovak Transport Minister Roman Hofbauer, bilingual road signs in ethnically mixed areas in southern Slovakia began to be removed. . . . The removal of bilingual signs evoked a sharp protest from the Hungarian minority. On 13 August 1993, László Sooky, Mayor of Marcelova, ordered a blockade of his town as a form of civil disobedience.[132]

As many as five thousand persons took part in a peaceful protest in Komárno on 27 August against Bratislava's minority policy .

Mečiar ignored the protests of Hungarian parties and proceeded with plans to Slovakize the names of ethnic Hungarian towns and villages, promote Slovak-language education in ethnic Hungarian municipalities through the vehicle of so-called bilingual schools (in which certain subjects would be taught in Slovak), and gerrymander electoral districts in order to reduce ethnic Hungarian strength in the parliament. These moves were slowed by Mečiar's removal from office on 11 March 1994. The Moravčík government set to work on a compromise bill regarding names of towns and villages, providing for bilingual identification of most municipalities but with exceptions for certain towns and villages where there were persuasive historical arguments against making any change. The HCDM accepted this law as an acceptable compromise, while Együttélés construed it as a defeat.

As already mentioned, the three ethnic Hungarian parties—the Hungarian Civic Party (led by László Nagy), the HCDM (led by Béla Bugár), and Együttélés (led by Miklós Duray)—had eventually ruled out territorial autonomy as a goal. But they were, nonetheless, agreed on the necessity of obtaining the right of self-administration in the spheres of culture and education.[133] In May there were reports that the Moravčík government had signed a secret agreement with leaders of the ethnic Hungarian parties; the agreement was said to have promised to end the promotion of bilingual education in areas inhabited by Hungarians and to transfer the care of schools and cultural institutions to community self-administrative bodies.[134] The coalition also promised to set up an independent department for ethnic minorities' schools within the framework of the Ministry of Education and Science.[135]

The public discourse about the rights of Hungarians evoked diverse responses from Slovaks. Some protested what they feared amounted to a "continuing policy of acquiescing to the demands of Hungarian politicians, whose aim is to achieve autonomy" and accused the latter of "chipping away at the teaching of Slovak in Hungarian schools."[136] Meetings were organized at which Hungarian demands were said "to pose a permanent threat to the language and ethnic sovereignty of Slovaks in their own state."[137] But Hungarians could, at the same time, take heart from a statement prepared by a student initiative group at the University of Bratislava and read to some fifteen thousand citizens in downtown Bratislava. Although not explicitly addressing the question of the civil rights of Hungarians, the statement emphasized as its central point that authentic democracy includes respect for the interests and perspectives of minorities.[138] Differences among Slovaks with regard to the representations of spokespersons for the Hungarian minority were also reflected in opinion poll data. A Focus poll conducted in May 1994, for example, found that 63 percent of Slovaks felt that Hungarians were entitled to bilingual signs in areas where they constituted 50 percent or more of the population, with 62 percent agreeing with the signs where Hungarians constituted between 20 and 49 percent of the local population. Even for districts where Hungarians constitute less than 1 percent of the local population, some 45 percent of Slovak respondents felt that bilingual signs were justified—a token of remarkable tolerance among ordinary citizens.[139] Moreover, as *Národná obroda* reported at the time, "the minority's demand to write Christian names and surnames in the[ir] native language is now encountering somewhat greater understanding among citizens of Slovak nationality."[140]

The sundry interrelated controversies affecting the rights of Slovakia's Hungarians were played out against the backdrop of negotiations between

Bratislava and Budapest concerning a so-called basic treaty. Bratislava wanted Budapest to forswear any irredentist notions vis-à-vis southern Slovakia, and in exchange Budapest wanted Bratislava to guarantee the collective rights of its citizens of ethnic Hungarian stock. A treaty worked out by late spring 1995 seemed to satisfy these desiderata, and in June 1995, the Hungarian parliament ratified the document. The Budapest daily newspaper *Magyar Hírlap* offered an optimistic prognosis at the time. "Although Slovakia has not yet ratified it," *Magyar Hírlap* opined, "the Hungarian-Slovak basic treaty has in practice come into force. Its principle, according to which the Hungarian Government has a say in whether Slovakia observes the rights of the Hungarian minority, is being applied in practice."[141]

But the high-level contacts between the respective governments proved to be little more than a formality. In spite of repeated and voluble protests on the part of both local ethnic Hungarian politicians and representatives of Budapest, Mečiar continued with policies viewed with trepidation and alarm by socially aware Hungarians. As early as March 1995, László Nagy, chair of the Hungarian Civic Party, accused the Mečiar regime of having developed plans "for abolishing the Hungarian[-language] school system."[142] A petition campaign in early 1995 registered the opposition of some forty-five thousand ethnic Hungarians to the introduction of classes with Slovak-language instruction in Hungarian schools, while some eleven thousand persons signed a subsequent petition in July protesting the government's dismissal of Anna Hechtova and László Kovacs from positions of responsibility in local schools.[143]

Hungarian protests notwithstanding, the Slovak parliament passed a school law in April 1995 stripping local authorities and schools of the right to appoint and recall school directors and giving it to the Ministry of Education in Bratislava.[144] The Mečiar government also rescinded other devolutionary measures implemented during the brief tenure of Moravčík and favorable to local authorities and pushed ahead with the promotion of bilingual education. Béla Bugar, chair of the HCDM, accused the government of having threatened Hungarian teachers with dismissal unless they supported the bilingual concept,[145] while Duna Television charged that the Slovak Ministry of Education had used intimidation tactics to pressure nursery school principals to cooperate and to hire ethnic Slovaks to teach in totally Hungarian nurseries. In despair, some parents talked of keeping their children out of school rather than expose them to systematic denationalization.[146]

At the same time that the school controversy escalated, the Ministry of Culture drafted a new law on the state language of the Slovak Republic, a bill tougher than the 1990 law. Among other things, the bill provided that all employees of state agencies, including those at the local level, should use Slovak in the performance of all their official functions, required that "public acts" by religious bodies (e.g., church weddings) be conducted exclusively in Slovak, and even prescribed that local ethnic Hungarian cultural events be introduced in Slovak, with Slovak informational brochures made available.[148] The bill further provided for the establishment of a supervisory agency to oversee the purity of the Slovak language and to impose fines as high as one million crowns ($40,000) for the use of Czechisms and Americanisms in Slovak speech; English words such as "pub," "drink," and "popcorn," hitherto commonplace in Slovak speech, would henceforth be illegal.[149] The bill was referred to the parliamentary Committee for Public Administration, Territorial Self-Administration, and Ethnic Minorities in August 1995. In heated exchanges on 23 August, László Szigeti, the only ethnic Hungarian serving on the committee, blasted the proposed law as unconstitutional, charging that the measures would deprive members of ethnic minorities of basic rights.[150] The following day, amid continuing polemics in committee discussion, Slovak deputies accused Miklós Duray, the Együttélés leader, of "trying to build an ethnic minority ghetto."[151] Duray introduced a proposal that the bill be withdrawn, calling its provisions "fascistic."[152] In reply, the HZDS issued a statement calling Duray's comments "grossly offensive and an abuse of free speech." The HZDS statement added that Duray's comments proved that the ethnic Hungarian leader was "disloyal" to the Slovak Republic.[153]

Matica Slovenská, the Slovak Cultural Society, pressed the parliament to adopt the controversial bill, which the parliament did in mid-November 1995. Leaders of the ethnic Hungarian parties met with Slovak president Kováč on 24 November and told him that they considered several sections of the language bill unconstitutional.[154] Two days later, Slovak National Party deputy Vít'azoslav Moric made a reply of sorts, declaring that "Hungarian political parties should not exist in Slovakia."[155]

In the final week of March 1996, the Slovak parliament passed three bills that, taken collectively, signaled a clear commitment to an authoritarian-nationalist line. The first bill, adopted on 22 March, rearranged Slovakia into eight administrative regions and seventy-nine counties. With boundaries bearing little resemblance to either historical demarcations or economic divisions, the restructuring had the effect of preventing Hungarians from consituting more than 30 percent of the population of any county.[156]

The second bill, adopted on 26 March, amended the penal code, authorizing penalties of up to two years' imprisonment for citizens convicted of "disseminating false information abroad damaging to the interests of the republic."[157] Stiff penalties were also prescribed for organizers of public rallies deemed to be subversive of the constitutional order or injurious to the territorial integrity of the country.[158] The bill was clearly aimed at ethnic Hungarian spokespersons; Duray, for one, would have been jailed for his earlier criticism of the language bill had the antisubversion amendment been on the books at the time. But the measure had potential consequences for other sectors of Slovak society as well. "The law can put pressure on journalists to practise self-censorship and create an environment of fear," said Karol Ježík, chief editor of the independent newspaper *Sme*.[159] Even as a parliamentary majority passed the bill, deputies from opposition parties shouted warnings that the measure would revive communist-style repression. The bill passed by the relatively narrow margin of 77 to 57.

The third bill was an addendum to the basic treaty with Hungary and was passed on 27 March in the same session that saw the belated ratification of the treaty. The interpretive addendum, adopted unilaterally without consultation with Hungarian authorities, held that the treaty with Hungary did not bind Bratislava to recognize collective rights for the Hungarian minority.[160] This addendum appeared to contradict the thrust of the treaty to which it had been appended.[161] A despondent Duray drew the inevitable conclusion from this triad of legislative acts. "Our present situation in Slovakia," he told Hungarian Radio, "can only be compared to two periods in history: the few years following 1945, which we call the era of repression of rights, and the fifties."[162]

Of these three bills, the amendment to the penal code aroused the most opposition. Deputies of the Democratic Union, the Christian Democratic Movement, the HCDM, and Együttélés expressed their opposition, vowing to kill the amendment before the end of the summer.[163] The Slovak (Catholic) Bishops' Conference, civic groups, judges, and certain trade unions also protested the amendment.[164] For his part, Slovak president Kováč refused to sign the bill, returning it to the parliament unsigned. But Mečiar expressed confidence that he could marshal enough votes to override the presidential veto.[165] Ironically, as the political stage was rocked with charges and counter-charges of threats to democracy and the constitutional order, most Slovaks remained ignorant of the controversial amendment. According to an April 1996 poll, 52 percent of Slovaks admitted they did not know about the amendment's provisions, 40 percent claimed to have a "rough idea" of its provisions, and only 8 percent said they had a detailed knowledge of the amendment's content. But in a finding that might well have surprised the bill's critics, of those claiming to have some knowledge of the amendment, 59 percent said the bill was necessary.[166]

Among those registering a strong protest was the Committee to Protect Journalists, whose executive chair, William Orme, sent a letter to President Kováč and Prime Minister Mečiar, warning that the bill would return Slovakia to conditions similar to those prevailing under Husák.[167]

Meanwhile, the government proposed an amendment to the law concerning the rights of Matica Slovenská, a patriotic cultural association that supported the ruling coalition. Under the terms of the proposal, the institutes for history and literature of the Slovak Academy of Sciences would be placed under the auspices of Matica Slovenská. The *Prague Post* noted that Matica Slovenská "stands for, among other things, historical exoneration of the clericofascist wartime leader Jozef Tiso, a whittling down of minority rights and freedoms, and a revival of Slovak nationalistic feeling" and warned that the measure would entrust the patriotic association with the right of oversight over all research and publications at the two institutes.[168] Dušan Kováč, the director of the Institute of History, spoke for many in warning, "During the last 60 years, we've tried everything to free ourselves of ideology. Now, the last six years of work will be completely destroyed, and we will become a machine for . . . propaganda."[169] Foes of authoritarianism have fought back, establishing a parliamentary organ for monitoring the secret service and offering the prospect of including opposition appointees in its ranks.[170]

In June 1996, Slovak president Michal Kováč paid a visit to Hungary, where the Budapest government impressed upon him the importance it attached to Bratislava's passing legislation to protect the language rights of Slovak Hungarians.[171] About two months later, Budapest returned to the theme, this time issuing a call for an assurance of autonomy for Slovakia's Hungarians.[172] The call did not have its intended effect, instead evoking protests from Bratislava.

Conclusion

As of 1995–96, the Hungarian minority in Slovakia numbered about 560,000 persons, or about 11 percent of the country's total population.[173] Both the absolute number and the percentage were eerily similar to the comparable figures for the proportion of Serbs in Croatia as of April 1991. But it was not until May 1995 that Slovaks started to worry that a comparison might go further than this. Specifically, on 20 May 1995, supporters of the Spartak Trnava and DAC Dunajská Streda soccer clubs clashed in what was described as "the first case of ethnically motivated violence in Slovakia."[174] Several Slovak papers observed, with concern, that the bloodshed in Croatia and Bosnia had started with similar incidents. Ondrej Dostál, a commentator for *Sme,* blamed the "fueling of ethnic intolerance, hatred, and bigotry" on "nationalistic politicians, to be found in large numbers particularly in the ruling coalition."[175] In a similar vein, František Buda, a commentator for the Bratislava daily *Pravda,* warned that "even the greatest fire originates from a small spark," cautioning about the dangers of an escalation with "far-reaching consequences."[176]

But just as in Yugoslavia, where the kindling of the fires of collective identity and the awakening of claims to collective rights began among the numerically predominant Serbs, the first appeal to collective rights in Slovakia was registered by nationalist-minded Slovaks, not by the minority Hungarians. But the Yugoslav tensions were sharpened by the fact that in the autonomous, and later independent, republics of Croatia and Bosnia-Herzegovina, ethnic Serb diasporas found themselves in the position of being in the minority. This allowed Serbian politicians simultaneously to experience feelings of threat and the exhilirating confidence of superior numbers. This combination is absent from the Slovak case, the moderation displayed by Budapest helping to keep Slovak fears from escalating too dangerously.

Yet the conclusion seems clear enough that the appeal to the collective rights of the Slovak nation has been part and parcel of a program of authoritarian state-building. One can scarcely imagine a would-be dictator constructing an authoritarian system on the basis of an appeal to individual rights. Indeed, the doctrines of collective rights and individual rights are mutually antagonistic; they pull in entirely different directions. This theme, to be developed more fully in the conclusion, provides a clue as to why the appeal to collective rights, whether in Slovakia or in Serbia or elsewhere, has too often been the grave of liberal democracy.

6

The Albanians of Kosovo

In 1992, the journal *Political Theory* published a debate between Chandran Kukathas, a professor at the Australian Defence Force Academy, and Will Kymlicka, a professor at the University of Ottawa. The subject of their debate was the question posed by Kukathas's opening volley: "Are there any cultural rights?"[1] By "cultural rights" Kukathas means special, differential rights thought to inhere in an ethnic or cultural subgroup existing within a larger society by virtue of that subgroup's cultural distinctiveness and subjective perception of need. It is clear that Kukathas's concept of cultural rights is similar to what I have termed "collective rights."

In his essay, Kukathas takes aim at Anthony Smith, Vernon Van Dyke, and Kymlicka. He charges Smith with disdain for liberalism in his embrace of ethnicity, quotes Van Dyke's claim that "liberalism cannot be trusted to deal adequately with the question of status and rights for ethnic minorities,"[2] and cites Kymlicka's complaint that liberalism, "as commonly interpreted, . . . gives no independent weight to our cultural membership, and hence demands equal rights of citizenship, regardless of the consequences for the existence of minority cultures."[3] As Kukathas notes, Van Dyke even attempts to provide a moral basis for his conclusions by arguing that "alongside the principle that individuals are right-and-duty-bearing units, a comparable principle should be accepted for the benefit of ethnic communities."[4]

In reply, Kukathas throws down the gauntlet. "What has to be denied," he tells us, "is the proposition that fundamental moral claims are to be attached to such groups and that the terms of political association must be established with these particular claims in mind."[5] Kukathas argues that (1) the boundaries and definitions of such groups are in flux, so any attribution of natural rights to such groups would risk reifying phenomena that cannot properly be reified; (2) such groups are partly shaped or, at times, actually created by legal and political institutions against which moral claims would founder on the reef of self-contradiction; (3) attributing special status (whether hegemonist or autonomist) to any given cultural groups qua group discriminates against smaller groups; and (4) the attribution of cultural rights to cultural or ethnic groups (whether hegemonist or autonomist) risks damage to the rights of individuals to define themselves according to criteria of their own choosing, whether language, religion, social class, region, philosophy, political orientation, or some other category of differentiation.[6] Kukathas concludes that while there is "no justification for breaking up such cultural communities, . . . this view does not give the cultural community any fundamental rights."[7]

Responding to Kukathas, Kymlicka appeals to pragmatic concerns, suggesting that guarantees of the rights of subgroups may be useful in enabling the individual members of subgroups to realize full equality as individuals. He states, "Special rights are needed to ensure that they are as able to work and live in their own culture as are the members of majority cultures by protecting them from decisions of the majority culture that could undermine the viability of their community."[8] It appears that for Kymlicka, every cultural phenomenon has an inherent and fundamental right to exist, with the result that the government is entrusted with a solemn duty to commit its tax-derived resources to furthering its role as a kind of custodian or curator for everything that exists.

In a final rejoinder, Kukathas accuses Kymlicka of missing the point. Kukathas allows that subgroups enjoy derivative rights—a point I have made earlier in this book—but insists that subgroups do not possess rights beyond those enjoyed by their members as individuals. Kukathas concludes: "If Kymlicka is suggesting that cultural minorities have different basic rights, I would say this is not defensible from the standpoint of liberal equality."[9]

This chapter will take up the question of the Albanians of Kosovo, noting the injustices to which they have been subjected by Slobodan Milošević and his minions, as well as the claims registered by politicians speaking on behalf of "the Serbian nation" or of "the Albanian nation," and assessing the validity of such claims in the light of the moral theory developed in this book. In so doing, it will provide a case study relevant to the Kukathas-Kymlicka debate.

The Context of Repression

With the signing, in Dayton, Ohio, of a preliminary peace accord, the presidents of Serbia, Croatia, and Bosnia brought at least a temporary halt to the most brutal warfare that Europe had witnessed since World War II. However, in the 140 pages of material that comprise this preliminary accord, there are only indirect and vague references to Serbia's internal minorities—the Hungarians of Vojvodina, the ethnic Muslims of Sandžak, and the Albanians of Kosovo. True, the accord does contain references to the need to guarantee human and civil rights in the region, but the Dayton accord is essentially an agreement relating to Bosnia. Yet if stability in the Balkans is to be assured, then other local problems will need to be addressed. The most pressing of these problems is the situation of the ethnic Albanians of Kosovo, a region in southwest Serbia. (The question of Croatia's indigenous Serbian population has, of course, been dramatically transformed by the flight, under duress, of the bulk of that population in the course of military campaigns during 1995.)

The processes of "ethnic cleansing" that have taken place in Bosnia-Herzegovina—during 1995, most prominently in Banja Luka and Bijeljina, though also in Cazinska Krajina (Bihać) and, albeit in the context of military action, in Slavonia and the Krajina—are well known. But there have also been parallel processes occurring within the Republic of Serbia itself, specifically the expulsion of non-Serbs from the Sandžak and the Vojvodina, and the imposition of a system of de facto apartheid in the heavily Albanian province of Kosovo in southern Serbia. Where the former cases are concerned, the international community has documentation that local Serbian authorities harassed and persecuted local non-Serbs to the extent that some sixty-nine thousand Muslims fled from the Sandžak between 1991 and summer 1993, and an estimated sixty thousand ethnic Hungarians and forty thousand Croats fled from Vojvodina by spring 1994.[10] Some three hundred thousand to four hundred thousand Albanians fled Kosovo between 1990 and 1995; about two hundred thousand of those who fled sought asylum in Germany.[11] (Naturally, since these flights under duress occurred in a society nominally at peace, they were not accompanied by mass graves, burned houses, and the like. Local authorities had no reason to burn the houses of non-Serbs, since they wished to take possession of the houses and turn them over to Serbian refugees from other regions.) Yet these processes provide a clue to the character of the Serbian regime. They also demonstrate that the Serbian regime has resorted to "ethnic cleansing" (genocide) not merely as a weapon of war but also as routine internal policy.

Belgrade's policies of ethnic cleansing and apartheid in Kosovo have entailed the mobilization of Serbs qua Serbs, and that process, which reversed the Tito-era policy of banning political appeals to national identity or culture, in turn required the wholesale embrace and exploitation of the doctrine of collective rights—in this case, of Serbs. This embrace is usually traced, in its incunabulum, to the 1986 Memorandum of the Serbian Academy of Sciences and Arts. Collectively authored, albeit under the guiding eye of Serb novelist Dobrica Ćosić (b. 1920), the Memorandum first articulated the claim that "all Serbs have the right to live in one state."[12] By 1990, Serbian president

Milošević was saying the same thing publicly, ominously highlighting its operative significance "in the event of the collapse of the Yugoslav federation."[13] The doctrine of the collective rights of the Serbian nation remained central to Serbian national ideology during the sanguinary struggle for Bosnia. Thus, for example, addressing a seminar for Serbian broadcast journalists, Momčilo Krajišnik, speaker of the Bosnian Serb Assembly, "stressed that the most important task facing Serb media was the creation of a single Serbian state, and that when it comes to the media, it was necessary to do *everything* to unify all Serbian areas."[14] Quite apart from the fact that this seemed to advocate the studied misrepresentation of facts to suit Serbian needs, in practice claims like Krajišnik's on behalf of Serbs' "right to live in one state" and the unification of "all Serbian areas" were used to justify the claims by Croatian Serbs (11.6 percent of the population of Croatia) and Bosnian Serbs (31.5 percent of the population of Bosnia-Herzegovina) that they should not be considered "minorities" within the republics in which they lived but sovereign parts of the sovereign Serbian nation, enjoying the right to attach themselves and their lands (as well as all non-Serbs who happened to live in their municipalities) to Serbia. This doctrine was applied not only in compact areas where Serbs constituted a local majority, but also in areas when local Serbs comprised as little as 20 percent of the local population (as in Eastern Slavonia) or less (as in Dubrovnik). That this claim involved a suspension of the claims of the Croatian and Bosnian governments to sovereignty over the people living within the borders bequeathed by the defunct SFRY was admitted by leading figures among the Croatian and Bosnian Serbs themselves.

The doctrine of collective rights is usually associated with a physical demographic presence, but at least one Serbian intellectual dispensed with this precondition and offered his view that "there is so much Serbian blood [that has been shed] and so many relics [in the province] that Kosovo will remain Serbian land, even if not a single Serb remains there."[15]

Covering 4,203 square miles, Kosovo enjoyed autonomous status from 1946 to 1989. The region is among the poorest in Europe. According to World Bank figures, Kosovo's per capita income amounted to only $662 in 1990 (the last year for which separate figures for Kosovo have been reported)—much less than the corresponding figure for Serbia ($2,238).[16] The population of Kosovo was officially estimated at 1,956,196 in 1991, including 1,596,072 Albanians and 194,190 Serbs.[17] Despite the clear preponderance of Albanians, Serbs, who constitute less than 10 percent of the local population, have been granted by the Milošević regime a virtual monopoly on positions of power and responsibility in the province, whether in administration, the judiciary, the police force, or even the economic sphere. In fact, since early 1989, a state of terror has prevailed in the province as Milošević and his minions have deprived the local majority Albanians of such elementary rights as the right to an education, the right to broadcast media in their own language, and the right to jobs. Segregation has been the norm in Kosovo since 1987, when Slobodan Milošević took the reins of power in Serbia. Kosovo, in effect, operates under conditions of apartheid.

Milošević has not spared his own beloved Serbs, however, and the Serbs may thank Milošević not only for a dramatic decline in their living standards, economic disarray produced by the war effort, and an intensifed shortage of medicines due to the prioritization of the military effort, but also for constricting freedoms of speech and assembly; snuffing out alternative media; persecuting Serbian opposition politicians such as Dobrica Ćosić, Vuk Drašković, and Vojislav Šešelj; marginalizing progressive political currents; creating conditions in which organized crime has grown rich and powerful in Serbia at the expense of honest Serbs; making hate-speech seem "normal"; and alienating the artistic and intellectual elite sufficiently that many of them have settled in the West in the years since 1991, thereby impoverishing Serbian culture. On balance, Milošević has done more than anyone else to injure the heterogeneous community of Serbs. It is conceivable that the Serbs themselves, at least those living in Serbia and experiencing his oppressions firsthand, may in time come to share Vuk Drašković's view of Milošević as "the greatest enemy of the Serbian people."

Sowing the Seeds of Trouble, 1912–86

But for the intervention of Britain, France, and Russia in 1913, Kosovo would have been assigned to Albania at the time that country was accorded diplomatic recognition. But Albania, which declared its independence of Ottoman Turkey only in 1912, was seen as a client of Austria-Hungary and Italy, and the other great powers wanted to keep the friends of their rivals small. Britain, France, and Russia therefore convened a conference in London that on 29 July 1913 recognized Albania within reduced borders: Kosovo and part of Metohija (including Prizren), despite their majority-Albanian population, were handed over to Serbia, a friend of France and Russia, while Montenegro (another friend of Russia's) received Peć, Djakovica, and Istok.[18] It was, thus, a great power veto of Kosovo's right of national self-determination that sowed the seed for all the problems that subsequently developed.

In interwar Yugoslavia, Belgrade had to suppress armed uprisings in Kosovo in 1918–20, and as early as 1918 the authorities shut down all Albanian-language schools in Kosovo in order to "Serbianize" the Albanians. Subsequently, Albanian access to even the Serbian-language schools was foreclosed, and Albanians were left with only the Islamic *medresas* to serve their educational needs. The authorities also carried out a massive colonization program, driving out as many as half a million Albanians in these years and turning over the confiscated lands to new settlers, mostly Serbs.[19]

The tables were turned during World War II, when Italian forces occupying Kosovo favored the Albanians. The Italian forces ejected an estimated seventy thousand to one hundred thousand of the newly arrived Serbian settlers and restored land to the Albanians.[20] By midsummer 1944, the communist partisans had overcome the Ballist forces in the southern part of Albania and begun pushing northward. Needless to say, as the communist partisans entered Kosovo at the end of 1944 with the intent of reannexing Kosovo to Yugoslavia, Albanians rose up to offer resistance. There were fierce battles between the Albanian resistance organization Balli Kombëtar and the Yugoslav communist army in January and February 1945, and the fighting in Kosovo continued until July 1945.[21] Even after being defeated on the battlefield, the Ballist resistance continued to operate underground for another two years, until repeated arrests and executions had decimated its ranks.[22] After Yugoslavia broke with the Soviet Union in June 1948, Albania became involved in the organization and equipping of terrorist groups operating in Kosovo.[23] About that time, the Yugoslav authorities passed a law forbidding Serb settlers who had moved to Kosovo during the interwar era but who had been expelled during the war from returning to the region. There was, of course, plenty of communist rhetoric about "brotherhood and unity." But despite such rhetoric, the communists introduced policies that, at first, differed very little from those of the interwar kingdom. For example, while Serbs accounted for only 23.5 percent of the population of Kosovo in 1956, some 58.3 percent of the local security forces and 60.8 percent of regular police were Serbs. The Albanians, who numbered 64.9 percent of the population at the time, accounted for 13.3 percent of the security forces and 31.3 percent of the regular police.[24] House searches were a routine phenomenon in Kosovo in the 1950s, as police confiscated all firearms and other weapons found in the homes of Albanians.[25] Ethnic Albanians in the Kosovar party apparatus repeatedly demanded republic status for Kosovo (which would have put Kosovo on the same legal footing with Croatia and Serbia, for example), but Tito always refused, leaving Kosovo as an "autonomous province" within the Republic of Serbia.

But conditions for the local Albanian majority gradually improved. In July 1966, Aleksandar Ranković was fired from his post as chief of the secret police; Ranković, a Serb hegemonist, had been deeply hostile to Albanian strivings for autonomy. In the wake of his removal, "new institutions were established in the field[s] of education, culture, and the media, which encouraged affirmation of the Albanian national identity."[26] After provincewide riots in November 1968, in particular, authorities granted a number of concessions, allowing more Albanians to be promoted to positions of authority and permitting the establishment of the independent University of Priština in 1969. The university adopted Albanian as the language of instruction.

In the 1970s, when Marshal Josip Broz Tito was still president of Yugoslavia, Kosovo enjoyed considerable autonomy as a constituent province, and Albanian cultural autonomy and political interests were protected. Local political power lay, appropriately, in the hands of the numerically preponderant Albanians. On the surface it appeared that Serb-Albanian frictions had finally eased, but materials published in Kosovo itself painted a less reassuring picture. Alongside underground organizations advocating the secession of the province from Yugoslavia were demonstrations by Albanian students at the University of Priština in December 1974, trials of eighty-one Kosovar Albanians for subversive activity 1976–80,[27] massive prison riots on the part of Albanian prisoners in spring 1978, and the wrecking of a police station by angry Albanian rioters in late 1979.[28] Although these events might have been sufficient to cause consternation in Belgrade, the federal authorities failed to see them in context and underestimated the potential for an ethnic explosion.

Then, in March 1981, less than a year after Tito died, the party press published statistics that showed that the much touted program of enabling Kosovo's economy to catch up with the rest of the country had failed. In fact, the party now conceded that Kosovo, always the poorest part of Yugoslavia, had slipped steadily backwards relative to the rest of Yugoslavia. On 11 and 25 March, there were disquieting disturbances at the University of Priština. A few days later, riots engulfed the entire province, from 1 to 3 April 1981. The demonstrators variously demanded either republic status for Kosovo within the Yugoslav federation or outright secession. These riots on the part of local Albanians had an anti-Serbian character.

The riots did not, however, awaken sympathetic sentiments in Belgrade. On the contrary, an anti-Albanian backlash took hold immediately thereafter, fueled by dramatic protest marches to Belgrade on the part of Kosovo's Serbian citizens, and waxed in strength over the next decade. It was this backlash that spawned the Serbian national awakening of the late 1980s and that brought Slobodan Milošević to the helm of the Serbian Communist Party in late 1987.

In the immediate aftermath of the riots, some one thousand persons were expelled from the local party organization, more than seven hundred Albanians were put behind bars by July 1982, and there were wholesale purges in the province's Albanian-language media. During the ensuing years, the security forces uncovered a number of underground organizations of Albanians, bringing charges against some fifty-two hundred Kosovar Albanians between April 1981 and September 1987.[29]

Meanwhile, rumors of alleged violent assaults on Serbs by Albanians and of Albanian vandalism of Serbian property began to circulate. But it was reports of a proliferation of rapes of Serbian women by Albanian men that inflamed the Serbian public, inspiring passage of a law that provided a harsher penalty for interethnic rape than for rape involving members of the same nationality.[30] Between April 1981 and December 1987, some 24,209 Serbs and Montenegrins left Kosovo, in most cases to take up residence in Serbia proper.[31] A 1992 report concluded that "in many cases, real and possible threats to women and female children were the main reason for [Serbs'] moving away, and there is no question that this, in all households, was an important aspect of indirect, psychological pressure suffered and of the social climate that led to people moving away."[32] Accompanying these reports were accusations that local authorities and judges, especially those of ethnic Albanian extraction, were taking an easygoing attitude when it came to prosecuting these cases.[33] For example, as early as 1984, two Albanian judges were fired for having allegedly dragged their feet in the prosecution of Albanians charged with crimes.[34]

The political climate in Serbia was increasingly poisoned by Serb-Albanian tensions in Kosovo, as the Serbian popular press played to the grandstands. Rural Serbs from Kosovo organized a series of dramatic marches on Belgrade beginning in March 1986, and "Kosovo" was increasingly on the lips of members of the Serbian Writers' Association and Serbian Orthodox clergy, who joined in referring to Kosovo as the "Serbian Jerusalem."

Serb Policies on Repression since 1987

But it was Slobodan Milošević who made Kosovo the centerpiece of his ideological appeal, promising Serbs that he would "save" the region. It was with the accession of Milošević to power at the end of 1987 that aggressive appeals started to be made to the historical legitimation of Serb rule of Kosovo that was supposedly afforded by the 1389 Battle of Kosovo. Under Milošević, publishers started to churn out books about the celebrated battle, and the Cyrillic alphabet gained a sudden ascendancy over the Latin alphabet favored by Tito and his immediate successors. With Milošević, the very alphabet assumed the character of a badge of pride, separating Serbs not only from Croats and Slovenes but also, more pointedly, from the Albanians, who also use the Latin alphabet.

On 28 June 1989, Milošević and his entourage, together with sundry Serbian Orthodox bishops, came to Kosovo to commemorate the six-hundredth anniversary of the battle in which King Lazar's army had faced a much larger Ottoman Turkish army. Then, as now, the battle was viewed as a clash between a Christian army and a Muslim army. But whereas King Lazar's forces included both Serbs and a certain number of Albanians, fighting shoulder to shoulder, Milošević preferred now to forget this detail and to focus instead on the Islamic religion that twentieth-century Albanians share with fourteenth-century Turks. Milošević also chose to play up the traditional portrayal of the battle as a defeat for the Serbs, rather than as a Pyrrhic victory that delayed the Ottoman advance while preparing the way for Serbia's subsequent reduction to vassal status—although other interpretations of the battle continued to be voiced in the Serbian academic community at least as late as 1940, if not later.[35] Kosovo, the great defeat, could now serve as a reminder of Serbian suffering, of the alleged victimization of Kosovo by Tito, and so forth. The entire republic was suffused with the myth of Kosovo. The very name seemed to breathe history, and more specifically, Serbian history. The battle would have a vast impact on the collective Serbian psyche, an impact that has, however, fluctuated over time, depending on the uses made of the battle by the authorities who happened to be in power at the time.

Thus, although Milošević and his collaborators did not create the myth of Kosovo, they reinterpreted it and manipulated it to stir up feelings of self-righteousness and hatred of non-Serbs and to give a powerful symbolic focus for their theme of Serbia as Job, suffering unjustly.[36] Given the complete absence of any parallel historical conflict between Serbs and Croats that could be exploited, the Milošević regime seized on the Kosovo myth to serve as the symbolic focus for a mobilization that was to set the Serbs as much against Croats and Bosnian Muslims as against the Albanians of Kosovo.

Within six months of seizing power, Milošević pushed through a bill declaring Serbo-Croatian the official language of Kosovo, thereby disallowing the use of Albanian for official business.[37] As early as July 1988, mass rallies of Serbs, orchestrated by a committee headed by Miroslav Solević,[38] demanded the abrogation of the autonomy of Kosovo and Vojvodina. In November 1988, Milošević engineered the resignation of the popular Azem Vllasi from the leadership of the Kosovar party apparatus and installed Rahman Morina as his "viceroy" in the province. The appointment triggered mass protests by local Albanians across Kosovo, who demanded the resignation of Morina and free elections. The province remained restless during the succeeding months, with the unrest assuming crisis proportions in February, when some one thousand miners at the Trepča zinc mine staged a hunger strike. In response, the authorities sent in the army and imposed emergency measures in the province.

That same month, the Serbian Assembly began to review a series of amendments to the Serbian constitution. These amendments were designed to curtail the powers of the two provinces. The army has maintained a strong and ostentatiously visible presence in Kosovo ever since. In March 1993, it was estimated that there were between forty thousand and sixty thousand Yugoslav army troops in Kosovo, alongside some forty thousand police officers.[39] Police strength was later boosted to sixty thousand.[40]

Kosovo's Assembly was scheduled to endorse the amendments on 23 March, with the vote in the Serbian Assembly set for 28 March. As the twenty-third approached, secret police met with the recalcitrant deputies to the Kosovar Assembly one by one, applying heavy pressure on them to vote "correctly."[41] In due course the assembly obediently voted 168 to 10, with 2 abstentions, to approve the amendments.[42] The amendments stripped provincial authorities of control over local police and civil defense, ended the autonomy of Kosovo's judicial system, and deprived the Kosovo Assembly of the right to participate in deliberations connected with any further constitutional changes affecting Kosovo.[43]

The entire province was now engulfed in mass protests involving as many as ten thousand persons at a time over the next six days. Paramilitary reinforcements were rushed to Kosovo from other parts of Serbia, and a dusk-to-dawn curfew was declared. Tanks patrolled the streets in several towns, helicopters sprayed tear gas on demonstrators, and police used truncheons to beat back protesters. At the end of the violence, at least twenty-four persons lay dead.[44] Violent clashes between local Albanians and Serbian security forces continued throughout the rest of 1989 and most of 1990; on 23 and 24 January 1990, for example, some forty thousand ethnic Albanians demonstrated in Priština, demanding the resignation of Rahman Morina and the restoration of parliamentary rule. In the course of the following month, at least thirty-four persons were killed.

In the meantime, on 24 December 1989, the Democratic League of Kosova was formed, under the chairmanship of Dr. Ibrahim Rugova; it was the first formal opposition party of Kosovar Albanians since World War II.

Milošević ignored the protests of the province's majority Albanians and inaugurated a campaign of aggressive Serbianization of the province, firing Albanians from all positions of responsibility and replacing them with Serbs. Within a matter of weeks, more than one hundred thousand Albanians lost their jobs. Many of them were also forced out of their apartments. At the same time, Milošević offered their jobs, together with free housing, higher wages, and other preferential treatment, to Serbs willing to move to Kosovo; many Serbs took advantage of this policy. The Serbian government also terminated Albanian-language instruction at the University of Priština, fired most of the faculty, and expelled the Albanian students. New faculty and students were imported from outside the province in order to convert the university into a purely Serbian institution.[45]

These policies, which already hinted at later Serbian policies of ethnic cleansing in Bosnia-Herzegovina, shocked the Albanians of Kosovo. On 2 July 1990, the Albanian members of the provincial assembly, most of whom had earlier been cowed into approving Milošević's constitutional changes, decided to stand up to Milošević and, in a bold move, declared Kosovo to be a self-governing unit within the Yugoslav federation.[46] That is to say, the assembly declared Kosovo's secession from Serbia, but not from Yugoslavia. On 5 July, the Serbian government replied with force, suspending the assembly and local government, issuing warrants for the arrest of assembly members, and shutting down local Albanian-language television and radio stations, together with the Albanian-language daily *Rilindja*.[47]

Undeterred, the Albanian deputies to the now-dissolved provincial assembly held a clandestine session in the town of Kaçanik on 7 September 1990 and proclaimed Kosovo a republic within the Yugoslav federation, approving a constitution.[48] In the ensuing crackdown, several deputies were arrested and jailed; the rest fled to Slovenia, Croatia, or abroad. Two weeks later, the Serbian Assembly adopted a new constitution for the Serbian Republic, scrapping what remnants of Kosovo's earlier autonomy had remained.[49]

The Belgrade authorities now escalated the conflict, helping to set up armed "self-defense" units among local Serbs and Montenegrins[50] and confiscating firearms from Albanians, even from those who possessed proper licenses.[51] Meanwhile, the firings of Albanians continued. Between 1990 and early 1995, some 130,000 Albanians were thrown out of work.[52] Judges, university rectors, and factory directors of Albanian ethnicity lost their jobs, as did Albanian physicians. In fact, during 1991 and 1992, 1,832 ethnic Albanian physicians and other medical personnel were dismissed from clinics and hospitals in Kosovo; the vacancies thus created were filled by Serbs.[53] Many Albanian families refused to take their children to see Serbian physicians; the result was a dramatic climb in infant mortality among Kosovo's Albanians. Indeed, by October 1995, infant mortality among Kosovo's Albanians stood at a staggering 17 percent—three times the figure recorded in the late 1980s.[54]

In autumn 1990, Serbian authorities shut down all Albanian-language education, from elementary school to university, and stationed police at neighborhood schools to turn back Albanian schoolchildren.[55] The children were allowed to return to school only in autumn 1994, and then only to strictly segregated schools. In municipalities with mixed populations, authorities completely sealed off the smaller, drabber sections of the school buildings (where the Albanian children would now have their classes) from the better maintained and better equipped sections for Serbs only.[56] School segregation, however, is only the tip of the iceberg. Segregation, in fact, permeates all levels of Kosovar society, from clubs and restaurants to which side of the street one walks on. Albanian men have even been known to rush out of an elevator when a Serbian woman enters, lest they be accused of rape.

In the second half of 1992, street names in Priština (the capital city) were Serbianized, and streets that had long borne the names of local Kosovar Albanian cultural and political figures were now renamed for Serbian figures.[57] In October 1995, after bulldozing a memorial to the victims of fascism in World War II, Serbian authorities erected in its place a monument to Vuk Karadžić, the nineteenth-century Serbian academician idolized by Serbs for his orthographic reform.[58]

As of early 1991, Kosovo seemed to be near the breaking point. But instead of escalating, tensions gave way to an eerie calm as local Albanians desisted from further mass protests. Three factors contributed to this development. The first was that the virtually unarmed Albanians were in no position to take on the heavily armed Serbs and did not want to give the Serbs (whether the authorities or such hotheads as might be found among the local Serbian population) an excuse for even greater repression. The second was the cautious moderation of Ibrahim Rugova, president of the (underground) Democratic League of Kosovo, who, as early as August 1990, had counseled against provoking a confrontation.[59] And third, the outbreak of the Serb-Croat war in July 1991 and the spread of hostilities to Bosnia in March and April 1992 convinced most Albanians that passive resistance was the wiser course.

But inevitably, Milošević's harsh policies destroyed the lingering loyalty to Yugoslavia that many Kosovar Albanians had professed. As Predrag Tasić has noted, separatism was a minority viewpoint among Kosovo's Albanians throughout the 1970s and up to the eve of Milošević's coup; it was Milošević's adoption of policies of repression, apartheid, and expulsion that made separatism mainstream thinking among the province's Albanians.[60] As early as February 1991, four months before Yugoslavia fell apart, a clandestine poll found that most Kosovar Albanians favored the merger of their province with Albania.[61] This finding was given dramatic confirmation on 26–30 September 1991, when the Albanian resistance held a referendum in Kosovo on the question of whether Kosovo should declare its independence. Some 87 percent of eligible citizens went to the polls, and of this number, 99.87 percent voted for independence.[62] Subsequently, in a 1994 poll conducted by the Albanian weekly *Koha,* some 78 percent of respondents expressed the desire to see Kosovo independent of Serbia.[63] By contrast, a poll taken among Serbs found that 83 percent of Serbs were completely opposed to any concessions to the Albanians of Kosovo, including the restoration of autonomy, while 13.9 percent were willing to offer the Albanians cultural, but not political, autonomy.[64]

In May 1992, underground Albanian political parties in Kosovo conducted elections, defying an official ban and braving police harassment.[65] Despite the ban, a vast majority of Kosovo citizens went to the polls, electing a shadow government headed by Ibrahim Rugova. The European Union quietly expressed concern that the simmering tensions in Kosovo would shortly reach a crisis stage,[66] but it proved even less able to formulate a policy to stabilize Kosovo than it had been to respond to the savagery of nationalist forces (especially those loyal to Radovan Karadžić) in Bosnia.

Changing Demographics

The Serbian "resettlement" program has been premised on the supposition that the creation of new "facts," even if primarily in the form of concentrated pockets of Serbs along the border with Albania[67] and in the vicinity of key towns such as Priština, can finesse Albanian aspirations toward independence and permanently change the diplomatic game. At first, most of Belgrade's rather limited success with this policy involved diverting Serbian refugees driven out of contested areas of Bosnia to Kosovo.[68] But despite clear favoritism toward incoming Serbs, the program bogged down. Some of those Serbs who had just settled in Kosovo left angrily, complaining that the government had failed to provide jobs and keep other promises. Some of these Serbs even sold their land to Albanians; Serbian law forbids Albanians to buy land from Serbs, but Serbs who have wanted to sell have gotten around this obstacle by entering into fictitious marriages that are soon abrogated by divorce agreements in which the Serbian partner deeds the land over to his spouse in return for a cash compensation.[69] Other Serbs and Montenegrins, lured from Albania by Belgrade's promises, became disgruntled with local living conditions and returned to Albania.[70] Those Serbs who remained became disconsolate. Therefore, in October 1994, local Kosovar Serbs—among them Kosta Bulatović, the leading figure in a series of petitions distributed between 1986 and 1989, and Miroslav Solević, the leading figure in the organization of the committee that had destabilized Kosovo and Vojvodina in 1988 and 1989—submitted to the authorities a petition signed by more than two thousand Serbs, demanding an acceleration of the resettlement program.[71]

Perhaps in response to this petition, Belgrade adopted a decree on 13 January 1995 reiterating the earlier offer of free land to Serbs willing to settle in Kosovo and adding the incentive of forty-year loans to enable them to build new houses.[72] The land has been obtained by force as local police issue ultimata to local Albanian residents to leave peaceably or be driven out.[73] Serbian officials have claimed that Greece has offered to provide assistance in constructing housing for Serbian settlers in Kosovo.[74]

Meanwhile, many Albanians have fled Kosovo. According to the Slovenian daily newspaper *Delo,* approximately twenty-five thousand fled from Kosovo to Italy between November 1994 and January 1995 alone.[75] Serbian warlord Željko Raznjatović (better known as "Arkan") has spelled out the vision that many Serbian politicians have nurtured for Kosovo, calling for the "expulsion of some 700,000 Albanians to Albania" and the confiscation of their property.[76]

Between 30 March and 1 April 1995, a large gathering of Serb intellectuals and scholars took place in Priština. The occasion was a symposium entitled "Population of FR Yugoslavia, with Special Focus on Kosovo and Metohija." The major work of this symposium was a drafting of a consensus declaration calling on the Belgrade government to adopt more resolute measures to change the ethnic composition of Kosovo and recommending, in particular, the outright expulsion of some four hundred thousand local Albanians (in addition to those who had already fled the province over the course of the preceding six years).[77]

Even the Church has become involved in the program to create a "Serbian" Kosovo. Alarmed at reports of a major drop in the birthrate among Serbs[78] and eager to reinforce the Serbian presence in the "Serbian Jerusalem, " the Serbian Orthodox Church started awarding medals in 1995 to Serbian mothers in Kosovo who give birth to the most children.[79]

Simultaneously, the Serbian authorities have pursued a genocidal policy designed to reduce the Albanian population. This policy, sustained without remission since 1990, has included: the frequent and recurrent harassment of Albanian civilians by the army and police, including fatal shootings of civilians;[80] the forcible ejection of Albanian civilians from their homes and villages;[81] the outright plundering of Albanian-run businesses, such as shops and restaurants, by Serbian "inspectors";[82] the raiding of Albanian homes on the pretext of searches for weapons;[83] and the arrest of those Albanians who had contact with CSCE representatives who were monitoring human rights violations in the province until Milošević and his minions expelled them in summer 1993.[84]

Serbian authorities have also targeted local intellectuals, journalists, former police of Albanian ethnicity, and Albanians with military experience for arrest on trumped-up charges and harassment.[85] As of July 1995, more than two hundred former policemen of Albanian nationality had been brought to trial on spurious charges; their confessions, according to Michael Wehninger, chargé d'affaires of the Austrian embassy in Belgrade, had been exacted under torture.[86] As Human Rights Watch explains, the arrests and detention of these persons served two related goals for Serbian authorities:

> First, by charging the former military officers with conspiring to overthrow [the Federal Republic of] Yugoslavia, police spread fear [among Serbs] that Albanians are planning an armed revolution. Second, should an uprising occur, the arrests effectively immobilize exactly those Albanians with the specific knowledge and skills necessary for plotting an armed rebellion.[87]

The repeated raids of the offices of the Democratic League of Kosovo (DLK) and the arrests of DLK officials,[88] as well as the sequestration of the facilities of the Albanological Institute in Priština,[89] serve the same purpose.

According to the Council for the Defense of Human Rights and Freedoms, Serbian authorities in 1994 alone murdered 17 Kosovar Albanians (either by shooting or as a result of police torture), physically abused another 8,551, and arrested at least 6,394. The Democratic League of Kosovo estimates that, counting attacks by armed Serbian civilians, Kosovar Albanians were subjected to almost 75,000 attacks of various kinds in the course of 1994.[90] In the first six and a half months of 1995, 10 Albanians, among them a nine-year-old child, died at the hands of Serbian police.[91] Albanian neighborhoods were even subjected to mortar bombardments from a locally stationed Serbian army installation in an incident that still has not been satisfactorily explained.[92]

Trials of Albanians are constantly being staged in Priština, with the defendants routinely convicted and sentenced on the basis of questionable evidence and confessions exacted through torture.[93] In the first nine months of 1995, about 294 Kosovar Albanians were sentenced on charges of endangering the territorial integrity of the Federal Republic of Yugoslavia.[94] In September 1995, for example, 10 ethnic Albanians were given prison terms ranging from six months to two and a half years on charges of "separatist activities," although the defense attorney protested that the authories had been unable to prove their case and had resorted to intimidation to extract confessions from the accused.[95] Given such conditions, it is not surprising that between 1990 and 1995—as mentioned at the outset—between 300,000 and 400,000 Albanians fled the province.[96]

Serbian officialdom has adopted a completely hypocritical attitude about the appalling conditions that Belgrade has created for Kosovo's Albanians. For example, addressing a gathering in Kosovo on 28 June 1995, Serbian parliamentary speaker Dragan Tomić "praised progress on conditions for ethnic Albanians since 1989."[97] As previously mentioned, some Serbian settlers from Albania had found even their privileged position so inferior to the conditions they had enjoyed in Albania that they preferred to return to Albania, rather than remain in Kosovo. Ignoring such convincing evidence, however, Margit Savović, a minister without portfolio in the Belgrade government who had special responsibility for human and minority rights, made so bold as to suggest, in a May 1995 interview, that the Serbs of Albania "would be more than satisfied to have only a part of what the Albanian minority in [the Federal Republic of] Yugoslavia is entitled to."[98] The evidence suggests a very different conclusion.

A Tide of Serb Refugees

In August 1995, after the collapse of the self-proclaimed "Krajina" rump in central Croatia, some 160,000 Serbian refugees streamed eastward, in the direction of Serbia. Milošević, who a few weeks earlier had visited Kosovo promising "a policy of national equality" and pledging himself to work for "a lasting and just" peace in the region,[99] now decided to resettle up to 20,000 of these Serb refugees in Kosovo.[100] Ibrahim Rugova immediately denounced the move as a "most serious and risky provocation," pointing out its effect in changing the local population structure.[101] The U.S., Albanian, and Egyptian governments also criticized Milošević's shipments of Croatian Serb refugees (incidentally, against their will) to the politically inflamed province.[102] Even the habitually pro-Serbian Greek foreign ministry issued a statement expressing concern that the move would raise tensions close to the Greek border and potentially cause the conflict to spread to the south.[103]

The Croatian Serbs, driven from the Krajina, arrived traumatized, bitter, nationalistic, and armed—a dangerous mixture to introduce into tension-ridden Kosovo. Moreover, as Yasushi Akashi, the UN Special Envoy to the Former Yugoslavia, admitted, the presence of war criminals among the Croatian Serb refugees added to the explosive risk entailed in this latest migratory movement.[104] "Kosovo today is pure dynamite," Marijan Tunaj, a spokesperson for the democratic League of Kosovo (LDK) in Aachen, Germany, warned in August 1995.[105]

Despite warnings from various quarters, Serbian authorities continued to direct a certain number of "Krajina" refugees to Kosovo. By late September, more than eleven thousand Serb refugees from Croatia had been settled in the province—most of them against their will.[106] In fact, no one in Kosovo was satisfied with this arrangement. Neither the refugees themselves,[107] nor the Albanians of Kosovo,[108] nor even local indigenous Serbs[109] wanted them there. Indigenous Serbs, for example, claimed that incoming Serbs were being given preferential placement in jobs.[110]

Meanwhile, there were reports that Serbian refugees were being accommodated in homes confiscated from local Albanians as well as in various public buildings.[111] Among those buildings opened to Serbian refugees was the

League of Prizren Museum in Prizren, which celebrated an important episode in the history of the Albanian people. Despite the importance the museum had for Albanians, Serbian authorities gave orders to the museum staff on 7 September to remove all exhibits within twenty-four hours and to vacate the premises.[112] While it is understandable that the Belgrade authorities have had to situate incoming refugees in various parts of the republic, including in Kosovo, the resentments stirred up on all sides in Kosovo have been difficult to deal with, and even a year later, a Swiss daily newspaper was talking of a "Krajina syndrome" among the Serbs of Kosovo.[113]

Kosovo's Mineral Wealth

In attempting to justify their denial of national self-determination to the Albanians of Kosovo, Belgrade authorities are fond of talking about monasteries and churches and graveyards (even while bulldozing the cemeteries of Albanians) and of indulging in nostalgic reverie about the battle of 1389.[114] While it is true that ordinary Serbs have been manipulated to the point that they take these arguments seriously, the real prize in Kosovo, as the Belgrade regime is well aware, is the province's mineral wealth.

Kosovo has enormous mineral reserves, most still unexploited. Kosovo's coal reserves are estimated to total 14 billion tons, "which, even if exploited to the maximum for the planned needs of the thermal power stations, could not be exhausted for 700 years."[115] Kosovo's coal reserves account for 70 percent of the coal reserves that Belgrade currently has at its disposal. Kosovo also has proven reserves of 120,300,000 tons of lead and zinc ore (50 percent of the total reserves of pre-1991 Yugoslavia) and 1,300,000 tons of manganese ore, plus additional reserves of cadmium, germanium, copper, bismuth, silver, gold, indium, gallium, barium, and bauxite, and it is the sole producer in the western Balkans of ferronickel. In addition, Kosovo possesses 84 million tons of magnesite (representing about 70 percent of the total reserves of pre-1991 Yugoslavia).[116] There is, in short, much more than mere historical sentiment involved in the new battle for Kosovo.

Despite persistent rumors of arms smuggling on the part of Kosovo's Albanians (at least some of these rumors originating with the Serbian authorities and Serbian media),[117] Ibrahim Rugova, the legitimate, albeit illegally elected, president of Kosovo, has continued to counsel against an uprising. "We have no choice," he told a Dutch journalist in October 1994.

> Serbian dominance is so complete that we will be exterminated if we resort to violence. We cannot even organize a protest demonstration, then we would be

beaten up or they would start shooting. The only remaining option is peaceful resistance. Rising up now would mean suicide.[118]

Western Policies

Where the United States and what is left of the Western alliance are concerned, the great temptation has been to opt for minimal responses—an approach that consistently looks safe in the short run but all too often proves to be explosively dangerous in the long run. The West missed its great opportunity to destroy Serbian military capabilities in 1992. At that time Russia was too self-absorbed to be capable of any coherent response to anything that might transpire in the Balkans. In the course of 1993, however, Moscow rediscovered foreign policy, and by early 1994 it had become immeasurably more complex to contemplate decisive military action against the nationalist forces loyal to Karadžić and supplied by Milošević. And yet, had such action been undertaken in 1992, the number of casualties could have been held to well under 100,000, instead of the 250,000 to 500,000 now dead, and the West could have imposed a dictated peace under which the wishes of local populations could have been respected. By 1996, however, the situation had become vastly more complex.

The Albanian government has made sure that Western governments have been aware of the problems affecting the people of Kosovo. President Sali Berisha of Albania met with President Clinton in September 1995 and raised the issue with him then, while Albanian foreign minister Alfred Serreqi met with the foreign ministers of Great Britain, France, Italy, Croatia, Bosnia, Slovenia, Mexico, and Iraq in the course of a few busy weeks that same month.[119] Berisha pleaded with U.S. assistant secretary of state Richard Holbrooke to keep the economic sanctions against Serbia in place until the issue of Kosovo had been resolved[120] and has repeatedly urged that the issue of Kosovo be included in any Yugoslav settlement.[121] But the Albanians have found it to be an uphill struggle. The British, for one, reiterated their position once more in October 1995 that it is for Serbia to decide what it wants to do in Kosovo.[122]

But two months later, after meeting with Ibrahim Rugova, German foreign minister Klaus Kinkel declared, "The international spotlight must now be turned to Kosovo and we must do all in our power to help the people there."[123] U.S. concurrence in this view seemed to be implied in the grant of audiences to Albanian foreign minister Alfred Serreqi by Assistant Secretary of State Rudolf Perina and Secretary of State Warren Christopher the following May; these conversations dealt almost entirely with the problem of Kosovo.[124]

President Rugova of Kosovo has made it clear that he considers political separation from Serbia the only acceptable solution. But there are well-respected Albanians in Kosovo, such as Behlul Beqaj and Adem Demaçi, who are said to be willing to work within the framework of the Federal Republic of Yugoslavia, provided that there is a willingness on Belgrade's part to reciprocate the spirit of compromise.[125] Moreover, despite more than five years of hate propaganda churned out by Belgrade, a recent poll found that 54.5 percent of citizens of Serbia (exclusive of Kosovo) considered it possible to live together with the Albanians in peace and harmony.[126] On the other hand, a USIA poll conducted in Kosovo in early 1996 found that 94 percent of local Albanians agreed with the statement "achieving independence from Serbia for Kosovo is a cause worth dying for."[127] One should not make too much of such polls, of course, but neither should one make too little of them.

Peace and social justice are inseparable. A state at war with a part of its own population is necessarily also dangerous to its neighbors, if only because of the possibility that those citizens most victimized by internal terror will seek to draw other powers into the imbroglio. While a democratic constitution is no guarantee of pacific policies,[128] a system characterized by apartheid, expulsion of innocent populations, wholesale confiscations of private property, and the beating and murder of minorities would, by most definitions, be considered an outlaw state. Yet Serbia has reached this stage by traversing a path defined, in part, by the Belgrade regime's appeal to the collective rights of Serbs and by subordinating those who are not members of the collectivity of Serbs to the doctrine of Serb collective rights.

A State of Semi-War?

In spring 1996, in the wake of Western moves to rehabilitate Serbia and reintegrate the Federal Republic of Yugoslavia into the international community, tensions in Kosovo rose dramatically. In early April, some thousand vendors at the Priština market went on collective strike to protest a sharp increase in taxes levied by Serbian authorities.[129] Two weeks later, on 21 April, a twenty-year-old Albanian student named Armend Daçi was shot by Zlatko Jovanović (a Serb) in Priština during a peaceful rally. The incident was immediately translated into ethnic terms, provoking attacks on Serbian police officers and citizens throughout the province on 22 April; the attacks left five Serbs dead and four wounded, three of them police.[130] Police responded by arresting some eighty Albanians. On 23 April 1996, some ten thousand Albanian women staged a mass demonstration in downtown Priština, to underline their concern over the shooting of Armend Daçi. It was the largest protest gathering in Kosovo since 1992.[131] Then, on 29 April, two armed Serbs entered an Albanian-owned bakery and opened fire.[132] *Naša borba*, the independent Serbian daily, reported that "Kosovo is in a state of semi-war following the series of attacks on the police and citizens through the province."[133] LDK leader Rugova, for his part, issued a statement characterizing the situation as "extremely dangerous" and appealing to Serb police and soldiers not to provoke the civilian population.[134] Within hours of Rugova's appeal, however, "hundreds of Serbian police and other military forces, including civilians and masked and armed groups backed by armoured vehicles, terrorized and raided" Albanian communities in Deve, Trstenik (Albanian name: Terstenik), Poklete i Vjeter, and the villages of Ri, Fushtice e Larte, and Nekof in the Glogovac (Gllogovc) commune.[135]

President Rugova and Prime Minister Bujar Bukoshi of Kosovo voiced their support in June 1996 for a compromise package, assuring the Serbian Orthodox Church of wide-ranging "sovereignty" and prerogatives within an independent Kosovo in an effort to reassure Orthodox Serbs concerning their religious freedom.[136] But even as these proposals were being made, tensions rose in the province as a result of a series of violent incidents involving bombings, shootings, and physical attacks between Serbs and Albanians.[137] In October, five Kosovar Albanians were convicted on what *Illyria* characterized as "fraudulent and . . . trumped-up charges" of hostile activity endangering the territorial integrity of the state.[138]

In spite of all the obstacles, some progress was made in summer 1996, specifically the agreement between Milošević and Rugova on a deal permitting Albanian students to return to "regular" secondary schools.[139] An agreement reestablishing cooperative relations between the universities of Priština and Tiranë was also reached.[140]

But opinions differ within the Albanian community as to what kind of arrangement would best accord with the needs of the Albanian inhabitants of Kosovo. For Rugova, independence and eventual attachment to Albania appears to be the most favorable option.[141] On the other hand, for Adem Demaçi, chair of Kosovo's human rights committee and a veteran political activist who spent twenty-seven years in prison in the communist era, independence should be realized within the framework of a confederal union with Serbia and Montenegro, with which republics Kosovo has been economically integrated for nearly eighty years.[142] On the other hand, partition of the province, which was being broached at one time by certain prominent Serbian figures, has never found advocates within the Albanian community and, as Dennison Rusinow has noted, no longer appears to be a likely or viable solution for the region's problems.[143] But whatever differences observers might have, most were prepared by spring 1996 to agree with Carl Bildt's assessment that Serbian stability and prosperity required that a democratic resolution to the issues in Kosovo be found.[144]

The example of Kosovo aptly illustrates the problems of the doctrine of collective rights. Premised as it is on the notion that there are rights attached to being a Serb or an Albanian, the doctrine necessarily pits collectivities, whether national or religious, against each other. And while one can, up to a point, distinguish between aggressive and defensive manifestations of this doctrine, the underlying thinking is the same, tending to embrace two central points: that there are rights enjoyed by the group qua group, and that the members of the group enjoy a right to live with like (i.e., a right of Serbs to live with Serbs, Albanians to live with Albanians, Orthodox with Orthodox, Muslims with Muslims). And while one can trace the history of this doctrine, it is impossible to identify moral grounds for its suppositions. By contrast, claims for individual and societal rights are founded upon secure moral groundwork elaborated in the era of the Enlightenment.[145]

Thus, it is not that the Belgrade regime has abused a morally justifiable doctrine of collective rights, but rather that the doctrine of collective rights upon which it has based its repressive policy is itself pernicious and morally void. The problem in Kosovo, to make it concrete, is not that either the Serbian nation or the Albanian nation has been served an unjust fate, but that individuals have been deprived of jobs, property, basic security, civil rights, health, and sometimes even their lives in the name of this doctrine. Certainly, among the rights enjoyed by individuals is the right to education in one's native language when one is living in an area with a large concentration of colinguals, but this right can be defended at the level of individual rights without recourse to the inflammatory doctrine of collective rights. Indeed, the relative success achieved by, let us say, Britain, in integrating the English, Scots, and Welsh into a harmonious community has been premised precisely on muting appeals to supposed collective rights. Or again, as the Swiss example illustrates, adequate protection for language rights and confessional rights can be secured without stirring up notions of basing group rights on collective identities and the doctrine of collective rights. This principle seems to have been understood by Rugova, who has taken pains to avoid a countermobilization of Albanians and who has concentrated his attention on highlighting Serbian policies of repression rather than on developing mythologies of Albanian historic rights with which to counter Serbian mythologies of historic rights.

A Fallback Right to Autonomy?

In order for groups to possess natural (i.e., inherent) rights to particular territory, there would have to be provision in the moral order, discernible by reason, that one group should live in one region and another group in another region. But, of course, the territorial divison of the world is largely arbitrary. Because of that, and because of the absence of a moral foundation for the putative principle of national self-determination, as well as because the principle of national self-determination is exposed to self-contradiction via the presentation of counterclaims consistent with the principle itself, the moral foundations of statehood have nothing whatsoever to do with the nationality principle, Woodrow Wilson notwithstanding. This conclusion should not surprise us, since it is entirely consistent with the writings of Hobbes, Locke, and Kant, the giants of classical liberalism.

In the context of Kosovo, this conclusion signifies that politicians are mistaken in supposing that one can speak coherently about either a Serbian "right" to hegemonic rule over the Albanians or to an Albanian "right" to autonomy. Both of these supposed rights are derived from the bogus doctrine of collective rights. But we are not left hanging in the void. On the contrary, the affirmation of the centrality of human rights, tolerance, social justice, equality, and basic freedoms provides a much surer and fairer basis than the doctrine of collective rights or its bastard offspring, the principle of autonomism, for resisting tyranny and working toward a better world.

I have argued thus far that there is no inherent right to autonomous status enjoyed by any groups anywhere. At the same time, I have argued that in conditions of tyranny, any self-designating group or any aggregate of inhabitants may organize to resist tyranny and may, on its own discretion, separate from the state gripped by tyranny. It may seem that this consideration might open up an exceptional case, a kind of fallback right to autonomy.

The argument for a fallback right to autonomy would run like this. Granted there is no absolute right to autonomy, but any group may, as is already conceded, separate from tyranny, in the process asserting its sovereignty. As a sovereign body, the group may, however, choose to affiliate with the state from which it might otherwise separate altogether on the basis of a grant of autonomy. Since it enjoys discretionary rights as a sovereign body, it may therefore be said to enjoy a right to autonomy.

The flaw in this argument has to do with a misconception about the nature of tyranny, which is a system characterized by the de facto nonrecognition of individual (and perhaps also societal) rights. The right to resist tyranny is, however, grounded in a (Lockean) concept of individual rights, so that the putative right to autonomy would be, on this argument, an extension of individual rights taken in aggregate. This leads to an absurdity, however, for what autonomists seek is to negotiate a recognition of their aggregated individual rights from a state that does not recognize such rights at all. Or, to bring the argument down to practice, it requires that an outlaw state behave in a law-abiding (or right-abiding) manner vis-à-vis the autonomous zone. Rights cannot be grounded on absurdity. Hence the attempt to found a right to autonomy on an appeal to individual rights fails.

An appeal to societal rights would be irrelevant, first, because autonomous status creates differential zones with differential rights, whereas the notion of societal rights refers to common rights simultaneously enjoyed by all citizens equally; and, second, because it is not in the nature of societal rights to specify juridical and administrative arrangements within a state. Moreover, the creation of an autonomous zone would risk diminishing such resistance to tyranny as might exist in the society and would therefore be interpreted as unfavorable for the prospects of the freedom of the citizenry as a whole.

That leaves only an appeal to collective rights to buttress the demand for autonomy, and it will not come as a surprise that it is exclusively on the basis of an appeal to collective rights that demands for autonomy tend to be registered. Yet, as we have already seen, there are no duty correlates for supposed specific collective rights, and hence there are no collective rights. This is why it is completely absurd to state either that "the Serbs" are entitled to rule Kosovo or that "the Albanians" are entitled to rule Kosovo. What may be said is that those people who have been living in Kosovo have human rights (i.e., individual rights) and societal rights, and have every right to defend those rights, with resort to secession if necessary. Thus, it appears that the right to secession does not create a right to autonomy.

But the argument remains incomplete, because thus far I have approached the question of a right to autonomy exclusively from the standpoint of natural rights, that is, from the standpoint of those rights generated by Univeral Reason. But there exists a second category of rights, namely, positive rights, that is, those rights created by positive or statutory law.[146] Such rights have no necessary moral dimension and may or may not have an absolute claim to respect; it is purely the force of the lawgiver that raises optional (morally innocuous) arrangements to the level of rights. And while I have suggested that there is no *natural* right to autonomy, groups of citizens and parties may, within the scope of the constitutional order, agree to create one or more autonomous zones as an act of positive law; such an act would create positive rights to autonomy, existing for as long as the legal arrangement continues.

If the grant of autonomy is discretionary and optional, can the same be said of the withdrawal or cancellation of autonomy? Here the analogy with gift giving is appropriate. One may choose to give a gift to person B or to refrain from doing so, but once the gift is given, it belongs to B and remains B's legitimate property. And if one wishes to reclaim possession of the gift, one is dutybound to reach a mutually satisfactory agreement with B to that effect. The same holds for autonomy, which creates a relationship of divided or shared sovereignty. By sharing sovereignty, the central government gives up certain

rights that it cannot reclaim unilaterally. This is why Belgrade's 1989 abrogation of Kosovo's autonomous status represents a clear violation of customary
notions of positive right. In essence, the Yugoslav constitutional order established in 1946 and subsequently modified had created a positive right of
autonomy in Kosovo that Belgrade had no right to abolish.

But there is an exception to this rule (of course), namely, if those to whom
autonomy is granted violate the terms of that grant, then the granter would be
fully entitled, under customary notions of positive law, to withdraw such
autonomy. The same principle applies to ethnic, religious, and cultural associations that, for example, do not possess any special natural rights but that,
upon registration with the authorities, may be granted status as legal persons,
thereby obtaining all the positive rights and privileges pertaining thereto. In
the case of religious organizations, there is usually an additional hurdle—a
requirement that the association in question demonstrate that its practices do
indeed have a "religious" character. This proof is typically required in conjunction with the extension of tax-exempt status to the association. When,
however, the authorities conclude, on the basis of reliable information, that the
association is not displaying practices and behaviors that conform to the norms
prescribed by law—as in the case of the German authorities' contention that
Scientology is not a bona fide religious association—they are entitled and
authorized to withdraw this status.

It is the distinctions between Natural Law (Universal Reason) and positive
law, and again between liberal systems and tyrannies, that render the discussion of the rights of associations and subgroups somewhat complex. The
heart of the matter is that under positive law, anything can be established or
disestablished, provided that the action taken is not contrary to Universal
Reason. Is this qualification mystical and ethereal? I think not. If it were, then
charges of genocide could be reduced to differences of opinion about what
sort of positive law accorded best with local interests—a position what would
reduce both the Nuremberg trials and the war crimes tribunal at the Hague to
absurdity.

Conclusion

Collective Rights in the Dialectic of History

The past two and a half centuries have been dominated by the concept of rights. Claims have been made on behalf of rights, wars have been launched in their defense, and constitutions have been drafted to enshrine and protect them. Of all the ideological concepts that suffuse societies, perhaps none is so taken for granted and allowed to go so unchallenged as that of rights. In the twentieth century, thanks in part to the rival but mutually reinforcing pronouncements by Woodrow Wilson and V. I. Lenin, the self-determination and self-administration of self-declared groups have been largely assumed to be natural rights. But there is no agreement as to how one may distinguish groups that may be said to enjoy such rights from those that do not, unless one opts to allow that any self-declared group may declare its "secession." But that principle, if taken literally, would sanction the indefinite and infinite splitting up of communities. If, for example, we allow that Bosnia-Herzegovina had a right to secede from the already defunct SFRY, then perhaps the Serbs of Bosnia had a right to secede from Bosnia-Herzegovina. But if so, then surely the Croats and Bosnian Muslims living within predominantly Serbian areas would enjoy the right to secede from these secessions, and most certainly, the Serbs living within these subsecessions would themselves enjoy the right of secession. One ends up with secessions from secessions from secessions from secessions. And of course, what is to prevent even local noncitizen residents from declaring that, as humans, they too enjoy the right to secede?[1] Appealing to the notion of majority rule does not, by itself, assist with the notion of self-determination, because one must first determine within which territory one will calculate one's majority.

But in practice, violent, aggravated forms of secessionism occur in some states and not in others. The Soviet Union and Yugoslavia are well-known cases of systems that fractured along ethnic lines, while the attempted secessions of Biafra and Katanga reflect parallel processes in Africa. On the other hand, neither the Welsh nor the Scottish have shown any inclination to enter into a separatist war, nor have the Basques of France, the Francophones or Italophones of Switzerland, or the Swedes of Finland. Why the difference? As these examples should readily suggest, the essential variable is *legitimacy*. Where a state is legitimate, the doctrine of collective rights is apt to have less resonance, while in illegitimate states, ethnic, confessional, cultural, and social cleavages can quickly be translated into lines of fissure and fracture. As I noted in a 1989 publication, "While multiethnic societies are not *necessarily* unstable, illegitimate regimes in multiethnic states *are.*"[2] Now it is certainly true that separatism may solve the problem for those separating from an illegitimate regime, assuming that the separatists can fashion a legitimate state to take its place. But those left under the illegitimate regime still confront the same problem, while the separation of disgruntled peripheries can only serve to weaken the resistance to illegitimate rule in the rump state. Serbia is a case in point. On 9 March 1991, Belgrade was rocked by massive riots; the demand on the part of the demonstrators was simple: democracy. Milošević responded by sending security forces against the demonstrators, crushing the incipient rebellion. More than five years later, in November 1996, demonstrators once again took to the streets of Belgrade, this time joined by rebels in Niš and in other Serbian towns.[3] On 25 November, more than one hundred thousand jeering protesters hurled eggs at state-run television headquarters and later threw rocks at regime buildings. Leaders of the opposition coalition Zajedno protested the government's annulment of local elections in some forty-four municipalities where Zajedno had outpolled the ruling socialists.[4] Zoran Žuković, an opposition leader, explained, "We are going through what Hungary, Czechoslovakia, Bulgaria, and Poland went through six years ago [in 1989–90]."[5] As Belgrade lived through the tenth day of demonstrations, on 28 November, opposition leader Vuk Drašković told an ITN journalist, "Milošević is the main enemy of the Serbian people, the Serbian nation."[6] With their demonstrations against the Belgrade regime, local Serbs were passing the same judgment on Milošević that the Slovenes, Croats, and Macedonians had passed in 1991. Perhaps Belgrade's rioting Serbs understood for themselves, as the dissidents of yesteryear constantly insisted, that there are no adequate substitutes for human rights or for legitimate politics.

Legitimacy

I have suggested in this book that legitimacy has something to do with the moral order and very little, if anything, with supposed rights of national self-determination. One does not have to be a Hegelian to associate democratic life with moral universalism. This association was, for example, central to Kant's understanding of liberal politics.[7] But there is more to legitimacy than just morality. Accordingly, I would like to outline a theory of political legitimacy by way of providing a framework within which to view the sundry cases taken up in this book.

Legitimacy, one might say, is a facet of the political or social order and, as such, bears a relation to the chief components of the social order in question. I have sketched out the chief alternatives among the components of a social order in table 7.1. As is clear from the table, I view social order as consisting of three principal components: moral orientation, political arrangement, and economic system. By moral orientation, I mean the dominant moral orientation of the system as reflected in the state ideology or practice, the educational system, and public opinion. While one would, in theory, expect to find societies to be very heterogeneous when it comes to moral orientation, I would argue that there is almost always (indeed, everywhere except in disintegrating societies) a modal or dominant moral orientation, whether it be moral universalism in either its religious or its secular-liberal strain, ethnarchy, conventionalism, or theocracy in either its religious or its secular-communist strain.

I make no claim for completeness in the itemization of alternative political arrangements, but I would argue that this list does include the principal alternatives of the past two centuries: monarchy (whether royal-elective, dynastic, or pseudoroyal), representative democracy, plutocracy, timocracy, and authoritarian one-party monopolies (such as found in communism or Naziism).

Table 7.1
The Components of a Social Order

Moral orientation	Political arrangement	Economic system

Moral univeralism
  (a) religious
  (b) secular (liberalism)
	Monarchy
	
	Representative democracy
		Capitalism
		
		Socialism

Ethnarchy (moral relativism)	Plutocracy Timocracy	Solidarism

Conventionalism
  (nominalism)
	Authoritarian one-party
	  monopoly	

Theocracy
  (a) religious
  (b) secular (e.g., communist)		

Note: A social order is composed of one option from each of the three categories: moral orientation, political arrangement, and economic system. The chart is not to be read across.

The chief economic systems are, rather obviously, capitalism, socialism, and, somewhat less obviously, solidarism. By solidarism, I mean a mixed economy in which the society is characterized by strong currents of mutual caring and mutual aid and in which the state plays an active role in assuring a basic equality of opportunity, providing corrective action where necessary (for example, through affirmative action), and curtailing the tendency of the rich to aggrandize their wealth indefinitely. Such a vision reflects certain ideas found in Kropotkin, Pope Leo XIII's *Rerum Novarum* (1891), and Pope John Paul II's *Sollicitudo Rei Socialis* (1988).

This scheme enumerates six alternative moral orientations, five alternative political arrangements, and three alternative economic systems. Tabulating all possible combinations of the relevant alternatives, one comes up with ninety possible permutations, which is to say, ninety theoretically possible alternative social orders. In fact, however, some of the combinations prove to be null sets. Some examples of null sets would be:

- moral universalism (either strain) + authoritarian one-party system + any economic system

- ethnarchy + solidarism + any political arrangement

- plutocracy + socialism + any moral orientation

- plutocracy + solidarism + any moral orientation

Other combinations are all too well known, such as:

- liberalism + monarchy + capitalism = constitutional monarchy

- ethnarchy + authoritarian one-party system + capitalism = fascism

- moral universalism (religious) + monarchy + solidarism = medievalism

- theocracy + authoritarian one-party rule + socialism = fundamentalism

- secular theocracy + authoritarian one-party rule + socialism = communism

- moral universalism (secular) + timocracy + capitalism = tutorial democracy

- moral universalism (secular) + representative government + capitalism = liberal democracy

- conventionalism + plutocracy + capitalism = corporate "democracy"

- moral universalism (secular) + representative democracy + socialism = social democracy

Less well known but potentially realizable are:

- moral universalism (secular) + representative government + solidarism = solidarist democracy

- moral univeralism (either strain) + monarchy + solidarism = solidarist monarchy

We can, moreover, identify pairings of special compatibility, for example, between moral universalism and solidarity, ethnarchy and authoritarianism, and plutocracy and capitalism, but that does not signify that the components cannot be brought into other combinations.

Now it is my contention that, among moral orientations, only moral universalism is legitimate or can provide a legitimate moral foundation for a state or social order and that, among economic systems, solidarism is best situated to provide the economic underpinnings for a legitimate social order. Among alternative political arrangements, only plutocracy is self-evidently inappropriate as a constitutive element in a legitimate social order.

Taking this theoretical vantage point, one might be inclined to judge that there has never been a legitimate system in all of history. However, this judgment must be tempered, since even objective criteria must be "read" in much the way that someone must read a gas meter. The doctrine of popular sovereignty (a central element in Locke's moral-political thinking) presumes that it is the citizenry of a state that is authorized to assess whether the state's behavior is in accord with the objective criteria provided by Universal Reason.[8] And since perception and assessment are "subjective," we may say that the process of legitimation involves both objective and subjective factors existing in mutual interdependence. On this basis, I would suggest that history has generated only three legitimate systems: feudalism, royal monarchy, and democracy (whether ancient democracy, liberal democracy, or social democracy, the last mentioned being, itself, a variant of liberal democracy).

Kantian Prudence

The fact that there is a moral standard against which one can measure the performance of states and that can define the optimal goals to set before ourselves does not create an immediate agenda. Kant himself urged that statesmen act prudently and avoid "premature measures."[9] In Kant's view, "Statesmen should wait until the time is right, until things have naturally proceeded to the point where their measures might succeed; before then, they are most likely to fail, thereby discrediting morality and perhaps unintentionally causing a great deal of suffering."[10] But "waiting" does not mean adopting a Machiavellian mode of action. On the contrary, what Kantianism entails is a prudent pursuit of moral ends, never losing sight of the fact that it is idealism that is apt to prove the most successful, while so-called realism is repeatedly shown to be pitiably unrealistic. Indeed, Kantianism is not merely a recipe for individual moral action but also a kind of roadmap for the moral refinement of the state. By making use of this roadmap, statesmen can make their contribution toward "a steadily advancing but slow development" of human culture and civilization.[11] If there were no possibility of such moral development, then, as Kant put it in *The Conflict of the Faculties,* "the whole traffic of our species with itself on this globe would have to be considered as a mere farcical comedy."[12]

Legitimacy and Revolution

There has been a certain amount of confusion concerning the concept of revolution, as revealed in the sudden popularity of a neologism, *refolution,* that many scholars have elected to use in referring to the events of 1989–90. In adopting this term, they wish to suggest that these events were, somehow, not quite *revolutionary.* Although the term originated with Timothy Garton Ash, Kazimierz Poznański is, perhaps, the clearest exponent of this school of thought, arguing that the transformation in Central and Eastern Europe beginning in 1989 was neither revolutionary in character nor suitably "portrayed as the triumph of an abused society."[13] On the contrary, according to Poznański, what occurred in 1989 and 1990 was that communist elites throughout the area chose to "negotiate" certain changes, that the transformation of 1989–90 constitutes proof that communism "accommodated considerable change," and that the whole point of the transformation was to enable "reformed" communist elites to grab control of capital stock for themselves.[14] He concludes that the postcommunist system "evolved" quite naturally out of communism and thus did not represent a decisive break with the past.[15] Since the systems "evolved," it follows that the cumulative changes cannot be "revolutionary," in Poznański's view. He fortifies his position with a highly exclusionary definition of revolution. In his view, "revolution is understood as a radical transformation of the social structure combined with a violent upheaval from below, i.e., from people who feel alienated and abused."[16]

"Since the collapse of the [communist] system was basically non-violent"[17] in Central and Eastern Europe, in Poznański's view, the violence in Romania in 1989–90, in Croatia in 1991–95, and in Bosnia in 1992–95 and the mass chaos in Albania in 1990–91 evidently not constituting sufficiently important countervailing evidence, and since he judges the transformations to have been "evolutionary" rather than "radical," Poznański concludes that Central and Eastern Europe did not experience a revolution beginning in 1989.

Robert Hayden appears to follow Poznański's lead but takes the Parmenidean line to an extreme. He denies that there has been any repluralization of Central and East European society, evidently believing that the communist-era organizational monopoly of all social institutions is still in place and arguing that, as of January 1996, Poland and Hungary remained under "communist" rule. [18] It is hard to account for Hayden's manifest concerns, but he writes further that even cautious optimism about the eventual prospects for the Czech Republic and Slovenia to realize something that might be termed "democratic rule" is unrealistic[19]—"wonderfully optimistic," as he wrote of the prospects for Slovenia and Macedonia in 1992.[20]

It would be fatuous for me to argue that the foregoing theory is "incorrect" (not to mention that such an approach would smack of Leninist modes of discourse), but I shall suggest that this approach is neither innocent nor useful. It is not innocent because it appears to be tied to a conspiratorial view of the transformation. It is not useful because it does not lead to any further conclusions, whether at the theoretical or the policy level.

I prefer to think of revolution as a change in any of the components of social order, that is, as a change in the principles of legitimation and order underpinning a political system. While change in even one of these components would qualify, to my mind, as revolutionary, a change in all three components simultaneously may be described as a comprehensive revolution. On this understanding, what occurred in Poland, the Czech Republic, Hungary, and Slovenia beginning in 1989 was a comprehensive revolution involving change from secular theocracy/authoritarian one-party monopoly/socialism to moral universalism/representative democracy/(incipient) capitalism.

Revolution does not have to occur in a flash. Few revolutions do. The French Revolution, for example, was evolutionary, growing out of the Estates General summoned by the king of France. The Russian Revolution was likewise "evolutionary," taking its start with the abdication of the czar, passing a crucial watershed with the Bolshevik seizure of power, but reaching its climax (the point at which it defined its character) only with the changes associated with the five-year plan period beginning in 1928. The Central and East European revolutions "of 1989" are no exception; far from having been accomplished within the space of a year or two, these revolutions are still unfolding. Revolutions are *always* evolutionary, and yet they are revolutions all the same.

I would suggest that this approach to revolution is more useful in that it avoids arbitrary time limits and shifts the focus from the means employed (violence) to the results obtained (a change in the ordering principles of state).

Rights

Different legitimating formulae entail different concepts of rights and, indeed, emphasize different bearers of rights. In order to obtain perspective on this subject, however, one might begin by distinguishing among different kinds of rights, legitimated at various levels. The major categories of rights (historically) are rights of kings (divine legitimation); rights of society (natural legitimation); rights of the collective (allegedly natural legitimation); and rights of the individual (divine, natural, or positive legitimation). My argument has been that the notion of collective rights is spurious. There are other rights, of course, such as the rights of corporations, the rights of the patient (in a medical procedure), the rights of the accused (in a trial), and so forth. But these do not concern me here—first, because they are derivative, and second, because they do not play a role in forming and shaping political systems.

But the aforementioned major categories of rights *do* play such a role, whether in conjunction with, or in antagonism to, each other. As is clear from the above, the claim for a right of kings to rule was always premised on divine grace, rendering it, thus, a divine right of kings. Nor was it only in the eighteenth century that this claim was first developed (as is commonly thought); rather, it was only then that this particular phraseology was developed. The concept itself can be found in the ancient Egyptian religio-polity, in ancient Rome, and in the Inca empire, among other places. And associated with this claim for a right of kings was an assumption that the concept also entailed divinely mandated duties for kings.

The claims for the rights of societies, collectivities, and individuals were all developed between the early eighteenth and mid-nineteenth centuries, so that the arguments on their behalf, which seemed new and even unexpected at the time of their origination, now seem ancient and beyond challenge. All three have been defended on the basis of *natural derivation,* linking them to concepts of Natural Law and natural right. In this form of legitimation, the right in question is seen as given by history, reason, progress, or natural morality. Of these three claimed rights, only individual rights have also been defended by appeal to divine grace or to the sanction of the law (positive right).

But historically, the relationship among these sundry "rights" has been uneasy. The doctrine of *collective rights* makes a claim on behalf of a national community or of a majority in that community and owes its development in the first place to Jean-Jacques Rousseau, whose idea of the General Will served as the central legitimating principle in his system. Indeed, Rousseau denied that someone who had been outvoted could claim to have lost, because the interests of the community were, in his eyes, identical with what the majority in the community thought they were and because the outcome of a vote merely informed those who lost that their assessment of what the majority wanted was inaccurate. One must beware of dismissing this formulation as merely curious; on the contrary, it is a key to understanding that for Rousseau, as for Treitschke and, for that matter, most advocates of collective rights, the individual has no legitimate basis for claims against her or his nation, and the interests of the national community always take precedence over those of the individual.

The notion of *societal rights,* traceable to Saint-Simon, Fourier, Owen, Marx, and others, has a rather different point of departure, namely, the right of society as a whole to certain outcomes, safeguards, etc. And whereas the doctrine of collective rights refers to the national community, thus excluding foreigners and other outsiders but, by extension, embracing expatriates and exiles from the homeland, the doctrine of societal rights refers to the naturally existing community, embracing all its members. And further, where the advocates of collective rights have focused on cultural and political claims (for language, cultural autonomy, territorial autonomy, etc.), the advocates of societal rights have instead emphasized economic and social claims (for equality of power and wealth, universal education, access to vital services such as health care, etc.). The reader should have no difficulty in associating the advocates of collective rights with nationalists, and the advocates of societal rights with socialists and social democrats.

Now it is not impossible to advocate more than one category of rights, but two qualifications are needed. First, there will typically be an emphasis on one category of rights or another (e.g., in Serbia an emphasis on collective rights, in present-day America an emphasis on individual rights). Second, the concentration of energy at one level is apt to pit one right against another. Or, to put it another way, an extreme nationalist, absorbed in the defense of the allegedly threatened nation, is apt to be disinclined to worry about the rights of individuals qua individuals—so that, at most, the extreme nationalist will be concerned with violations of the rights of individuals qua members of the favored nation, while individual members of other nations have, by definition, lesser claims.

Political systems are always founded upon some concept of rights or another, whether a rarefied, simple doctrine or a hybrid doctrine. Thus, the advocacy of rights has profound consequences for the evolutionary course of any system. In times of political transition, as in Eastern Europe since 1989, the advocacy of rights plays a heightened role in influencing and shaping the formation of states. More specifically, insofar as liberal democracy is premised on notions of the primacy of individual rights (a notion stated explicitly in both Hobbes and Locke and carried over into *The Federalist Papers*), an emphasis on collective rights is apt to prove subversive of liberalism.

All three modern doctrines (collective, societal, and individual rights) have an appeal in contemporary Eastern Europe. The pre-1989 socialist system was, of course, premised on a particular interpretation of societal rights, and in the first two or so years after the collapse of communism, the advocates of collective rights and individual rights dominated the political stage. But as the recent electoral victories of reformed communist parties demonstrate (as noted in chapter 2), the claims on behalf of societal rights have by no means been delegitimated in the region. On the contrary, for many persons they offer the promise of a welcome security.

The doctrine of collective rights typically takes the form of heightened nationalism, but it may also take the form of claims on behalf of a particular religious community. Thus, in Poland the Catholic Church has claimed to possess a right to dictate its moral agenda, through the vehicle of secular law, to all citizens of Poland and has claimed that its younger members have a right to obtain religious instruction at state schools. These claims derive from a doctrine of collective rights, but in this case, the source of legitimation is divine, indicating that this is a hybrid claim entirely different in character and content from the old *cuius regio eius religio.*

What is especially striking about the three major cases under review, however, is that the escalation of tensions between nationality groups or between confessional groups started in each case with heightened group consciousness within the dominant group. In Poland, non-Catholics and liberal Catholics did not begin protesting against the Church until the Church began to push its agenda. In Slovakia, the Hungarians of southern Slovakia did not begin talking of territorial autonomy and local control of schools until the Mečiar government began to eliminate physical evidence of Hungarian inhabitation (as in the names of towns and villages) and to take action to eliminate local control of schools. And in Kosovo, the local Albanians had, to a considerable extent, reconciled themselves to life in Yugoslavia and did not begin to talk of secession until Slobodan Milošević took power in Serbia and initiated a series of measures reducing the Albanians to the status of second-class citizens. The consistency of this pattern suggests, in turn, that the doctrine of collective rights lends itself rather more to an offensive exploitation than to defensive uses. But what has happened in southern Slovakia and Kosovo, as in Vojvodina, the Sandzak, western Macedonia and Transylvania, is that members of the repressed nationality group have replied in kind by embracing the selfsame doctrine in whose name their rights are being violated. Thus, for example, when representatives of Vojvodina Hungarians from northern Serbia met with the Hungarian state leadership in Budapest in October 1995 to work out a strategy whereby autonomy for Vojvodina might be restored, they were accepting the principle that nationality groups enjoy collective rights distinct and apart from the rights enjoyed by the individual members of such groups.[21] This principle, in turn—as already noted—conjures up the ill-considered notion that the supposed rights of the nationality group (or religious group) may come into conflict with the rights of individuals. The Czech government has shown some recognition of the threat of this doctrine by passing an amendment to the criminal code on 29 June 1995. Under the amendment, the maximum penalty for hate-motivated murder was increased from fifteen years to life imprisonment, and for other hate-related crimes, from three years to five years. Ladislav Body, the Czech parliament's only Romany deputy, called for even more effective measures, challenging the notion that there is a right of hate speech—a right seemingly acknowledged in the south Bohemian town of Pisek in 1994 when a judge allowed skinheads accused of causing the death of a seventeen-year-old Romany to wear uniforms with fascist insignia in court.[22]

Hegemonism versus Autonomism

I have examined eight cases in which conflicts have been stoked by appeals to the (discrete) collective rights of one or another group or religious association. In these cases, a consistent pattern emerges: in every case but one, where hegemonist impulses arise on the part of the dominant group, autonomist impulses appear in response among members of the subordinated group. In the cases of Hungarians in southern Slovakia and Transylvania and Albanians in Kosovo and Macedonia, intergroup tensions arose against the background of a history of conquest and variably overt or latent irredentism. In the cases of Serbs in Croatia and Turks in Bulgaria, the population distributions could be identified as side-effects of the Ottoman conquest (the former having arisen in connection with the creation of the Military Frontier in Croatia).

But although the histories of these sundry interactions are, at times, complex, the conflicts were rekindled, in the postcommunist era, in diverse ways. In Slovakia, Hungarian autonomism appeared as a response to Slovak hegemonism. Likewise in Kosovo, although Albanian autonomism could be interpreted as an attachment to the status Albanians had enjoyed from 1946 to 1989, separatism flared up among Kosovar Albanians directly in reaction to Serbian assertions, under Milošević, of hegemonic rights. In Transylvania and Bulgaria, by contrast, autonomism among the Hungarians and Turks was stronger in earlier years, but again arose in reaction to actual tendencies of hegemonism.

The case of the Serbs in Croatia is somewhat more complex, because the Serbs enjoyed a history of autonomy over a period of centuries in Habsburg times, and the memory of these years could be revived and harnessed to justify a renewed appeal for autonomous status. As shown in chapter 3, Serbian autonomism in Croatia flared up in 1989 as a projection of Serbian hegemonism within the Republic of Serbia. Countervailing Croatian tendencies of hegemonism arose in simultaneous response to Serb hegemonism in Serbia and Serb autonomism in Croatia.

The cases of Macedonia and Poland have displayed particular features. In Macedonia, Albanian autonomism has been associated with perceptions of cultural threat, to be sure; yet one looks in vain for symptoms of nationalist hegemonism on the part of Macedonia's coalition government. If the Macedonian case supplies an example of autonomism in the absence of hegemonism, Catholic theocratic currents in Poland illustrate the phenomenon of hegemonism without autonomism. Moreover, given that the non-Catholics of Poland do not inhabit any specific or discrete region of Poland, it is difficult to imagine how the religious dispute could provoke autonomist demands.

Then there is Bosnia, which during 1990–95 was taken down the road to war by followers of Radovan Karadžić, who had been inflamed by hegemonic appeals to the doctrine of collective rights. Partitioned Bosnia follows schemata associated with illusions about so-called collective rights; individual rights are repeatedly violated, in the name of the collective rights of now one nation, now the other, while the West looks on, smiling in arrogance and ignorance, seemingly oblivious to the consequences of building states on the foundations of hatred and intolerance. It is as if the West wants to test the nationalist proposition that democracy may be built without regard for individual rights. Indeed, by endorsing Dayton, the West has returned to Treitschke, the German historian who, it will be recalled from chapter 1, scorned notions of conscience, demanded absolute obedience to the dictates of regimes (without allowing individuals to make any independent assessment of those regimes), and advised that one was human only secondarily and derivately. It was this philosophy that Hannah Arendt criticized in her brilliant book *Eichmann in Jerusalem*. But for Treitschke and—so it seems—for the West as well, one is, in the first place, a Serb or a Croat or a Muslim, and only derivatively a human being enjoying certain rights. But there is more: if one's humanity derives from one's membership in a national community, then any appeals to individual rights must depend on their compatibility with the collective rights of the nation, and then, indeed, the supposed rights of individuals to return to their homes must be subordinated to the interests of the nation that controls the area. The Dayton accords, at least as they have been carried out and enforced, could be better termed the Treitschke accords.

The Problems with Autonomism

Observers frequently display a certain complacency about autonomy, usually opining that there is nothing inappropriate about having people running their own affairs. Phrased that way, autonomism seems unobjectionable, even democratic. But autonomism involves an element of self-contradiction by asserting simultaneously that a given state is authorized to rule over a certain group of people and that that group of people is authorized to disassociate itself, in part, from that selfsame state. And while the creation of purely administrative subunits, such as the county system in the United States, presents no such problems, not being associated in any way with the doctrine of collective rights (so that no one argues that the people of a certain region are "entitled" by nature to their own county), autonomism, in the sense in which I have used the term throughout this book, creates fissures, or fault lines, through which the communities living within separate autonomous zones can grow steadily farther apart and along which the system will be inclined, given sufficiently prolonged and intense crisis, to break apart, as the Soviet and Yugoslav cases demonstrate.

There are also some differences between the three cases included in this book and the other cases mentioned here. In the cases of Poland, Slovakia, and Kosovo, the dominant group's assertion of the doctrine of collective rights has dominated the political agenda and thus has directly threatened the construction of liberal democracy. In the cases of Macedonia and Bulgaria, the dominant group has not generated nationalist politicians capable of distorting the government's agenda along nationalist lines; in these cases, therefore, nationalism has not stimulated as acute a sense of threat as in the other societies or so directly threatened the construction of liberal democracy. In the case of Transylvania, by contrast, nationalist politicians Gheorghe Funar (head of the Romanian National Unity Party and mayor of Cluj-Napoca) and Vadim Tudor (head of the Greater Romania Party and member of the senate) have openly played the nationalist card. Funar, who had earlier earned notoriety for having adopted measures to erase the memory of Hungarian influence in Transylvania, presided over the unveiling in March 1996 of a commemorative plaque memorializing "the bloody repression led by the Hungarian landowners, during which more than 40,000 Romanians were killed and 230 villages set on fire and destroyed."[23]

Of course, nationalists claim that their doctrine is fully compatible with democracy. They claim merely to be engaged in the project of protecting the national culture within the framework of democracy and in accord with the wishes of the population (the General Will). In the course of carrying out this project, therefore, they seek to equate the cultural community with the political community. But, as George Schöpflin has observed,

> The idea of making the two coincide—the kernel of the nationalist principle—raised enormous practical difficulties for the definition of both culture and politics. Thus nationalists tended to go for the simplest, most "self-evident" criteria, above all language, and to argue that the speakers of a particular language constituted a cultural community, that this was "the nation" and consequently the nation should be recognized as an independent unit of politics, viz., as a state.[24]

Quite apart from the practical and logistical difficulties associated with this notion (extending even to so basic a matter as determining to which language group peoples in border areas, who are often bilingual and may also speak a local hybrid language, should be thought to belong), there is the more basic question as to just why language in particular should be thought to be the transcendent variable in determining what constitutes a natural community. On the (unnecessary) assumption that some common quality may determine the boundaries of a community, one could look to religion, music, or even cuisine to set the boundaries of a state, and anyone familiar with the dispersion of these aspects of culture will know that each would dictate rather different borders. Discarding that assumption, one might propose to draw state borders on the basis of more practical considerations, for example, natural economic zones, traditional or historical or existing borders, dynastic claims, and so forth. But even that project is still founded on the assumption that the drawing of boundaries dividing states is in and of itself not merely an unavoidable practical matter but positively desirable—and the latter has (as far as I know) never been proved.

What occurs when the political community is identified with a single cultural community (however defined)? As Schöpflin explains, when

> political organization is erected on the foundation of cultural community ... non-members of that community are automatically disqualified from membership of both political and cultural units. When political rights are derived from culture, as they logically are in the construction of nation-states, and when the codes of political behavior are determined by reference to national homogeneity, cultural (ethnic) minorities begin from a very poor position.[25]

The same principle applies in cases of religious hegemony.

Part of the problem clearly lies with the leaders. To take the example of Serbia, had Latinka Perović and Marko Nikezić been able to continue in office in the early 1970s, there is at least a chance that they might have been able to consolidate the tradition of Serbian liberalism and political moderation that they represented and that the chauvinistic appeals later made by persons like Dobrica Ćosić and Slobodan Milošević might have fallen on deaf ears. The "what ifs" of history serve to remind us that political outcomes are the product of a finite number of variables among which, at times, one particular factor is determinative.

Contemporary Eastern Europe has by no means resolved the two-hundred-year-old struggle between advocates of societal rights, collective rights, and individual rights. Nor has any other part of the world. Not only has history not reached some sort of "end," but in fact history admits of no teleological end, consisting, rather, of a spiral-like evolution in which the same conflicts and battles are ever fought afresh, albeit with some discernible shifts. But the struggle is played out differently from society to society, with advocates of collective rights stronger in some societies than in others and with advocates of societal rights stronger in some societies than in others. And this struggle, I would argue, has played, and will continue to play, a pivotal role in the political evolution of Eastern Europe and of the entire world.

Notes

Introduction

1. I am referring here to the arguments made by spokespersons for the Croatian Serbs between 1990 and 1995. On this, see my introduction ("The Roots of Discord and the Language of War") to *Beyond Yugoslavia: Politics, Economics, and Culture in a Shattered Community,* ed. Sabrina P. Ramet and Ljubiša S. Adamovich (Boulder, Colo.: Westview Press, 1995), 5–6.

2. As I defined it in my essay, "Delegitimation and Relegitimation in Yugoslavia and After" (unpublished manuscript, 1994), 1.

3. Ibid.

4. Guglielmo Ferrero, *The Principles of Power,* trans. Theodore R. Jaeckel (New York: G. P. Putnam's Sons, 1942).

5. See Frank M. Coleman, *Hobbes and America: Exploring the Constitutional Foundations* (Toronto: University of Toronto Press, 1977).

6. Benedict R. O'Gorman Anderson, *Imagined Communities: Reflections on the Origin and Spread of Nationalism* (London and New York: Verso, 1991).

7. Gaines Post, *Studies in Medieval Legal Thought,* excerpted in *Renaissance Man—Medieval or Modern?* ed. Brian Tierney, Donald Kagan, and L. Pearce Williams, 3d ed. (New York: Random House, 1976), 42–44.

8. Susan Reynolds, *Kingdoms and Communities in Western Europe, 900–1300* (Oxford: Clarendon Press, 1984), 59–64. See also Robert C. Palmer, *The County Courts of Medieval England, 1150–1350* (Princeton: Princeton University Press, 1982). Moreover, as J. R. Maddicott notes in an article devoted to county courts and county affairs in fourteenth-century England, while it is not clear "that there was anything remotely 'democratic' about the county court," legal proceduralism was already highly developed and, moreover, had to reckon with "the activities of a newly articulate political public." J. R. Maddicott, "The County Community and the Making of Public Opinion in Fourteenth-Century England," *Transactions of the Royal Historical Society* (London), 5th ser., 28 (1978): 30, 42.

9. J. M. Kelly, *A Short History of Western Legal Theory* (Oxford: Clarendon Press, 1992), 135.

10. Quoted in ibid.

11. Ognyan Minchev, "Foreign Policy and Ethnic Issues Confronting Bulgaria Today" (lecture presented at the University of Washington, 19 April 1996).

12. See Immanuel Kant, *Groundwork of the Metaphysic of Morals,* trans. H. J. Patton (New York: Harper & Row, 1964); and John Locke, *Two Treatises of Government,*

ed. Peter Laslett, rev. ed. (New York: Mentor Books, 1965), *First Treatise,* para. 101, and *Second Treatise,* paras. 57, 63.

13. Bernard Yack, "The Problem with Kantian Liberalism," in *Kant and Political Philosophy: The Contemporary Legacy,* ed. Ronald Beiner and William James Booth (New Haven: Yale University Press, 1993), 234.

14. Russell Hardin, *Morality within the Limits of Reason* (Chicago: University of Chicago Press, 1988), 11–12.

15. On the moral relativism implicit in Western policy responses to Bosnia, see Daniele Conversi, "Moral Relativism and Equidistance in British Attitudes to the War in the Former Yugoslavia," in *This Time We Knew: Western Responses to Genocide in Bosnia,* ed. Thomas Cushman and Stjepan G. Meštrović (New York: New York University Press, 1996); and Thomas Cushman, *Critical Theory and the War in Bosnia,* Donald W. Treadgold Papers, no. 13 (Seattle: Henry M. Jackson School of the University of Washington, in press).

16. Dennis F. Thompson, *The Democratic Citizen: Social Science and Democratic Theory in the Twentieth Century* (London: Cambridge University Press, 1970), as quoted in Julie Mostov, "Women and the Radical Right: Ethnocracy and Body Politics," in "The Radical Right in Central and Eastern Europe," ed. Sabrina P. Ramet (unpublished manuscript).

17. Coleman, *Hobbes and America,* esp. chap. 3.

18. As Coleman notes, the legal tradition underpinning the American system, not recognizing the existence of societal rights, also does not accept the notion of an objective moral system that one might call Natural Law and therefore relies exclusively on notions of the enforcement of positive law, seen as the outcome of the politicking among individuals and their parties and political groupings. See Coleman, *Hobbes and America,* 49.

19. Kossuth Radio Network (Budapest), 17 September 1995, trans. in Foreign Broadcast Information Service (FBIS), *Daily Report* (East Europe), 18 September 1995, 74.

20. Serbian Radio (Belgrade), 5 May 1993, trans. in *BBC Summary of World Broadcasts,* 7 May 1993.

21. Radovan Karadžić, interviewed by Yelena Kalyadina, *Komsomskaya pravda* (Moscow), 17 May 1995, 7, trans. in FBIS, *Daily Report* (East Europe), 19 May 1995, 9.

22. See Locke, *Two Treatises of Government, Second Treatise,* para. 63.

23. Radovan Karadžić, interviewed by Elena Yoncheva, *168 Chasa* (Sofia), 30 October–5 November 1995, 17–18, trans. in FBIS, *Daily Report* (East Europe), 3 November 1995, 20.

24. Joseph Raz, "Autonomy, Toleration, and the Harm Principle," in *Justifying Toleration: Conceptual and Historical Perspectives,* ed. Susan Mendus (Cambridge: Cambridge University Press, 1988), 157, 165.

25. The relation between liberal presuppositions and nationalist claims has recently been discussed in philosophic circles. See Omar Dahbour, "Introduction: National Identity as a Philosophical Problem"; Judith Lictenberg, "How Liberal Can National-

ism Be?"; and Darrel Moellendorf, "Liberalism, Nationalism, and the Right to Secede"; all in *Philosophical Forum* 28, nos. 1–2 (Fall/Winter 1996–97).

26. Andrei Simić, "Obstacles to the Development of a Yugoslav National Consciousness: Ethnic Identity and Folk Culture in the Balkans," *Journal of Mediterranean Studies* 1, no. 1 (1991): 31.

27. Sabrina P. Ramet, *Balkan Babel: The Disintegration of Yugoslavia from the Death of Tito to Ethnic War,* 2d ed. (Boulder, Colo.: Westview Press, 1996), 322.

28. James Madison, *Federalist Paper No. 10,* in *The Federalist Papers,* by Alexander Hamilton, James Madison, and John Jay (New York: Mentor Books, 1961), 78.

29. James Madison, *Federalist Paper No. 51,* in *The Federalist Papers,* by Hamilton, Madison, and Jay, 323–24.

30. David Lucas, *Ethnic Bipolarism in Slovakia, 1989–1995*, Donald W. Treadgold Papers, no. 11 (Seattle: Henry M. Jackson School of International Studies of the University of Washington, 1996), 17, summarizing Donald L. Horowitz, *Ethnic Groups in Conflict* (Berkeley and Los Angeles: University of California Press, 1985), esp. 346–49.

31. Oscar Jászi, *The Dissolution of the Habsburg Monarchy* (Chicago: University of Chicago Press, 1929).

32. Diana T. Meyers, *Inalienable Rights: A Defense* (New York: Columbia University Press, 1985), 116.

33. Ibid., 119.

34. Ibid., 117.

35. Locke, *Two Treatises of Government, Second Treatise,* para. 63.

36. See, e.g., Sabrina P. Ramet, *Nationalism and Federalism in Yugoslavia, 1962–1991,* 2d ed. (Bloomington: Indiana University Press, 1992); Sabrina P. Ramet, "War in the Balkans," in *Foreign Affairs* 71, no. 4 (Fall 1992); and Ramet, *Balkan Babel.*

37. *NIN,* no. 1939 (28 February 1988): 8. In 1987, Milošević took over as president of the Serbian party organization and shortly thereafter set in motion processes designed to reverse the natural demographic trends.

38. John Keane, *Reflections on Violence* (London: Verso, 1996), 125–27.

39. Immanuel Kant, *The Metaphysics of Morals,* trans. Mary Gregor (Cambridge: Cambridge University Press, 1991), 130–33, 176–77.

40. It was Giovanni Gentile, a twentieth-century fascist, who first claimed Hegel for fascism. And even if most observers are sagacious enough to realize that such a conflation is clearly erroneous, many writers (such as Karl-Heinz Ilting and Karl Popper) have, all the same, viewed Hegel as an authoritarian or totalitarian thinker. Other scholars have pointed out the errors in such a construal and have made a strong case for viewing Hegel as a democrat. See, e.g., Jan Drydyk, "Hegel's Politics: Liberal or Democratic?" *Canadian Journal of Philosophy* 16, no. 1 (March 1986): esp. 101, 105–7, 109–10, 120–22; Richard Bellamy, "Hegel and Liberalism," *History of European Ideas* 8, no. 6 (1987): esp. 693, 694–95, 701, 704, 705; and Reinhardt Albrecht, *Hegel und die Demokratie* (Bonn: Bouvier Verlag Herbert Grundmann, 1978), esp. 17–40, 92–103.

41. Quoted in Drydyk, "Hegel's Politics," 121–22.

Chapter 1

This chapter is a revised version of a piece originally published in *Acta Slavica Iaponica* (Hokkaido University, Sapporo) 13 (1995). Reprinted by permission.

1. See the monthly issues of the American Bar Association's newsletter, *The Central and East European Law Initiative*. See also Sabrina P. Ramet, "Balkan Pluralism and Its Enemies," in *Orbis* 36, no. 4 (Fall 1992): 563, for a few examples.

2. Joseph Rothschild, *East Central Europe between the Two World Wars* (Seattle: University of Washington Press, 1974), 87.

3. Figures for 1924, given in "Jugoslavija," in *Enciklopedija Jugoslavije,* vol. 4 (Zagreb: Leksikografski zavod FNRJ, 1960), 639.

4. Bruce F. Pauley, *The Habsburg Legacy, 1867–1939* (San Francisco: Holt, Rinehart & Winston, 1972), 115.

5. On Czechoslovak-Hungarian relations in the interwar era, see Helmut Slapnička, "Die böhmischen Länder und die Slowakei 1919–1945," in *Handbuch der Geschichte der Böhmischen Länder,* vol. 4, ed. Karl Bosl (Zagreb and Stuttgart: Anton Hiersemann, 1970), 49–50, 57.

6. *Economist* (London), 17 April 1993, 50.

7. *Der Spiegel* (Hamburg), 17 May 1993, 183.

8. On Greece, Russia, and China, see *Seattle Post-Intelligencer,* 17 November 1992, sec. A, p. 2; on Greece, see also *Neue Zürcher Zeitung,* 17 November 1992, 2; on Libya, see *Der Spiegel,* 24 January 1994, 110–13; on Romania, see *Vjesnik* (Zagreb), 16 April 1993, 48.

9. See Anton Logoreci, *The Albanians: Europe's Forgotten Survivors* (London: Victor Gollancz, 1977), 58–62.

10. When, in June 1993, Albanian authorities deported a Greek Orthodox cleric who had been distributing propaganda calling for Greek annexation of southern Albania, the Greek government protested loudly and within a matter of weeks deported more than 12,500 Albanians. See *Süddeutsche Zeitung* (Munich), 26–27 June 1993, 7; and *Frankfurter Allgemeine,* 30 June 1993, 3.

11. Antony Polonsky, *Politics in Independent Poland, 1921–1939* (Oxford: Clarendon Press, 1972), 7–8.

12. Ibid., 52.

13. Hugh Seton-Watson, *Eastern Europe between the Wars, 1918–1941,* 3d ed. (Hamden, Conn.: Archon Books, 1962), 179.

14. Alex N. Dragnich, *The First Yugoslavia: Search for a Viable Political System* (Stanford, Calif.: Hoover Institution Press, 1983), 15.

15. Blagota Gardasević, "Organizaciono ustrojstvo i zakonodavstvo pravoslavne crkve izmedju dva svetska rata," in *Srpska Pravoslavna Crkva 1920–1970: Spomenica o 50-godišnjici vaspostavljanja Srpske Patriaršije* (Belgrade: Kosmos, 1971), 37–41.

16. For discussion of Romania's problems of integration, see Irina Livezeanu, *Cultural Politics in Greater Romania: Regionalism, Nation Building, and Ethnic Struggle, 1918–1930* (Ithaca: Cornell University Press, 1995), 135.

17. *Süddeutsche Zeitung,* 19 October 1993, 6.

18. *International Herald Tribune,* 29–30 May 1993, 4, Tokyo edition.

19. A June 1993 poll found that "only 22 percent of West Germans and 11 percent of Easterners say they feel a common identity" with each other. *International Herald Tribune,* 28 June 1993, 1, Tokyo edition.

20. On Stamboliski, see John D. Bell, *Peasants in Power: Alexander Stamboliski and the Bulgarian Agrarian National Union, 1899–1923* (Princeton: Princeton University Press, 1977). On Radić, see Ivan Muzić, *Stjepan Radić u Kraljevini Srba, Hrvata i Slovenaca* (Ljubljana: Narodna in univerzitetna knjižnica, 1987). On Tărănism in Romania, see Armin Heinen, *Die Legion 'Erzengel Michael' in Rumänien: Soziale Bewegung und politische Organisation* (Munich: R. Oldenbourg Verlag, 1986), 172–74.

21. Josef Korbel, *Twentieth-Century Czechoslovakia: The Meaning of Its History* (New York: Columbia University Press, 1977), 16.

22. István Deák, "Historical Foundations," in *Ungarn,* Südosteuropa–Handbuch, vol. 5, ed. Klaus Detlev Grothusen (Göttingen: Vandenhoeck & Ruprecht, 1987), 47, 49.

23. Quoted in Wacław Jedrzejewicz, *Piłsudski: A Life for Poland* (New York: Hippocrene Books, 1982), 276–77.

24. Jan Tomasz Gross, *Polish Society under German Occupation: The Generalgouvernement, 1939–1944* (Princeton: Princeton University Press, 1979), 24.

25. On this point, see Joseph Raz, "Autonomy, Toleration, and the Harm Principle," in *Justifying Toleration: Conceptual and Historical Perspectives,* ed. Susan Mendus (Cambridge: Cambridge University Press, 1988).

26. Heinrich von Treitschke, *Politics,* vol. 1, trans. Blanche Dugdale and Torben de Bille (New York: Macmillan, 1916), 104.

27. Ibid., 9.

28. On the "tri-named people," see Ivo Banac, *The National Question in Yugoslavia: Origins, History, Politics* (Ithaca: Cornell University Press, 1984), 161–62.

29. See Sabrina P. Ramet, *Social Currents in Eastern Europe: The Sources and Consequences of the Great Transformation,* 2d ed. (Durham, N.C.: Duke University Press, 1995), chap. 18.

30. As Katherine Verdery argues. See her *What Was Socialism, and What Comes Next?* (Princeton: Princeton University Press, 1996), 92.

31. For details and further discussion, see Sabrina P. Ramet, "The Serbian Church and the Serbian Nation," in *Beyond Yugoslavia: Politics, Economics, and Culture in a Shattered Community,* ed. Sabrina P. Ramet and Ljubiša S. Adamovich (Boulder, Colo.: Westview Press, 1995).

32. One of the remarkable patterns in post-1989 Eastern Europe involves the political rehabilitation of precommunist figures, including collaborators. Among those who have been rehabilitated since 1989 are Admiral Miklós Horthy in Hungary, Msgr. Jozef

Tiso in Slovakia, Croatian Peasant Party leader Vlatko Maček, Croatian fascist leader Ante Pavelić, and Chetnik leader Draža Mihailović in Serbia. On Horthy, see *Süddeutsche Zeitung,* 6 September 1993, 6; and *Der Spiegel,* 13 September 1993, 162, 164; on Tiso, see *Der Spiegel,* 6 September 1993, 176; on Maček, see *Vjesnik,* ,31 July 1993, 14–15; on Pavelić and Mihailović, see Ramet, *Social Currents in Eastern Europe,* chap. 17.

33. On the Károlyi and Kun governments, see Zsuzsa L. Nagy, "Revolution in Hungary (1918–1919)," in *A History of Hungary,* ed. Ervin Pamlenyi, trans. László Boros et al.; translation rev. by Margaret Morris and Richard E. Allen (Budapest: Corvina, 1973); and Oscar Jászi, *Revolution and Counter-Revolution in Hungary* (1924; reprint New York: Howard Fertig, 1969); also Rudolf L. Tökés, *Béla Kun and the Hungarian Soviet Republic: The Origins and Role of the Communist Party of Hungary in the Revolutions of 1918–1919* (New York: Frederick A. Praeger, 1967).

34. Polonsky, *Politics in Independent Poland,* 317–21.

35. Ibid., 331.

36. Seton-Watson, *Eastern Europe between the Wars,* 165.

37. For an account of the period of unstable parliamentary government up to the proclamation of the royal dictatorship in Yugoslavia, see Branislav Gligorijević, *Parlament i političke stranke u Jugoslaviji (1919–1929)* (Belgrade: Narodna knjiga, 1979); and John R. Lampe, *Yugoslavia as History: Twice There Was a Country* (Cambridge: Cambridge University Press, 1996), chap. 5.

In 1938, the czar reintroduced elections but without parties. See Robert J. McIntyre, *Bulgaria: Politics, Economics, and Society* (London: Pinter, 1988), 39–40.

38. Victor S. Mamatey, "The Development of Czechoslovak Democracy, 1920–1938," in *A History of the Czechoslovak Republic, 1918–1948,* ed. Victor S. Mamatey and Radomir Luza (Princeton: Princeton University Press, 1973), 101.

39. Pauley, *Habsburg Legacy,* 119.

40. For details and documentation, see *MTI Econews,* 15 December 1990, on Nexis; Hungarian TV (Budapest), 16 August 1992, trans. in *BBC Summary of World Broadcasts,* 22 August 1992; Hungarian Radio (Budapest), 9 January 1993, trans. in *BBC Summary of World Broadcasts,* 12 January 1993; Hungarian Radio, 21 January 1994, trans. in *BBC Summary of World Broadcasts,* 24 January 1994; *MTI Econews,* 10 April 1994, on Nexis; and *MTI Econews,* 12 September 1994, on Nexis.

41. For details and documentation, see *MTI Econews,* 17 March 1996, on Nexis; Reuter, 18 March 1996, on Nexis; MTI news agency (Budapest), 18 March 1996, in *BBC Monitoring Service: Eastern Europe,* 20 March 1996; Hungarian Radio, 18 March 1996, trans. in *BBC Monitoring Service: Eastern Europe,* 20 March 1996; and Reuter, 29 April 1996, on Nexis.

42. Korbel, *Twentieth-Century Czechoslovakia,* 69; Dragnich, *First Yugoslavia,* 21, 36; and Heinen, *Die Legion 'Erzengel Michael,'* 266.

43. Sabrina P. Ramet, *Social Currents in Eastern Europe: The Sources and Meaning of the Great Transformation* (Durham, N.C.: Duke University Press, 1991), 315.

44. In the parliamentary elections of October 1991, more than twenty political parties obtained representation in the Polish parliament, rendering coalition governments

unstable. Wałęsa, who had criticized the election law in its draft form, obtained revisions to it in the summer of 1993, resulting in a smaller number of parties obtaining representation in the September 1993 elections. For background, see *International Herald Tribune,* 2 June 1993, 2, Tokyo edition; and Sabrina P. Ramet, "The New Poland: Democratic and Authoritarian Tendencies," *Global Affairs* 7, no. 2 (Spring 1992).

45. On this subject, see Peter F. Sugar, ed., *Native Fascism in the Successor States, 1918–1945* (Santa Barbara, Calif.: ABC-Clio, 1971).

46. See Dov B. Lungu, *Romania and the Great Powers, 1933–1940* (Durham, N.C.: Duke University Press, 1989), 115–16.

47. See Walter Laqueur, *Fascism: Past, Present, Future* (New York: Oxford University Press, 1996); and Sabrina P. Ramet, "The Radical Right in Eastern Europe" (unpublished manuscript).

48. *Süddeutsche Zeitung,* 23 June 1993, 7. See also *Vjesnik,* 14 June 1993, 8; and *Süddeutsche Zeitung,* 24 June 1993, 8.

49. On the character of the Milošević regime, see Branka Magaš, *The Destruction of Yugoslavia: Tracking the Break-up, 1980–1992* (London: Verso, 1993); on the character of the Tudjman government, see Dijana Plestina, "Democracy and Nationalism in Croatia: The First Three Years," in *Beyond Yugoslavia,* ed. Ramet and Adamovich.

50. See *Süddeutsche Zeitung,* 7 September 1993, 7.

51. Seton-Watson, *Eastern Europe between the Wars,* 141.

52. Ibid., 266.

53. Quoted in Polonsky, *Politics in Independent Poland,* 186.

54. Romania is a prime example. See Trond Gilberg, *Nationalism and Communism in Romania: The Rise and Fall of Ceausescu's Personal Dictatorship* (Boulder, Colo.: Westview Press, 1990), esp. 194–95, 239–42.

55. Alexis de Tocqueville, *The Old Regime and the French Revolution* (Garden City, N.Y.: Doubleday, 1955), xiii, quoted in Ken Jowitt, "The Leninist Legacy," in *Eastern Europe in Revolution,* ed. Ivo Banac (Ithaca: Cornell University Press, 1992), 213.

56. Jowitt, "Leninist Legacy," 215.

57. Public opinion poll reported in *Nowa Europa* (Warsaw), 1 September 1992, trans. in Foreign Broadcast Information Service (FBIS), *Daily Report* (East Europe), 9 September 1992, 23.

58. Banac, *National Question,* 162.

59. Seton-Watson, *Eastern Europe between the Wars,* 77, 180.

60. Ibid., 77; and Banac, *National Question,* 299–300, 320.

61. Polonsky, *Politics in Independent Poland,* 140–41.

62. Stephen Fischer-Galati, *Twentieth-Century Rumania* (New York: Columbia University Press, 1970), 31.

63. Logoreci, *The Albanians,* 69.

64. Banac, *National Question,* 299.

65. Seton-Watson, *Eastern Europe between the Wars,* 344.

66. Polonsky, *Politics in Independent Poland,* 141; and Gross, *Polish Society,* 19.

67. Polonsky, *Politics in Independent Poland,* 35.

68. Ibid., 335.

69. In June 1993, the "Serbian Krajina Republic" in Croatia voted to join Serbia. See the report in the *Times* (London), 21 June 1993, 9.

70. On Romania, see *Frankfurter Allgemeine,* 19 June 1993, 12; on Slovakia, see *Süddeutsche Zeitung,* 4 January 1994, 5; and *International Herald Tribune,* 11 January 1994, 5.

71. See *Süddeutsche Zeitung,* 27 July 1993, 6.

72. On Istria, see *Vjesnik,* 28 July 1993; and *Glas Istre* (Pula), 2 June 1993, 3–4.

73. Jászi, *Revolution and Counter-Revolution,* 7.

74. Polonsky, *Politics in Independent Poland,* 53.

75. Heinen, *Die Legion 'Erzengel Michael,'* 45.

76. Seton-Watson, *Eastern Europe between the Wars,* 139.

77. Ibid., 75.

78. Ibid., 124–25.

79. On this point, see Yeshayashu Jelinek, *The Parish Republic: Hlinka's Slovak People's Party, 1939–1945* (Boulder, Colo.: East European Monographs, 1976).

80. For discussion, see Ghita Ionescu and Ernest Gellner, eds., *Populism: Its Meaning and National Characteristics* (London: Weidenfeld & Nicolson, 1969).

81. On Germany's increasing problems with ethnocentrism and right-wing extremism, see Thomas Assheuer and Hans Sarkowicz, *Rechtsradikale in Deutschland: Die alte und die neue Rechte* (Munich: C. H. Beck'sche Verlagsbuchhandlung, 1990); Wolfgang Benz, ed., *Rechtsextremismus in Deutschland* (Frankfurt am Main: Fischer Taschenbuch Verlag, 1994); Thomas Lillig, *Rechtsextremismus in den neuen Bundesländern* (Mainz: Hausdrückerei der Universität Mainz, 1994); and Sabrina P. Ramet, "The Radical Right in Germany," *In Depth* 4, no. 1 (Winter 1994): 43–68.

82. Details in Ramet, "Radical Right in Central and Eastern Europe."

83. It might be thought that these differences reflect a concession to "linear thinking." But in fact they serve to highlight the way cycles shift and evolve, so that no cycle ever exactly replicates any other.

Chapter 2

This chapter is a revised and updated version of an article of the same title, originally published in *Current History,* vol. 95, no. 599 (March 1996). Reprinted by permission.

1. For data, see Sabrina P. Ramet, *Social Currents in Eastern Europe: The Sources and Consequences of the Great Transformation,* 2d ed. (Durham, N.C.: Duke University Press, 1995), 375.

2. *New Europe* (Athens), 10–16 March 1996, 21, and ibid., 5–11 May 1996, 22.

3. *New York Times,* 26 October 1994, sec. A, p. 5.

4. Slovenia's growth rate slowed by a rather less dramatic 0.5 percent.

5. *New Europe,* 12–18 November 1995, 13.

6. Ibid., 21–27 January 1996, 16; and *Neue Zürcher Zeitung,* 29 December 1995, 9.

7. *New Europe,* 27 October–2 November 1996, 10.

8. *European* (London), 18 November 1994, 20.

9. *Neue Zürcher Zeitung,* 3 November 1995, 9.

10. For example, in August 1994, when Western banks agreed to write off half of Poland's $13 billion commercial debt. See *Boston Sunday Globe,* 28 August 1994, 26.

11. *New Europe,,* 28 January–3 February 1996, 17; and 28 April–4 May 1996, 19.

12. *Euromoney Central European,* 1 July 1995, on Nexis; and *New Europe,* 15–21 October 1995, 24.

13. *Reuters European Business Report,* 7 June 1995, *Business Eastern Europe,* 12 June 1995, and *Business Eastern Europe,* 19 June 1995—all on Nexis; and *New Europe,* 22–28 October 1995, 24.

14. Jože Mencinger, "Economics of Disintegration—From Slovenia's Perspective," *Balkan Forum* 3, no. 4 (December 1995): 195.

15. *New Europe,* 28 April–4 May 1996, 25; and 19–25 May 1996, 25.

16. *Romania Libera* (Bucharest), 24 February 1994, 3, trans. in Foreign Broadcast Information Service (FBIS), *Daily Report (East Europe)*, 3 March 1994, 30.

17. Details in Ramet, *Social Currents,* 380.

18. *Balkan News International and East European Report* (Athens), 5–11 March 1995, 17. See also *Die Welt* (Bonn), 11 May 1995, sec. 2, p. IV.

19. *New Europe,* 11–17 February 1996, 32. See also *Neue Zürcher Zeitung,* 28 December 1995, 12.

20. *New Europe,* 15–21 September 1996, 38; and *Neue Zürcher Zeitung,* 1 November 1996, 9.

21. On Bulgaria, see *New Europe,* 24–30 December 1995, 29.

22. *European,* 25 November–1 December 1994, 12.

23. *New Europe,* 22–28 October 1995, 35; and 17–23 December 1995, 32.

24. *Neue Zürcher Zeitung,* 2 July 1996, 11.

25. *New Europe,* 4–10 February 1996, 31.

26. Ibid., 17–23 March 1996, 31.

27. See *Neue Zürcher Zeitung,* 7 June 1996, 11; and *New Europe,* 28 July–3 August 1996, 6.

28. *New Europe,* 12–18 May 1996, 35; 19–25 May 1996, 34; 4–10 August 1996, 35; and 11–17 August 1996, 36.

29. Quoted in *New Europe,* 12–18 May 1996, 35.

30. Ibid., 21–27 April 1996, 1.

31. Ibid., 2–8 June 1996, 2, 35.

32. *Balkan News and East European Report* (Athens), 28 May–3 June 1995, 6.

33. *Illyria* (The Bronx), 6–8 May 1996, 1. See also *New Europe,* 17–23 March 1996, 39.

34. *New Europe,* 20–26 October 1996, 32.

35. Ibid., 10–16 December 1995, 5; and 25 February–2 March 1996, 38.

36. *Neue Zürcher Zeitung,* 30 April 1996, 10; and *New Europe,* 3–9 December 1995, 35; and 21–27 January 1996, 35.

37. *New Europe,* 17–23 March 1996, 38.

38. Ibid., 4–10 August 1996, 25; and 20–26 October 1996, 31.

39. Ibid., 28 January–3 February 1996, 22; and 4–10 February 1996, 22.

40. Ibid. 24–30 December 1995, 22.

41. Ibid., 7–13 April 1996, 44; 16–22 June 1996, 27; and 30 June–6 July 1996, 27.

42. Ibid., 19–25 November 1995, 33. See also *Vreme International.* 24 August 1996, 8–9.

43. *New Europe,* 5–11 May 1996, 39.

44. *New York Times,* 9 July 1996, sec. A, p. 6; also *New Europe,* 19–25 May 1996, 38.

45. *New York Times,* 9 July 1996, sec. A, p. 6.

46. *New Europe,* 17–23 November 1996, 1.

47. Quoted in *New York Times,* 9 July 1996, sec. A, p. 6.

48. On Poland, see *Nowa Trybuna Opolska* (Opole), 6 October 1994, 1, 15, trans. in FBIS, *Daily Report (East Europe),* 18 October 1994, 26; *Życie Warszawy* (Warsaw), 18 October 1994, 2, trans. in FBIS, *Daily Report (East Europe),* 18 October 1994, 27; *Wprost* (Poznań), 12 February 1995, 11, trans. in FBIS, *Daily Report (East Europe),* 13 February 1995, 19; and *Balkan News and East Europe Report,* 18–24 June 1995, 30. On Romania, see *Romania Libera,* 25 July 1994, 3, trans. in FBIS, *Daily Report (East Europe),* 1 August 1994, 26.

49. Quoted in *Rzeczpospolita* (Warsaw), 17 January 1995, 12, trans. in FBIS, *Daily Report (East Europe),* 26 January 1995, 14. On Romania, see *Romania Libera,* 13 March 1995, 3, trans. in FBIS, *Daily Report (East Europe),* 17 March 1995, 21.

50. Central and East European Law Initiative, *CEELI Update* 5, no. 1 (Spring 1995): 1, 3–15; ibid., 5, no. 2 (Summer 1995): 1, 3–17; ibid., 5, no. 3 (Fall 1995): 1, 3–17; and ibid, 6, no. 1 (Spring 1996): 3–4.

51. *Bar Bulletin,* November 1995, 19.

52. On Budapest, see *New York Times,* 3 February 1995, sec. A, p. 6. On Bucharest, see *Christian Science Monitor,* 29 November 1995, 15. On Albania, see *Balkan News International and East Europe Report,* 12–18 March 1995, 6.

53. Regarding Serbia, see Desimir Tosić, "Jednopartijska vladivina," *Vreme International* (Belgrade), 2 March 1996, 48–49. Regarding Croatia, see Mirjana Kasapović, "Transition and Neoinstitutionalism: The Example of Croatia," *Croatian Political Science Review* 30, no. 2 (1993): 71–80.

54. Thomas Carothers, "Romania: Projecting the Positive," *Current History* 95, no. 599 (March 1996): 119–20.

55. Most recently in March 1995. See *Demokratsiya* (Sofia), 28 March 1995, 3, trans. in FBIS, *Daily Report* (East Europe), 4 April 1995, 3. See also the discussion in Albert P. Melone, "The Struggle for Judicial Independence and the Transition toward Democracy in Bulgaria," *Communist and Post-Communist Studies* 29, no. 2 (June 1996).

56. For details, see Douglas E. Schoen, "How Milošević Stole the Elections," *New*

York Times Magazine, 14 February 1993. See Srečko Mihailović, "The Parliamentary Elections of 1990, 1992, and 1993," in *Challenges of Parliamentarism: The Case of Serbia in the Early Nineties,* ed. Vladimir Goati (Belgrade: Institute of Social Sciences, 1995), 69–91.

57. *Globus* (Zagreb), 10 November 1995, 5–6; *Neue Zürcher Zeitung,* 4 January 1996, 1; *Christian Science Monitor,* 2 April 1996, 6; and *New Europe,* 31 March–6 April 1996, 27.

58. *Illyria,* 3–5 June 1996, 3.

59. *New Europe,* 5–11 May 1996, 1; and *Illyria,* 9–11 May 1996, 3. The government denied the allegations.

60. *New York Times,* 30 May 1996, sec. A, p. 6.

61. *Christian Science Monitor,* 10 June 1996, 6. See also *Times* (London), 3 June 1996, on AmeriCast.

62. Jakub Karpiński, "Politicians Endanger Independence of Polish Public TV," *Transition,* 19 April 1996, 28–29.

63. *New Europe,* 25 February–2 March 1996, 36.

64. *Večernje novosti* (Belgrade), 22 December 1993, 6, trans. in FBIS, *Daily Report (East Europe),* 28 December 1993, 27.

65. *Vjesnik* (Zagreb), 14 July 1994, 5, trans. in FBIS, *Daily Report* (East Europe), 29 July 1994, 39; *Feral Tribune* (Zagreb), 18 March 1996, *Glede and unatoč* supplement, 19–22; and *New Europe,* 5–11 May 1996, 3.

66. *New Europe,* 21–27 April 1996, 40; and *Guardian,* 3 May 1996, 13.

67. *New Europe,* 9–15 June 1996, 19.

68. Reuter, 14 June 1996, on Nexis; and *New Europe,* 29 September–5 October 1996, 25. See also *Globus* (Zagreb), 17 May 1996, 3–4, 7, and 21 June 1996, 14.

69. Dan Ionescu, "Tele-Revolution to Tele-Evolution in Romania," *Transition,* 19 April 1996, 42.

70. *New Europe,* 7–13 July 1996, 28.

71. See Andrei Skolkay, "Slovak Government Tightens Its Grip on the Airwaves," *Transition,* 19 April 1996, 18–19; and *New Europe,* 17–23 November 1996, 6, 15.

72. Kossuth Radio Network (Budapest), 6 December 1993, trans. in FBIS, *Daily Report* (East Europe), 6 December 1993, 24.

73. *New Europe,* 7–13 January 1996, 14; and Zsofia Szilagyi, "Hungary Has a Broadcast Media Law, at Last," *Transition,* 19 April 1996, 22–23.

74. Khorizont Radio Network (Sofia), 6 November 1995, trans. in FBIS, *Daily Report* (East Europe), 6 November 1995, 5.

75. *New Europe,* 15–21 September 1996, 36.

76. BTA news agency, 5 September 1996, in *BBC Monitoring Service: Eastern Europe,* 7 November 1996.

77. *Koha Jone* (Lezha), 20 May 1994, 5, trans. in FBIS, *Daily Report* (East Europe), 1 June 1994, 3; and *New Europe,* 3–9 March 1996, 39.

78. *Gazeta Shqiptare* (Tiranë), 24 June 1994, 1, trans. in FBIS, *Daily Report* (East Europe), 29 June 1994, 1.

79. *Aleanca* (Tiranë), 19 November 1994, 4, trans. in FBIS, *Daily Report* (East

Europe), 22 November 1994, 2. See also *Gazeta Shqiptare* (Tiranë), 11 January 1995, trans. in FBIS, *Daily Report* (East Europe), 27 January 1995, 3.

80. Ghia Nodia, "Nationalism and Democracy," in *Nationalism, Ethnic Conflict, and Democracy,* ed. Larry Diamond and Marc F. Plattner (Baltimore: Johns Hopkins University Press, 1994), 8.

81. See Sabrina P. Ramet, *Balkan Babel: The Disintegration of Yugoslavia from the Death of Tito to Ethnic War,* 2d ed. (Boulder, Colo.: Westview Press, 1996), esp. chaps. 12–13.

82. Radio Romania Network (Bucharest), 17 June 1995, trans. in FBIS, *Daily Report (East Europe),* 19 June 1995, 50.

83. Duna TV (Budapest), 16 June 1995, trans. in FBIS, *Daily Report* (East Europe), 19 June 1995, 51.

84. John Mueller, "Minorities and the Democratic Image," *East European Politics and Societies* 9, no. 3 (Fall 1995): 515.

85. For details and discussion, see Ramet, *Social Currents in Eastern Europe,* 2d ed., chap. 18.

86. *Slobodny Piatok* claimed that almost 50 percent of Slovaks were living below the minimum subsistence level, while Rozhlasova Stanica radio station claimed that 20 percent of Slovak households were "on the edge of poverty." See *Slobodny Piatok* (Bratislava), 25 August 1994, 13, trans. in FBIS, *Daily Report (East Europe),* 26 September 1994, 10; and Rozhlasova Stanica Slovensko Network (Bratislava), 23 April 1995, trans. in FBIS, *Daily Report* (East Europe), 24 April 1995, 14. On Romanians, see Reuter News Service, 22 June 1995, on Nexis.

87. *Süddeutsche Zeitung* (Munich), 10–11 December 1994, 7; *Neue Zürcher Zeitung,* 14 December 1994, 3, and 18–19 March 1995, 2; and *Balkan News and East Europe Report,* 21–27 May 1995, 32.

88. *Gazeta Wyborcza* (Warsaw), 8 November 1995, 15, trans. in FBIS, *Daily Report* (East Europe), 20 November 1995, 58.

89. *Salt Lake Tribune,* 24 December 1995, sec. A, p. 14. The number of violent crimes in Slovakia more than doubled between 1989 and 1993, rising from a total of 829 to 1,847, dropping in 1994 to 1,205.

90. *New York Times,* 12 January 1995, sec. A, p. 6; confirmed in Balkan *News and East Europe Report,* 11–17 June 1995, 48. On robbery victims, see Reuter, 1 August 1996, on Nexis. See also *European,* 6–12 January 1995, 4.

91. On Macedonia, see *Vreme International,* 23 March 1996, 23. On Albania, see *Vreme* (Belgrade), 28 September 1996, 58–59. On all other countries mentioned, see *Washington Times,* 25 March 1996, sec. A, p. 19. On Romania, see also *Evenimentul Zilei* (Bucharest), 10 November 1995, 3, trans. in FBIS, *Daily Report* (East Europe), 15 November 1995, 56.

92. This has been reported in many sources, including *MTI Econews,* 28 March 1996, on Nexis.

93. On the Poles, see *European,* 30 September–6 October 1994, 13. On the Bulgarians, see *European,* 6–12 January 1995, 4.

94. For example, regarding Poland, see *Rzeczpospolita,* 18 July 1995, 1, trans. in

FBIS, *Daily Report* (East Europe), 18 July 1995, 57; and *Życie Warszawy*, 25 August 1995, 2, trans. in FBIS, *Daily Report* (East Europe), 28 August 1995, 57.

95. *Süddeutsche Zeitung*, 22 June 1993, 6.

96. *Denni Telegraf* (Prague), 3 May 1995, 1–2, trans. in FBIS, *Daily Report* (East Europe), 10 May 1995, 11.

97. Quoted in *Prague Post*, 15–21 February 1995, 1, in FBIS, *Daily Report* (East Europe), 31 March 1995, 10.

98. MTI (Budapest), 17 May 1996, in *BBC Monitoring Service: Eastern Europe*, 18 May 1996; and *Süddeutsche Zeitung*, 18–19 May 1996, 6.

99. *Balkan News and East European Report*, 16–22 July 1995, 33.

100. *New Europe*, 29 September–5 October 1996, 19.

101. *New York Times*, 19 December 1995, A6.

102. Deutsche Presse-Agentur, 23 July 1995, on Nexis.

103. See, e.g., *Christian Science Monitor*, 18 September 1995, 7.

104. Deutsche Presse-Agentur, 29 October 1995, on Nexis. For a report on one of these exercises, see *Die Welt* (Bonn), 24 February 1996, 6.

105. ATA (Tiranë), 2 May 1996, in *BBC Monitoring Service*, 4 May 1996.

106. *Illyria*, 8–10 July 1996, 1.

107. *New Europe*, 12–18 January 1997, 5. See also statements about the Czech Republic by U.S. secretary of defense William Perry and French president Jacques Chirac, in *New Europe*, 24–30 September 1995, 16, and ibid., 19–25 November 1995, 21. On Slovenia, see ibid., 5–11 November 1995, 24. NATO Secretary General Javier Solana, in a visit to Ljubljana on 1 May 1996, praised Slovenia's role in the NATO Partnership for Peace program but refrained from offering the Slovenian government any concrete assurances.

108. *Neue Zürcher Zeitung*, 20–21 April 1996, 4.

109. See, e.g., the report in *New Europe*, 17–23 March 1996, 3.

110. *Neue Zürcher Zeitung*, 19 April 1996, 3. See also *Rzeczpospolita*, 23 October 1995, 7, trans. in FBIS, *Daily Report* (East Europe), 2 November 1995, 38–41.

111. *New Europe*, 18–24 August 1996, 15.

112. *New Europe*, 5–11 May 1996, 3.

113. *Die Welt*, 11 January 1996, 1, 6.

114. *Süddeutsche Zeitung*, 16 February 1995, 8.

115. *Neue Zürcher Zeitung*, 11 April 1996, 3.

116. *Neue Zürcher Zeitung*, 2–3 March 1996, 3.

117. See the report in CTK, 24 April 1996, in *BBC Monitoring Service*, 25 April 1996.

118. *Süddeutsche Zeitung*, 27–28 April 1996, 6.

119. According to unnamed Western officials, as cited in CTK, 30 April 1996, on Nexis.

120. *Neue Zürcher Zeitung*, 23 May 1995, 7; and *Balkan News and East Europe Report*, 28 May–3 June 1995, 12.

121. Details in Ramet, *Balkan Babel*, chap. 12 and epilogue.

Chapter 3

1. G. M. Tamás, "Ethnarchy and Ethno-Anarchism," *Social Research* 63, no. 1 (Spring 1996): 172.

2. Ibid., 171.

3. Norman Davies, *God's Playground: A History of Poland,* vol. 2 (New York: Columbia University Press, 1982).

4. Para. 21, quoted in Alan Sked, *The Decline and Fall of the Habsburg Empire, 1815–1918* (Harlow, Essex: Longman Group, 1989), 143.

5. Norberto Bobbio, *Thomas Hobbes and the Natural Law Tradition,* trans. Daniela Gobetti (Chicago: University of Chicago Press, 1993), 154.

6. Ibid., 96, 114–25, 154, and passim.

7. Johan Heilbron, *The Rise of Social Theory,* trans. Sheila Gogol (Minneapolis: University of Minnesota Press, 1995), 96–99.

8. Bobbio, *Thomas Hobbes,* 66, 79.

9. Ibid., 23–25.

10. Zeev Sternhell with Mario Sznajder and Maia Asheri, *The Birth of Fascist Ideology: From Cultural Rebellion to Political Revolution,* trans. David Maisel (Princeton: Princeton University Press, 1994), chap. 1.

11. See Hannah Arendt, *Eichmann in Jerusalem: A Report on the Banality of Evil* (New York: Viking Press, 1963).

12. E. J. Hobsbawm, *Nations and Nationalism since 1780,* rev. ed. (Cambridge: Cambridge University Press, 1992), 102.

13. Robert M. Hayden, "Constitutional Nationalism in the Formerly Yugoslav Republics," *Slavic Review* 51, no. 4 (Winter 1992): 655.

14. Cited in Jacques Rupnik, "The Reawakening of European Nationalisms," *Social Research* 63, no. 1 (Spring 1996): 42.

15. See also Pedro Ramet, "Kantian and Hegelian Perspectives on Duty," *Southern Journal of Philosophy* 21, no. 2 (Summer 1983).

16. Reasoning attributed to Jeremy Bentham by L. W. Sumner, *The Moral Foundation of Rights* (Oxford: Clarendon Press, 1987), 113.

17. Ibid., 113–26.

18. Loren E. Lomasky, *Persons, Rights, and the Moral Community* (Oxford: Oxford University Press, 1987), 104–5. For a presentation of diverse views about Universal Reason, see Robert P. George, ed., *Natural Law, Liberalism, and Morality: Contemporary Essays* (Oxford: Clarendon Press, 1996).

19. Virginia Held, *Rights and Goods: Justifying Social Action* (New York: Free Press, 1984), 119.

20. Sumner, *Moral Foundation,* 163.

21. Ibid., 129.

22. Ibid., 130.

23. Ibid., 130.

24. See Max Stirner, *The Ego and His Own,* trans. Steven T. Byington, ed. James J. Martin (New York: Libertarian Book Club, 1963).

25. Irina Livezeanu, *Cultural Politics in Greater Romania: Regionalism, Nation Building, and Ethnic Struggle, 1918–1930* (Ithaca: Cornell University Press, 1995), 135.

26. Ibid., 151.

27. Ibid., 138–39.

28. Quoted in ibid., 143.

29. Quoted in ibid., 223.

30. "A Chronology of Transylvanian History," in *Transylvania: The Roots of Ethnic Conflict,* ed. John F. Cadzow, Andrew Ludanyi, and Louis J. Elteto (Kent, Ohio: Kent State University Press, 1983), 32.

31. "Methods of Rumanianization Employed in Transylvania," in *Witnesses to Cultural Genocide: First-Hand Reports on Rumania's Minority Policies Today* (New York: American Transylvanian Federation and the Committee for Human Rights in Rumania, 1979), 60–61.

32. Ibid., 61.

33. Elemér Illyés, "Education and National Minorities in Contemporary Rumania," in *Transylvania,* ed. Cadzow, Ludanyi, and Elteto, 249.

34. Ibid., 252.

35. "Chronology of Transylvanian History," 33.

36. Bulcsu Veress, "The Status of Minority Rights in Transylvania: International Legal Expectations and Rumanian Realities," in *Transylvania,* ed. Cadzow, Ludanyi, and Elteto, 275.

37. György Lázár, "Memorandum," in *Witnesses to Cultural Genocide,* 112–13.

38. Ibid., 115.

39. Ibid., 113–16, 129.

40. Tom Gallagher, *Romania after Ceauşescu: The Politics of Intolerance* (Edinburgh: Edinburgh University Press, 1995), 56, 85.

41. Georg Brunner, *Nationality Problems and Minority Conflicts in Eastern Europe* (Gütersloh: Bertelsmann Foundation Publishers, 1996), 64.

42. Ibid.

43. See Radio Romania Network (Bucharest), 19 May 1995, trans. in Foreign roadcast Information Service (FBIS), *Daily Report* (East Europe), 22 May 1995, 66.

44. Duna TV (Budapest), 22 December 1993, trans. in FBIS, *Daily Report* (East Europe), 23 December 1993, 19. For a detailed discussion of the Hungarian minority in Romania, see Michael Shafir, "The Hungarian Democratic Federation of Romania: Actions, Reactions, and Factions" (unpublished manuscript, 1995).

45. "Transcript of an Interview with Bishop László Tökeś of the Hungarian Reformed Church in Romania on the Current Situation of Ethnic Hungarians in Romania" (telephone interview by Joseph Pungur, Calgary–Budapest, 8 November 1995), 2.

46. *AZI* (Bucharest), 5 August 1995, 5, trans. in FBIS, *Daily Report* (East Europe), 17 August 1995, 38–39; *Adevarul* (Bucharest), 16 August 1995, 1–2, trans. in FBIS, *Daily Report* (East Europe), 25 September 1995, 48–52; *Evenimentul zilei* (Bucharest), 4 September 1995, 5; and Kossuth Radio Network (Budapest), 9 September 1995, trans. in FBIS, *Daily Report* (East Europe), 11 September 1995, 57.

47. *Adevarul* (16 August 1995), 1–2, trans. in FBIS, *Daily Report* (East Europe), 25 September 1995, 50–51.

48. "Interview with Bishop László Tökeś," 1.

49. Quoted in Andrew Ludanyi, "Ideology and Political Culture in Rumania: The Daco-Roman Theory and the 'Place' of Minorities," in *Transylvania,* ed. Cadzow, Ludanyi, and Elteto, 231.

50. Ibid.

51. Kemal H. Karpat, "Introduction: Bulgarian Way of Nation-Building and the Turkish Minority," in *The Turks of Bulgaria: The History, Culture, and Political Fate of a Minority* (Istanbul: Isis Press, 1990), 2.

52. L. S. Stavrianos, *The Balkans since 1453* (New York: Holt, Rinehart & Winston, 1958), 107.

53. Zachary T. Irwin, "The Fate of Islam in the Balkans: A Comparison of Four State Policies," in *Religion and Nationalism in Soviet and East European Politics,* ed. Pedro Ramet, rev. ed. (Durham, N.C.: Duke University Press, 1989), 397.

54. R. J. Crampton, "The Turks in Bulgaria, 1878–1944," in *Turks of Bulgaria,* ed. Karpat, 43–44.

55. John Georgeoff, "Ethnic Minorities in the People's Republic of Bulgaria," in *The Politics of Ethnicity in Eastern Europe,* ed. George Klein and Milan J. Reban, (Boulder, Colo.: East European Monographs, 1981), 72.

56. Crampton, "Turks in Bulgaria," 47.

57. Valeri Stojanov, "Die türkische Minderheit Bulgariens bis zum Ende des Zweiten Weltkrieges," *Österreichische Osthefte* (Vienna) 36, no. 2 (1994): 285.

58. Crampton, "Turks in Bulgaria," 52.

59. Georgeoff, "Ethnic Minorities," 73.

60. Crampton, "Turks in Bulgaria," 55.

61. Ibid., 61.

62. Ibid., 65–66.

63. Ibid., 68.

64. Ibid., 68–69.

65. Ibid., 69.

66. Ibid., 70.

67. Stojanov, "Die türkische Minderheit," 291.

68. Irwin, "Fate of Islam," 399.

69. Ibid., 400.

70. Marie Gaille, "Reshaping National Memory: The Policy of Bulgarian Government toward the Ethnic Turks in Bulgaria from 1984 to 1989," *Balkan Forum* 4, no. 2 (June 1996): 192–93.

71. Ibid., 193; and Karpat, "Introduction," 18. See also Pedro Ramet, "The Interplay of Religious Policy and Nationalities Policy in the Soviet Union and Eastern Europe," in *Religion and Nationalism,* ed. Ramet, 32.

72. "News in Brief," *Religion in Communist Lands* 5, no. 4 (Winter 1977): 272.

73. Ramet, "Interplay," 32.

74. Gaille, "Reshaping National Memory," 199.

75. Regarding 1956, see Karpat, "Introduction," 14; regarding 1984, see Amnesty International, *Bulgaria: Continuing Abuse of Ethnic Turks* (New York: Amnesty International, February 1989), 1.

76. Karpat, "Introduction," 17.

77. Amnesty International, *Bulgaria: Continuing Abuse,* 1–2.

78. Quoted in ibid., 2–3.

79. Brunner, *Nationality Problems,* 45.

80. Ibid., 76.

81. Reuter, 31 October 1996, on Nexis.

82. Reuter, 9 August 1996, on Nexis.

83. BTA (Sofia), 1 March 1996, in *BBC Monitoring Service: Eastern Europe,* 5 March 1996.

84. *Trud* (Sofia), 19 July 1996, trans. in *BBC Monitoring Service: Eastern Europe,* 22 July 1996.

85. BTA, 5 February 1991, two reports, in FBIS, *Daily Report* (East Europe), 6 February 1991, 15–16.

86. As cited in *Duma* (Sofia), 10 October 1996, 1, trans. in *BBC Monitoring Service: Eastern Europe* (12 October 1996).

87. BTA, 18 March 1996, in *BBC Monitoring Service: Eastern Europe* (20 March 1996.

88. *Duma,* 10 October 1996 , 1, trans. in *BBC Monitoring Service: Eastern Europe,* 12 October 1996.

89. *Standard News* (Sofia), 4 August 1996, 3, trans. in *BBC Monitoring Service: Eastern Europe*, 7 August 1996.

90. Ibid.

91. Stavrianos, *The Balkans since 1453,* 502.

92. Michael Schmidt-Neke, *Entstehung und Ausbau der Königsdiktatur in Albanien (1912–1939)* (Munich: R. Oldenbourg Verlag, 1987), 31–32.

93. Paul Robert Magocsi, *Historical Atlas of East Central Europe* (Seattle: University of Washington Press, 1993), 142–43.

94. Hugh Poulton, *Who Are the Macedonians?* (Bloomington: Indiana University Press, 1995), 125–26.

95. Ibid., 126.

96. Quoted in ibid., 127.

97. Ibid., 128.

98. Ibid., 129.

99. Ibid., 130.

100. Teuta Arifi, "Albanian Society in Macedonia and Montenegro," *Harriman Review* 9, no. 3 (Summer 1996): 42.

101. Mirče Tomovski, "Albanian Society in Macedonia and Montenegro," in *Harriman Review* 9, no. 3 (Summer 1996): 47.

102. Ibid.

103. Risto Lazarov, "The Albanians in Macedonia: Co-Citizenship or . . . ?," *Balkan Forum* 3, no. 2 (June 1995): 31–32.

104. Quoted in Zvonimir Jankuloski, "'Nationality' (Minority) Protection in Macedonia: A Question of Human Rights or Politics," *Balkan Forum* 4, no. 2 (June 1996): 156.

105. Quoted in ibid., 156, 157.

106. Further details in Sabrina P. Ramet, "All Quiet on the Southern Front? Macedonia between the Hammer and the Anvil," *Problems of Post-Communism* 42, no. 6 (November/December 1995): 32.

107. Quoted in Lazarov, "Albanians in Macedonia," 30.

108. Quoted in ibid.

109. Details in Ramet, "All Quiet," 32–33.

110. Quoted in Lazarov, "Albanians in Macedonia," 30.

111. Exact figures in Sabrina P. Ramet, *Balkan Babel: The Disintegration of Yugoslavia from the Death of Tito to Ethnic War,* 2d ed. (Boulder, Colo.: Westview Press, 1996), 233.

112. Exact figures in ibid.

113. Quoted in *A Threat to "Stability": Human Rights Violations in Macedonia* (New York: Human Rights Watch/Helsinki, 1996), 36 n, my emphasis.

114. Lazarov, "Albanians in Macedonia," 36.

115. *Threat to "Stability,"* 35–37.

116. Ibid., 37.

117. See *Balkan News and East European Report* (Athens), 16–22 July 1995, 18.

118. For details, see *Flaka e Vëllazërimit* (Skopje), 3 October 1995, 5, trans. in FBIS, *Daily Report* (East Europe), 11 October 1995, 53.

119. Details in *Illyria* (The Bronx), 21–23 October 1996, 3.

120. Ibid., 30 September–2 October 1996, 2.

121. Gunther E. Rothenberg, *The Military Border in Croatia 1740–1881: A Study of an Imperial Institution* (Chicago: University of Chicago Press, 1966), 4, 8.

122. Ibid., 8.

123. Ferdo Šišić, *Pregled povijesti Hrvatskog naroda* (Zagreb: Nakladni Zavod M.H., 1975), 310.

124. From a report by the Duke of Sachsen-Hildburghausen, as quoted in Rothenberg, *Military Border,* 10.

125. Wayne S. Vucinich, "The Serbs in Austria-Hungary," in *Austrian History Yearbook,* vol. 3, pt. 2 (1967), 10.

126. Ibid., 10–11.

127. Rothenberg, *Military Border,* 13.

128. Vucinich, "The Serbs," 14.

129. Rothenberg, *Military Border,* 18–19.

130. Robert Pick, *Empress Maria Theresa: The Earlier Years, 1717–1757* (New York: Harper & Row, 1966), 241.

131. Rothenberg, *Military Border,* 29.

132. Ibid., 122.

133. Ibid., 166.

134. Vucinich, "The Serbs," 21.

135. Drago Roksandić, *Srbi u Hrvatskoj, od 15. stoljeća do naših dana* (Zagreb: Vjesnik, 1991), 121.

136. Ivo Banac, *The National Question in Yugoslavia: Origins, History, Politics* (Ithaca: Cornell University Press, 1984), 183. But, regarding certain manifestations of Greater Serbian hegemonism at that time, see Charles Jelavich, "The Issue of Serbian Textbooks in the Origins of World War I," *Slavic Review* 48, no. 2 (Summer 1989).

137. Banac, *National Question,* 183.

138. Ibid., 185.

139. Ibid., 189.

140. Ibid., 225.

141. As cited in Aleksa Djilas, *The Contested Country: Yugoslav Unity and Communist Revolution, 1919–1953* (Cambridge: Harvard University Press, 1991), 126.

142. Vladimir Žerjavić, *Gubici stanovništva Jugoslavije u drugom svjetskom ratu* (Zagreb: Jugoslavensko Viktimološko Društvo, 1989), 61–66.

143. See Stella Alexander, "Croatia: The Catholic Church and the Clergy, 1919–1945," in *Catholics, the State, and the European Radical Right, 1919–1945,* ed. Richard J. Wolff and Jorg K. Hoensch (Boulder, Colo.: Social Science Monographs, 1987), esp. 53–54. See also Ivan Mužić, *Pavelić i Stepinac* (Split: Logos, 1991).

144. See esp. Milovan Djilas, *Wartime,* trans. Michael B. Petrovich (New York: Harcourt Brace Jovanovich, 1977); Fikreta Jelić-Butić, *Ustaše i NDH* (Zagreb: S. N. Liber & Školska knjiga, 1977); Bogdan Krizman, *Ustaše i Treći Reich,* 2 vols. (Zagreb: Globus, 1983); Walter R. Roberts, *Tito, Mihailović, and the Allies, 1941–1945* (Durham, N.C.: Duke University Press, 1987); and Jozo Tomašević, *The Chetniks: War and Revolution in Yugoslavia, 1941–1945* (Stanford, Calif.: Stanford University Press, 1975). Also of interest is Fikreta Jelić-Butić, *Četnici u Hrvatskoj, 1941–1945* (Zagreb: Globus, 1986).

145. Djilas, *Contested Country,* 172.

146. Roksandić, *Srbi u Hrvatskoj,* 156.

147. Djilas, *Contested Country,* 173.

148. Discussed in Sabrina P. Ramet, *Nationalism and Federalism in Yugoslavia, 1962–1991,* 2d ed. (Bloomington: Indiana University Press, 1992), chap. 7.

149. Quoted in Dennison Rusinow, "The Yugoslav Peoples," in *Eastern European Nationalism in the Twentieth Century,* ed. Peter F. Sugar (Washington, D.C.: American University Press, 1995), 341.

150. This paragraph summarizes the information given in Ramet, *Nationalism and Federalism,* 237.

151. Quoted in Laura Silber and Allan Little, *The Death of Yugoslavia* (London: Penguin Books and BBC Books, 1995), 92.

152. Quoted in ibid., 102.

153. Ibid., 102–3.

154. Ibid., 103.

155. Ibid., 104.

156. Cited in ibid., 147.

157. "Nationalism Has Triumphed," interview with Žarko Puhovski, *Uncaptive Minds* 8, no. 2 (Summer 1995): 77 n.

158. "It Is Not Too Late," interview with Milorad Pupovac, *Uncaptive Minds* 8, no. 2 (Summer 1995): 88–89.

159. "Nationalism Has Triumphed," 76.

160. *Civil and Political Rights in Croatia* (New York: Human Rights Watch/ Helsinki, 1995), 19.

161. *Borba* (Belgrade), 17 February 1993, 8, trans. in FBIS, *Daily Report* (East Europe), 12 March 1993, 59–60.

162. *Feral Tribune* (Split), 7 November 1994, as summarized in FBIS, *Daily Report* (East Europe), 28 November 1994, 53.

163. *Borba*, 17 February 1993, 8, trans. in FBIS, *Daily Report* (East Europe), 12 March 1993, 60.

164. *Civil and Political Rights,* 18.

165. "Nationalism Has Triumphed," 77.

166. One American congressman declared that the people of Bosnia had been fighting each other for fifteen hundred years, apparently unaware that the people of Bosnia had not yet settled in that part of the world at that time, while Sir Crispin Tickell, a British self-appointed pundit, claimed that the hatreds between the peoples of "Yugoslavia" extended back "thousands of years"—a curious claim, given that there was no Yugoslavia before 1918 and no South Slavs before the seventh century. See Michael A. Sells, *The Bridge Betrayed: Religion and Genocide in Bosnia* (Berkeley and Los Angeles: University of California Press, 1996), 128.

167. For some examples, see David Owen's solipsistic fantasy, *Balkan Odyssey* (London: Victor Gollancz, 1995).

168. For details and documentation, see *Northwestern Bosnia: Human Rights Abuses during a Cease-Fire and Peace Negotiations* (New York: Human Rights Watch/Helsinki, February 1996).

169. *Bosnia-Hercegovina: A Failure in the Making—Human Rights and the Dayton Agreement* (New York: Human Rights Watch/Helsinki, June 1996), 3.

170. Ibid., 7. For an update, see *Boston Sunday Globe,* 3 November 1996, sec. A, p. 2.

171. *Washington Post,* 26 October 1996, on AmeriCast; and *New York Times,* 7 November 1996, sec. A, p. 6.

172. *Failure in the Making,* 27.

173. Ibid.; confirmed in *Neue Zürcher Zeitung,* 14–15 September 1996, 3.

174. According to World Bank figures, industrial production in both the Muslim-Croatian Federation and the Bosnian Serb Republic remains, as of October 1996, at about 10 percent of prewar levels. See *New York Times,* (27 October 1996), 6.

175. For details, see *New York Times,* (7 October 1996), A4.

176. *International Herald Tribune,* 11 October 1996, 5, Paris edition; and *Washington Post,* 2 November 1996, on AmeriCast.

177. Renata Salecl, "See No Evil, Speak No Evil: Hate Speech and Human Rights," in *Radical Evil,* ed. Joan Copjec (London: Verso, 1996), 159.

178. As I have argued at some length in *Social Currents in Eastern Europe: The Sources and Consequences of the Great Transformation,* 2d ed. (Durham, N.C.: Duke University Press, 1995), chap. 1.

179. Bobbio, *Thomas Hobbes,* 123, 139; and Kimberly Hutchings, *Kant, Critique, and Politics* (London and New York: Routledge, 1996), 46.

180. And hence Kant's concept of society as a *"rational* community"—which provides a response to nationalists' appeal to an *"affective* community." See Bernard Yack, "The Problem with Kantian Liberalism," in *Kant and Political Philosophy,* ed. Ronald Beiner and William James Booth (New Haven: Yale University Press, 1993), 126–27.

181. Quoted in ibid., 235.

182. Quoted in Gallagher, *Romania after Ceauşescu,* 26–27.

Chapter 4

1. On the repluralization of Polish society in the course of the 1980s, see *Reinventing Polish Society: Poland's Quiet Revolution, 1981–1986* (New York: Helsinki Watch, 1986); Roman Dumas, "Poland's 'Independent Society,'" *Poland Watch,* no. 8 (1986); and Sabrina P. Ramet, "Underground Solidarity and Parallel Society," chap. 4 in *Social Currents in Eastern Europe: The Sources and Consequences of the Great Transformation,* 2d ed. (Durham, N.C.: Duke University Press, 1995). On the role of the Catholic Church in communist-era Poland, see Vincent C. Chrypinski, "Church and Nationality in Postwar Poland," in Pedro Ramet, ed., *Religion and Nationalism in Soviet and East European Politics,* rev. ed. (Durham, N.C.: Duke University Press, 1989); Vincent C. Chrypinski, "The Catholic Church in Poland, 1944–1989," in *Catholicism and Politics in Communist Societies,* ed. Pedro Ramet (Durham, N.C.: Duke University Press, 1990); and Ramet, "Church and Dissent in Praetorian Poland," chap. 7 in *Social Currents.*

2. See Sabrina P. Ramet, "The New Church-State Configuration in Eastern Europe," *East European Politics and Societies* 5, no. 2 (Spring 1991): 249–50; also *Frankfurter Allgemeine,* 6 May 1989, 12, and 18 May 1989, 6.

3. Jan Łopuszański, interview with Zbigniew Lipiński, in *Nowy Swiat* (Warsaw), 20 November 1992, 3, trans. in Foreign Broadcast Information Service (FBIS), *Daily Report* (East Europe), 30 November 1992, 28.

4. Opinion poll conducted by the OBOP Center for Public Opinion Research, reported in PAP (Warsaw), 20 October 1989, in FBIS, *Daily Report* (East Europe), 2 November 1989, 74; *Christian Science Monitor,* 26 May 1993, 9; and *Süddeutsche Zeitung* (Munich), 11–12 February 1995, 9.

5. *Times* (London), 1 June 1991, on Nexis.

6. Małgorzata Fuszara, "Legal Regulation of Abortion in Poland," *Signs* 17, no. 1 (Autumn 1991): 127.

7. PAP, 7 November 1992, in FBIS, *Daily Report* (East Europe), 16 November 1992, 28.

8. Fuszara, "Legal Regulation," 127.

9. *In These Times,* 10–16 April 1991, 9.

10. Rebecca Pasini, "Piety amid Politics: The Roman Catholic Church and Polish Abortion Policy," in *Problems of Post-Communism* 43, no. 2 (March–April 1996), 38.

11. Ibid., 41.

12. PAP, 30 November 1992, in FBIS, *Daily Report* (East Europe), 1 December 1992, 30.

13. Quoted in Pasini, "Piety amid Politics," 41.

14. PAP, 7 December 1992, in *BBC Summary of World Broadcasts,* 10 December 1992).

15. PAP, 19 December 1992, in *BBC Summary of World Broadcasts,* 22 December 1992).

16. PAP, 7 January 1993, in FBIS, *Daily Report* (East Europe), 7 January 1993, 4.

17. PAP, 15 February 1993, in FBIS, *Daily Report* (East Europe), 16 February 1993, 34–35.

18. *Warsaw Voice,* 29 May 1994), on Nexis.

19. Quoted in *Chicago Tribune,* 11 June 1994, 1.

20. Quoted in Reuter German News Service, 31 May 1994, on Nexis.

21. PAP, 14 April 1994, on Nexis.

22. PAP, 25 August 1994, on Nexis.

23. *Guardian,* 3 September 1994, 10.

24. Quoted in Agence France Presse (Paris), 30 March 1995, on Nexis.

25. *Gazeta Wyborcza* (Warsaw), 4 May 1995, 3, trans. in *Polish News Bulletin,* 4 May 1995, on Nexis.

26. *Süddeutsche Zeitung,* 22–23 September 1990, 12.

27. *In These Times,* 10–16 April 1991, 9.

28. Ewa Nowakówska, in *Polityka* (Warsaw), 2 November 1996, 18, summarized in *Polish News Bulletin,* 7 November 1996, on Nexis.

29. *Wall Street Journal,* 22 November 1994, sec. A, p. 1.

30. Quoted in ibid.

31. *Süddeutsche Zeitung,* 31 December 1992, on Nexis.

32. Article 18.2 of the Law on Radio and Television Broadcasting, as published in *Dziennik Ustaw* (Warsaw), 29 January 1993, trans. in U.S. Department of Commerce, *Central and Eastern European Legal Texts,* 29 January 1993.

33. Andrzej Korboński, "Poland Six Years After: The Church" (paper presented at the annual meeting of the American Association for the Advancement of Slavic Studies, Washington, D.C., 26–29 October 1995), 5, citing *Gazeta Wyborcza,* 31 December 1992–1 January 1993, and *Ład,* 30 May 1993.

34. *Wrost* (Warsaw), 18 April 1993, 75–76, trans. in JPRS, *East Europe Report* 17 (May 1993): 10–11. For further discussion of the broadcasting law, see Sabrina P. Ramet, *Nihil Obstat: Religion, Politics, and Social Change in Eastern Europe and Russia,* chap. 12 (Durham, N.C.: Duke University Press, in press).

35. Quoted in *New York Times,* 31 December 1992, 6.

36. *Polish News Bulletin,* 11 October 1995, on Nexis.

37. Agence France Presse, 23 May 1995, on Nexis.

38. Quoted in *Warsaw Voice,* 16 July 1995, on Nexis.

39. Andrzej Korboński, "A Concordat—But No Concord," *Transition* 1, no. 9 (9 June 1995): 15.

40. PAP, 28 December 1993, in FBIS, *Daily Report* (East Europe), 30 December 1993, 19–20; and *Polskie Radio First Program* (Warsaw), 15 September 1995, trans. in FBIS, *Daily Report* (East Europe), 15 September 1995, 50–51.

41. *Warsaw Voice,* 9 January 1994, on Nexis; and *Gazeta Wyborcza,* 28 January 1994, trans. in *Polish News Bulletin,* 3 February 1994, on Nexis.

42. *Gazeta Wyborcza,* 20 June 1994), 3, trans. in *Polish News Bulletin,* 20 June 1994, on Nexis.

43. PAP, 28 December 1993, in FBIS, *Daily Report* (East Europe), 30 December 1993, 20.

44. Quoted in Korboński, "Concordat–But No Concord," 16.

45. *Polskie Radio First Program,* 26 July 1995, trans. in FBIS, *Daily Report* (East Europe), 27 July 1995, 38.

46. *Polskie Radio First Program,* 15 September 1995, trans. in FBIS, *Daily Report* (East Europe), 15 September 1995, 50.

47. Survey data from October 1995, as reported in PAP, 27 October 1995, on Nexis.

48. *Gazeta Wyborcza,* 14–15 October 1995, 2, trans. in *Polish News Bulletin,* 16 October 1995, on Nexis.

49. PAP, 17 October 1995, on Nexis; and Reuter News Service, 18 October 1995, on Nexis.

50. Polish Radio 1 (Warsaw), 24 January 1996, trans. in *BBC Monitoring Service,* 25 January 1996.

51. *Süddeutsche Zeitung,* 15 March 1996, on Nexis.

52. See, e.g., *Süddeutsche Zeitung,* 4 July 1996, on Nexis; and Polish Radio 3 (Warsaw), 11 August 1996, trans. in *BBC Monitoring Service: Eastern Europe,* 13 August 1996.

53. For discussion and analysis, see *Neue Zürcher Zeitung,* 14–15 September 1996, 7.

54. *Gazeta Wyborcza,* 1 August 1994, trans. in FBIS, *Daily Report* (East Europe), 2 August 1994, 36–37.

55. On point 1, see *Gazeta Wyborcza,* 11 August 1994), 1, trans. in FBIS, *Daily Report* (East Europe), 11 August 1994, 26; on point 2, see PAP, 24 October 1994, trans. in FBIS, *Daily Report* (East Europe), 25 October 1994, 21; on point 3, see *Gazeta Wyborcza,* 29 December 1994, 3, trans. in *Polish News Bulletin,* 30 December 1994, on Nexis.

56. TVP Television Second Program Network (Warsaw), 23 February 1995, trans. in FBIS, *Daily Report* (East Europe), 24 February 1995, 17.

57. Bishop Tadeusz Pieronek, interview with *Rzeczpospolita,* 31 October–1 November 1996), 3, excerpted in *Polish News Bulletin,* 7 November 1996, on Nexis.

58. Reuter News Service, 27 March 1995, on Nexis.

59. Reuter News Service, 4 April 1995, on Nexis; and PAP, 4 April 1995, trans. in FBIS, *Daily Report* (East Europe), 5 April 1995, 31.

60. *Trybuna* (Warsaw), 2–3 May 1995, 7–8, trans. in FBIS, *Daily Report* (East Europe), 9 June 1995, 51.

61. Article 38.1, trans. in ibid., 53.

62. Quoted in Reuter News Service, 30 June 1995, on Nexis.

63. *Rzeczpospolita,* 4 June 1996, 5, trans. in *Polish News Bulletin,* 12 June 1996, on Nexis.

64. Third Program Radio Network (Warsaw), 26 August 1995, trans. in FBIS, *Daily Report* (East Europe), 28 August 1995, 56; and *Warsaw Voice,* 10 December 1995, on Nexis.

65. Reuter News Service, 20 November 1995, on Nexis. In an interview with *Gazeta Wyborcza,* Cardinal Glemp explained, "I am surprised that the term 'neo-paganism' should elicit resentment. Indeed, 'neo-paganism' is the appropriate receptacle for such attitudes and there is nothing pejorative in it, or at least it is no more pejorative a term than 'non-believer' or 'atheist.'"*Gazeta Wyborcza,* 27 November 1995, 1, trans. in *Polish News Bulletin,* 30 November 1995, on Nexis.

66. Quoted in PAP, 17 September 1995, trans. in FBIS, *Daily Report* (East Europe), 18 September 1995, 60.

67. *Gazeta Wyborcza,* 22 November 1995, 4, trans. in *Polish News Bulletin,* 22 November 1995, on Nexis.

68. *Gazeta Wyborcza,* 6 November 1995, 5, trans. in FBIS, *Daily Report* (East Europe), 7 November 1995, 33.

69. *Die Woche* (Hamburg), 27 October 1995, 30.

70. *Polish News Bulletin,* 11 October 1995, on Nexis.

71. Quoted in *New York Times,* 23 November 1995, sec. A, p. 5.

72. Quoted in *National Catholic Reporter,* 15 December 1995, 18.

73. *Polskie Radio First Program Network,* 23 November 1995, trans. in FBIS, *Daily Report* (East Europe), 27 November 1995, 75.

74. See, e.g., PAP, 22 January 1996, on Nexis; and *Rzeczpospolita* (Warsaw), 23 January 1996, 1, trans. in *Polish News Bulletin,* 23 January 1996, on Nexis.

75. UPI, 15 February 1996, on Nexis.

76. *Rzeczpospolita,* 14 March 1996, 1, trans. in *Polish News Bulletin,* 14 March 1996, on Nexis.

77. *Rzeczpospolita,* 17 April 1996, 1, trans. in *Polish News Bulletin,* 17 April 1996, on Nexis.

78. *Życie Warszawy,* 16 April 1996, 2, trans. in *Polish News Bulletin,* 16 April 1996, on Nexis.

79. Reuter News Service, 1 March 1996, on Nexis.

80. These charges are reported respectively in *Gazeta Wyborcza,* 9 August 1996, 3, trans. in *Polish News Bulletin,* 9 August 1996, on Nexis; and PAP, 20 August 1996, on Nexis.

81. PAP, 30 August 1996, trans. in *BBC Summary of World Broadcasts*, 31 August 1996.

82. *Chicago Tribune*, 1 October 1996, 6.

83. *Przeglad Tygodniowy*, 2 October 1996, 3, excerpted in *Polish News Bulletin*, 7 November 1996, on Nexis.

84. *Polish News Bulletin*, 3 October 1996, on Nexis; and *Neue Zürcher Zeitung*, 5–6 October 1996, 2; see also *Süddeutsche Zeitung*, 5–6 October 1996, 7.

85. *Chicago Tribune*, 25 October 1996), 3.

86. PAP, 23 October 1996, in *BBC Monitoring Service: Eastern Europe*, 25 October 1996; *Times* (London), 25 October 1996, on AmeriCast, 27 October 1996; and *Chicago Tribune*, 25 October 1996, 3.

87. *Polish News Bulletin*, 27 November 1996, on Nexis.

88. Primate Glemp, quoted in PAP, 1 September 1996, trans. in *BBC Summary of World Broadcasts*, 3 September 1996.

89. *Polish News Bulletin*, 27 November 1996, on Nexis.

90. CBOS polls, summarized in *Polish News Bulletin*, 25 November 1996, on Nexis.

91. Quoted in PAP, 20 November 1996, in *BBC Monitoring Service: Eastern Europe*, 22 November 1996).

92. Quoted in *Polish News Bulletin*, 21 November 1996, on Nexis.

93. *Życie Warszawy*, 25 November 1996, 2, summarized in *Polish News Bulletin*, 25 November 1996, on Nexis.

94. *Polish News Bulletin*, 15 November 1996, on Nexis; and *Polish News Bulletin*, 27 November 1996, on Nexis.

95. *Gazeta Wyborcza*, 29 December 1992, 3, trans. in *Polish News Bulletin*, 29 December 1992, on Nexis.

96. *Polityka*, 20 April 1996, 20, trans. in *Polish News Bulletin*, 24 April 1996, on Nexis.

97. UPI, 6 February 1996, on Nexis.

98. *Nowa Europa*, no. 30 (12–14 February 1993), trans. in *Polish News Bulletin*, 22 February 1993, on Nexis; and PAP 20 April 1996, on Nexis.

99. Bishop Tadeusz Pieronek, interview with *Rzeczpospolita*, 31 October–1 November 1996, excerpted in *Polish News Bulletin*, 7 November 1996, on Nexis.

100. *Chicago Tribune*, 1 October 1996, 6; confirmed in *National Catholic Reporter*, 8 November 1996, 12.

101. *National Catholic Reporter*, 8 November 1996, 12.

102. *Chicago Tribune*, 1 October 1996, 6.

103. *World Paper*, June 1996, on Nexis.

104. Agnieszka Wolk-Laniewska, in *Przeglad Tygodniowy*, 18 September 1996, 1, excerpted in *Polish News Bulletin*, 7 November 1996, on Nexis.

105. Joseph Cardinal Ratzinger, interview with Vittorio Messori, *Ratzinger Report*, trans. Salvator Attanasio and Graham Harrison (San Francisco: Ignatius Press, 1985), 61–62.

Chapter 5

This chapter is a revised and expanded version of a piece originally published in *Nationalities Papers* 22, no. 1 (Spring 1994). Reprinted by permission.

1. *La Stampa* (Torino), 10 June 1992, 7; and *Welt am Sonntag* (Bonn), 21 June 1992, 2.

2. CSTK (Prague), 26 June 1992, in Foreign Broadcast Information Service (FBIS), *Daily Report* (East Europe), 30 June 1992, 13. The poll was taken by the Prague-based Institute for Public Opinion Research. A similar poll conducted in April by Bratislava's Center for Social Analysis reached similar results, showing only 17 percent of Slovaks favoring outright independence, as reported in *New York Times,* 22 June 1992, sec. A, p. 3.

3. *Mladá Fronta Dnes* (Prague), 29 June 1991, 1, 2, trans. in FBIS, *Daily Report* (East Europe), 3 July 1991, 11.

4. E. K. Francis, *Interethnic Relations: An Essay in Sociological Theory* (New York: Elsevier, 1976), 404.

5. Edward Taborsky, *Communism in Czechoslovakia, 1948–1960* (Princeton: Princeton University Press, 1961), 41–42.

6. Regarding the Hungarians' demands, see Galia Golan, *Reform Rule in Czechoslovakia: The Dubček Era, 1968–1969* (Cambridge: Cambridge University Press, 1973), 96–98. Regarding the specifics of Slovakia during the Prague Spring, see Alexander Dubček, *Hope Dies Last: The Autobiography of Alexander Dubček,* ed. and trans. Jiří Hochman (New York and Tokyo: Kodansha International, 1993), chaps. 14–22.

7. Among the best works on the history of Czechs and Slovaks 1918–89 are Josef Korbel, *Twentieth-Century Czechoslovakia: The Meanings of Its History* (New York: Columbia University Press, 1977); Carol Skalnik Leff, *National Conflict in Czechoslovakia: The Making and Remaking of a State, 1918–1987* (Princeton: Princeton University Press, 1988); Eugen Steiner, *The Slovak Dilemma* (Cambridge: Cambridge University Press, 1973); and Sharon L. Wolchik, *Czechoslovakia in Transition: Politics, Economics, and Society* (London: Pinter Publishers, 1991).

8. There are, by contrast, only twenty-three thousand Hungarians living in the Czech lands, according to official statistics. *Magyar Hírlap* (Budapest), 17 October 1990, 2, trans. in FBIS, *Daily Report* (East Europe), 23 October 1990, 20.

9. Edith Oltay, "Hungarian Minority in Slovakia Sets Up Independent Organizations," in Radio Free Europe (RFE), *Report on Eastern Europe,* 16 March 1990, 18–20.

10. CTK (Prague), 30 May 1991, in FBIS, *Daily Report* (East Europe), 3 June 1991, 15.

11. *Občansky Deník* (Prague), 19 August 1991, 7, trans. in FBIS, *Daily Report* (East Europe), 26 August 1991, 14.

12. *Daily Telegraph* (London), 2 March 1991, 10.

13. *Frankfurter Allgemeine,* 30 June 1990, 5.

14. Edith Oltay, "Hungarians in Slovakia Organize to Press for Ethnic Rights," in RFE, *Report on Eastern Europe,* 1 June 1990, 23.

15. This is also the view of *Národná obroda* (Bratislava), 24 July 1991, 3, trans. in FBIS, *Daily Report* (East Europe), 1 August 1991, 13.

16. Peter Martin, "The Hyphen Controversy," in RFE, *Report on Eastern Europe,* 20 April 1990, 14.

17. *New York Times,* 21 April 1990, 4.

18. Bratislava Domestic Service, 20 November 1990, trans. in FBIS, *Daily Report* (East Europe), 21 November 1990, 21.

19. Ibid., 22.

20. Jan Obrman, "The Issue of Autonomy for Moravia and Silesia," in RFE, *Report on Eastern Europe,* 12 April 1991, 17.

21. Bratislava Domestic Service, 20 November 1990, 22. (See note 18.)

22. CTK, 12 September 1990, in FBIS, *Daily Report* (East Europe), 19 September 1990, 37.

23. CTK, 18 June 1991, in FBIS, *Daily Report* (East Europe), 20 June 1991, 20.

24. CTK, 16 July 1991, in FBIS, *Daily Report* (East Europe), 19 July 1991, 12–13.

25. CTK, 10 August 1990, in FBIS, *Daily Report* (East Europe), 13 August 1990, 20. Regarding the Tiso regime, see Yeshayahu Jelinek, *The Parish Republic: Hlinka's Slovak People's Party, 1939–1945* (Boulder, Colo.: East European Monographs, 1976).

26. CTK, 27 August 1990, in FBIS, *Daily Report* (East Europe), 29 August 1990, 25; also Bratislava Domestic Service, 26 August 1990, trans. in FBIS, *Daily Report* (East Europe), 28 August 1990, 22.

27. CTK, 3 April 1991, in FBIS, *Daily Report* (East Europe), 5 April 1991, 14; also CTK, 13 March 1991, in FBIS, *Daily Report* (East Europe), 14 March 1991, 15.

28. Quoted in CTK, 19 August 1990, in FBIS, *Daily Report* (East Europe), 20 August 1990, 18.

29. See *Vjesnik* (Zagreb), 28 October 1990, 24; and *Lidové noviny* (Prague), 14 November 1990, 3, trans. in FBIS, *Daily Report* (East Europe), 20 November 1990, 24.

30. *Národná obroda,* 12 November 1990, 2, trans. in FBIS, *Daily Report* (East Europe), 16 November 1990, 21.

31. CTK, 26 November 1990, in FBIS, *Daily Report* (East Europe), 29 November 1990, 21.

32. CTK, 14 November 1990, in FBIS, *Daily Report* (East Europe), 19 November 1990, 33.

33. CTK, 8 August 1991, in FBIS, *Daily Report* (East Europe), 9 August 1991, 14.

34. CTK, 21 March 1991, in FBIS, *Daily Report* (East Europe), 25 March 1991, 22; *Pravda* (Bratislava), 23 March 1991, 3, trans. in FBIS, *Daily Report* (East Europe), 27 March 1991, 18; *Der Spiegel* (Hamburg), 15 April 1991, 200, 202; and *Hospodárské noviny* (Prague), 12 June 1991, 3, trans. in FBIS, *Daily Report* (East Europe), 14 June 1991, 16.

35. *Národná obroda,* 3 January 1991, 3, trans. in FBIS, *Daily Report* (East Europe), 9 January 1991, 13; and *Hospodárské noviny,* 21 January 1991, 5.

36. MTI (Budapest), 17 September 1990, in FBIS, *Daily Report* (East Europe), 19 September 1990, 38.

37. *Pravda* (Bratislava), 29 January 1991, 2, trans. in FBIS, *Daily Report* (East Europe), 5 February 1991, 23.

38. *Süddeutsche Zeitung* (Munich), 27–28 October 1990, 2.

39. *Lidové noviny,* 8 November 1990, 2, trans. in FBIS, *Daily Report* (East Europe), 16 November 1990, 23.

40. Quoted in *Mladá Fronta Dnes,* 27 August 1990, 1–2, excerpted in FBIS, *Daily Report* (East Europe), 5 September 1990, 21.

41. CTK, 30 July 1991, in FBIS, *Daily Report* (East Europe), 31 July 1991, 18.

42. *Rudé právo,* 15 June 1991, 1, 5, trans. in FBIS, *Daily Report* (East Europe), 20 June 1991, 19.

43. Quoted in CTK, 14 November 1990, in FBIS, *Daily Report* (East Europe), 14 November 1990, 19.

44. *Financial Times,* 15 November 1990, 2.

45. CTK, 14 November 1990, in FBIS, *Daily Report* (East Europe), 14 November 1990, 20.

46. Quoted in *Frankfurter Allgemeine,* 11 December 1990, 8.

47. See the full text in *Smena* (Bratislava), 2 March 1991, 4, trans. in FBIS, *Daily Report* (East Europe), 13 March 1991, 17.

48. From the complete text, as carried by Prague Domestic Service, 14 March 1991), trans. in FBIS, *Daily Report* (East Europe), 15 March 1991, 17.

49. CTK, 18 March 1991, in FBIS, *Daily Report* (East Europe), 22 March 1991, 14.

50. *Süddeutsche Zeitung,* 16–17 March 1991, 7; also Jiri Pehe, "Growing Slovak Demands Seen as Threat to Federation," in RFE, *Report on Eastern Europe,* 22 March 1991, 8–9.

51. Prague Television Service in Slovak, 14 August 1990, trans. in FBIS, *Daily Report* (East Europe), 16 August 1990, 11.

52. CTK, 5 October 1990, in FBIS, *Daily Report* (East Europe), 10 October 1990, 24.

53. The complete text of the law was published in *Národná obroda,* 27 October 1990, 2, trans. in FBIS, *Daily Report* (East Europe), 30 October 1990, 14–15.

54. Prague Domestic Service, 25 October 1990, trans. in FBIS, *Daily Report* (East Europe), 26 October 1990, 20.

55. *Lidové noviny,* 6 November 1990, 2, trans. in FBIS, *Daily Report* (East Europe), 9 November 1990, 11; and *Lidové noviny,* 10 November 1990, 3, trans. in FBIS, *Daily Report* (East Europe), 15 November 1990, 29.

56. See *Verejnost'* (Bratislava), 31 October 1990, 3, trans. in FBIS, *Daily Report* (East Europe), 16 November 1990, 24–25.

57. *Mladá Fronta Dnes,* 28 February 1991, 2, trans. in FBIS, *Daily Report* (East Europe), 5 March 1991, 26.

58. *Neue Zürcher Zeitung,* 8 March 1991, 2.

59. See, for example, *Zemedelske noviny* (Prague), 15 March 1991, 1, 4, trans. in

FBIS, *Daily Report* (East Europe), 21 March 1991, 15; and *Národná obroda,* 15 March 1991), 13, trans. in FBIS, *Daily Report* (East Europe), 22 March 1991, 13.

60. CTK, 25 March 1991, in FBIS, *Daily Report* (East Europe), 26 March 1991, 28–29.

61. *Verejnost',* 14 March 1991, 3, trans. in FBIS, *Daily Report* (East Europe), 19 March 1991, 22–23.

62. *Vancouver Sun,* 25 March 1991, sec. A, p. 5.

63. Prague Domestic Service, 24 April 1991, trans. in FBIS, *Daily Report* (East Europe), 25 April 1991, 13.

64. CTK, 8 August 1991, in FBIS, *Daily Report* (East Europe), 9 August 1991, 14.

65. *Rudé právo,* 27 July 1991, 2, trans. in FBIS, *Daily Report* (East Europe), 5 August 1991, 19.

66. CTK, 14 August 1991, in FBIS, *Daily Report* (East Europe), 20 August 1991, 18; CTK, 15 August 1991, in FBIS, *Daily Report* (East Europe), 16 August 1991, 9; and *Smena,* 15 August 1991, 1–2, trans. in FBIS, *Daily Report* (East Europe), 19 August 1991, 11.

67. A poll taken in early May 1991 found that 82 percent of Slovaks opposed the recall of Mečiar from the prime ministership and the appointment of Čarnogurský to that post. See CTK, 30 May 1991, in FBIS, *Daily Report* (East Europe), 3 June 1991, 15.

68. *Slovenský Denník* (Bratislava), 13 May 1991, 1, 2, trans. in FBIS, *Daily Report* (East Europe), 15 May 1991, 10.

69. Interview with *Liberation,* reprinted in *Lidové noviny,* 24 July 1991, 1–2, trans. in FBIS, *Daily Report* (East Europe), 29 July 1991, 12.

70. Excerpt from an article by V. Mečiar for *Za Demokratické Slovensko,* no. 14, reprinted in *Národná obroda,* 13 September 1991, 13, trans. in FBIS, *Daily Report* (East Europe), 19 September 1991, 16.

71. Ibid.; see also *Nové Slovo,* no. 20, reprinted in *Národná obroda,* 10 July 1991, 13, trans. in FBIS, *Daily Report* (East Europe), 12 July 1991, 11.

72. *Lidové noviny,* 16 July 1991, 1, summarized in FBIS, *Daily Report* (East Europe), 22 July 1991, 11.

73. *Neue Zürcher Zeitung,* 15 November 1991, 1.

74. Ibid., 1 November 1991, 4.

75. Ibid., 25 October 1991, 2.

76. Ibid., 8 November 1991, 2: and 20 November 1991, 3.

77. *Times* (London), 16 September 1991, 24.

78. *Financial Times,* 15 November 1991, 3.

79. *Neue Zürcher Zeitung,* 30 November 1991, 3.

80. Ibid., 24 January 1992, 3.

81. *Hodpodárške noviny,* 11 February 1992, 4, trans. in FBIS, *Daily Report* (East Europe), 14 February 1992, 7.

82. CSTK (Prague), 14 February 1991 and CSTK, 18 February 1992, both trans. in FBIS, *Daily Report* (East Europe), 19 February 1992, 3; and *Neue Zürcher Zeitung,* 21 February 1992, 4.

83. *Verejnost'*, 31 January 1992, 2, trans. in FBIS, *Daily Report* (East Europe), 6 February 1992, 5.

84. *Financial Times,* 9 June 1992, 2.

85. *Wall Street Journal,* 22 June 1992, A9.

86. *Financial Times,* 9 June 1992, 2.

87. *Salzburger Nachrichten,* 12 June 1992, 4.

88. *Financial Times,* 11 June 1992, 3; and *New York Times,* 25 June 1992, A7.

89. CSTK, 8 June 1992, in FBIS, *Daily Report* (East Europe), 9 June 1992, A14.

90. *Financial Times,* 17 June 1992), 2.

91. *Die Presse* (Vienna), 13 June 1992, 2, and 16 June 1992, 3; and *Die Furche* (Vienna), 18 June 1992, 1.

92. Rozhlasova Stanica Slovensko Network (Bratislava), 19 June 1992, trans. in FBIS, *Daily Report* (East Europe), 22 June 1992, 12–17.

93. *Frankfurter Allgemeine,* 10 June 1992, 15.

94. *Die Welt* (Bonn), 18 June 1992, 6.

95. *Wall Street Journal,* 26 June 1992), A14.

96. *Kurier* (Vienna), 18 June 1992, 3.

97. *Financial Times,* 30 June 1992, 3.

98. Stanice Ceskoslovensko Radio (Prague), 3 July 1992, trans. in FBIS, *Daily Report* (East Europe), 7 July 1992, 18.

99. Mečiar has scarcely mended his ways. For example, upon being returned to power, Mečiar presented a prize to a magazine that has repeatedly printed anti-Semitic cartoons and lambasted U.S. billionaire George Soros for being a Jew. See *New Europe* (Athens), 13–19 August 1995, 23.

100. *European* (London), 30 September–6 October 1994, 8.

101. *New York Times,* 7 March 1995), A12.

102. Adam Lewin, "The Electoral Appeal of Vladimir Mečiar and Its Role in the 1992 Slovak Elections" (master's thesis, University of Washington, 1996), 7.

103. *Salzburger Nachrichten,* 15 November 1995), 7, trans. in FBIS, *Daily Report* (East Europe), 16 November 1995, 12.

104. Eurobarometer poll reported in CTK (Prague), 22 March 1996, on Nexis.

105. Poll conducted by the Institute for Public Opinion Research, reported by CTK, 18 March 1996, trans. in *BBC Monitoring Service,* 19 March 1996.

106. On NATO, see CTK, 19 March 1996, on Nexis.

107. For discussion of this party, see Frank Cibulka, "The Radical Right in Slova-kia," in "The Radical Right in Central and Eastern Europe," ed. Sabrina P. Ramet (unpublished manuscript).

108. Regarding the ZRS, see *Slovenská Republika* (Bratislava), 27 November 1995, 2, trans. in FBIS, *Daily Report* (East Europe), 30 November 1995, 12–13. See also *Süddeutsche Zeitung,* 11–12 November 1995, 9; and CTK, 20 March 1996, in *BBC Summary of World Broadcasts,* 21 March 1996.

109. *Prognosis Weekly* (Prague), 19–25 January 1995, 4, in FBIS, *Daily Report* (East Europe), 27 February 1995, 11, citing the views of "others."

110. *New York Times,* 10 November 1994, sec. A, p. 14.

111. See, e.g., *Pravda* (Bratislava), 29 April 1994, 2, trans. in FBIS, *Daily Report* (East Europe), 3 May 1994, 10; *Republika* (Bratislava), 3 May 1994, 3, trans. in FBIS, *Daily Report* (East Europe), 11 May 1994, 8; and *Pravda,* 4 May 1994, 3, trans. in FBIS, *Daily Report* (East Europe), 9 May 1994, 14–15.

112. Rozhlasova Stanica Slovensko Network, 8 November 1994, trans. in FBIS, *Daily Report* (East Europe), 9 November 1994, 14.

113. *Prognosis Weekly,* 16 November 1994, 5, trans. in FBIS, *Daily Report* (East Europe), 9 December 1994, 14.

114. Ibid.

115. *Neue Zürcher Zeitung,* 11–12 March 1995, 2; and *Süddeutsche Zeitung,* 25–26 March 1995, 7.

116. *Prague Post,* 17 January 1995, 4, in FBIS, *Daily Report* (East Europe), 27 February 1995, 12.

117. *Frankfurter Allgemeine,* 25 January 1995, 33, trans. in FBIS, *Daily Report* (East Europe), 6 March 1995, 12.

118. The poll was conducted among four thousand persons and found that 15.2 percent of Slovaks prefer the Czech private television station Nova, while another 3.4 percent prefer to watch the Czech public channel CT1. Adding the 7.3 percent of Slovak citizens watching Hungarian MTV, one finds that 25.9 percent of Slovak citizens prefer to watch television broadcasts from outside their own country. CTK, 2 April 1996, on Nexis.

119. *European* (London), 16–22 June 1995, 8.

120. *Economist* (London), 30 September–6 October 1995, 62.

121. *Domino Ekeft* (Košice), 20 April 1995, 2, trans. in FBIS, *Daily Report* (East Europe), 11 May 1995, 9.

122. *Sme* (Bratislava), 27 October 1995, 2, trans. in FBIS, *Daily Report* (East Europe), 1 November 1995, 12.

123. CTK, 27 March 1996, on Nexis.

124. *Mladá Fronta Dnes* (Prague), 6 October 1995, 1, 8, summarized in FBIS, *Daily Report* (East Europe), 12 October 1995, 15.

125. Quoted in *Sme,* 18 July 1995, 8, excerpted in FBIS, *Daily Report* (East Europe), 26 July 1995, 11.

126. Ibid.

127. Extracts quoted in *New Europe* (Athens), 12–18 November 1995, 13.

128. Ibid.

129. CTK, 24 March 1996, on Nexis.

130. David Lucas, *Ethnic Bipolarism in Slovakia, 1989–1995,* Donald W. Treadgold Papers, no. 11 (Seattle: Henry M. Jackson School of the University of Washington, November 1996), 60.

131. Quoted in ibid., 61.

132. Ibid., 66.

133. *Pravda* (Bratislava), 24 September 1994, 1, 5, trans. in FBIS, *Daily Report* (East Europe), 4 October 1994, 14.

134. *Republika* (Bratislava), 10 May 1994, 1–12, trans. in FBIS, *Daily Report* (East Europe), 12 May 1994, 7.

135. *Sme* (Bratislava), 7 June 1994, 1–2, trans. in FBIS, *Daily Report* (East Europe), 10 June 1994, 4.

136. *Slovenská Republika* (Bratislava), 1 August 1994, 1–2, trans. in FBIS, *Daily Report* (East Europe), 8 August 1994, 11.

137. *Slovenská Republika,* 25 May 1994, 3, trans. in FBIS, *Daily Report* (East Europe), 1 June 1994, 15.

138. Rozhlasova Stanica Slovensko Network, 17 November 1994, trans. in FBIS, *Daily Report* (East Europe), 18 November 1994, 10.

139. Reported in *Národná obroda,* 25 June 1994, 3, trans. in FBIS, *Daily Report* (East Europe), 29 June 1994, 10.

140. Ibid., 9.

141. *Magyar Hírlap* (Budapest), 26 July 1995, 7, trans. in FBIS, *Daily Report* (East Europe), 27 July 1995, 13.

142. Quoted in *Uj Szo* (Bratislava), 1 February 1995, 1, 4, trans. in FBIS, *Daily Report* (East Europe), 9 March 1995, 11.

143. *Sme,* 6 February 1995), 5, trans. in FBIS, *Daily Report* (East Europe), 9 February 1995, 2; and *Pravda* (Bratislava), 18 July 1995, 2, trans. in FBIS, *Daily Report* (East Europe), 20 July 1995, 4.

144. *Beszelo* (Budapest), 27 April 1995, 21–23, trans. in FBIS, *Daily Report* (East Europe), 2 May 1995, 5.

145. *Kurier,* 8 July 1995, 3, trans. in FBIS, *Daily Report* (East Europe), 10 July 1995, 7.

146. Duna TV (Budapest), 23 August 1995, trans. in FBIS, *Daily Report* (East Europe), 24 August 1995, 11.

147. *Sme,* 30 June 1995, 1–2, trans. in FBIS, *Daily Report* (East Europe), 5 July 1995, 12.

148. *Nepszabadsag* (Budapest), 7 July 1995, 1, 3, trans. in FBIS, *Daily Report* (East Europe), 11 July 1995, 14; New Europe (Athens), 19–25 November 1995, 14; and *Sme,* 7 July 1995, 2, trans. in FBIS, *Daily Report* (East Europe), 11 July 1995, 10.

149. CTK, 14 November 1995, on Nexis.

150. CTK, 23 August 1995, in *BBC Monitoring Service,* 25 August 1995.

151. Kossuth Radio Network (Budapest), 24 August 1995, trans. in FBIS, *Daily Report* (East Europe), 24 August 1995, 8.

152. TASR News Agency (Bratislava), 25 August 1995, in *BBC Summary of World Broadcasts,* 28 August 1995.

153. Slovakia 1 Radio (Bratislava), 25 August 1995, trans. in *BBC Monitoring Service,* 28 August 1995.

154. Slovakia 1 Radio, 24 November 1995, trans. in *BBC Monitoring Service,* 27 November 1995.

155. CTK, 26 November 1995, in *BBC Monitoring Service,* 28 November 1995.

156. Deutsche Presse-Agentur (Hamburg), 23 March 1996, on Nexis; and CTK, 22 March 1996, in *BBC Monitoring Service,* 25 March 1996.

157. Quoted in *Independent* (London), 27 March 1996, 11.

158. Ibid.

159. Quoted in *New Europe,* 17–23 March 1996, 13.

160. CTK, 26 March 1996, on Nexis; also Duna TV, 27 March 1996, trans. in *BBC Monitoring Service,* 29 March 1996).

161. As a result of pressure from many sides, Bratislava later agreed to drop the controversial addendum. See *New Europe,* 19–25 May 1996, 15.

162. Hungarian Radio (Budapest), 2 April 1996, trans. in *BBC Monitoring Service,* 4 April 1996.

163. CTK, 28 March 1996, on Nexis; and CTK, 29 March 1996, on Nexis.

164. Deutsche Presse-Agentur, 26 March 1996, on Nexis; and CTK, 26 March 1996, on Nexis.

165. *New Europe,* 14–20 April 1996, 15; CTK, 18 April 1996, on Nexis; CTK, 22 April 1996, on Nexis; and CTK, 25 April 1996, on Nexis.

166. CTK, 23 April 1996, on Nexis. Very similar results were obtained in a follow-up poll a month later. See CTK National News Wire, 23 May 1996, on Nexis.

167. Slovakia 1 Radio (Bratislava), 10 May 1996, trans. in *BBC Monitoring Service: Eastern Europe,* 13 May 1996.

168. *Prague Post,* 1 May 1996, on Nexis.

169. Quoted in ibid.

170. CTK National News Wire, 18 June 1996, on Nexis.

171. *New Europe,* 16–22 June 1996, 19.

172. Ibid., 11–17 August 1996, 19.

173. CTK, 23 August 1995, in *BBC Monitoring Service,* 25 August 1995.

174. FBIS Editorial Report, in FBIS, *Daily Report* (East Europe), 31 May 1995, 18.

175. Quoted from *Sme,* 26 May 1995, 4, in ibid., 19.

176. Quoted from *Pravda* (Bratislava), 27 May 1995, 1, in ibid., 19.

Chapter 6

An earlier draft of this chapter was originally published in *Brown Journal of World Affairs* 3, no. 1 (Winter/Spring 1996).

1. Chandran Kukathas, "Are There Any Cultural Rights?" *Political Theory* 20, no. 1 (February 1992): 105–39.

2. Quoted in ibid., 106.

3. Quoted in ibid., 107.

4. Vernon Van Dyke, "The Individual, the State, and Ethnic Communities in Political Theory," *World Politics* (April 1977), quoted in ibid., 108–9.

5. Kukathas, "Cultural Rights," 110.

6. Ibid., 110, 112, 114, 116.

7. Ibid., 117.

8. Will Kymlicka, "The Rights of Minority Cultures: Reply to Kukathas," *Political Theory* 20, no. 1 (February 1992): 141–42.

9. Chandran Kukathas, "Cultural Rights Again: A Rejoinder to Kymlicka," *Political Theory* 20, no. 4 (November 1992): 675.

10. "Abuses Continue in the Former Yugoslavia: Serbia, Montenegro, and Bosnia-Hercegovina," *Human Rights Watch Helsinki* 5, no. 11 (July l993): 6–7, 13; Commission on Security and Cooperation in Europe, *Sandžak and the CSCE* (Washington: April 1993), 1, 6; "Human Rights Abuses of Non-Serbs in Kosovo, Sandžak, and Vojvodina," *Human Rights Watch Helsinki* 6, no. 6 (May 1994), 7; and MTI (Budapest), 9 September 1993, in Foreign Broadcast Information Service (FBIS), *Daily Report* (East Europe), 10 September 1993, 12. For compatible but earlier estimates of the numbers being driven out of Vojvodina and the Sandžak, see MTI, 10 November 1991, on Nexis; and *Washington Post,* 11 November 1992, sec. A, p. 1.

11, The number of Albanians to have fled Kosovo is reported in *Rilindja* (Zofingen), 22 February 1995, 5, trans. in FBIS, *Daily Report* (East Europe), 24 February 1995, 43; confirmed in *Neue Zürcher Zeitung,* 6 March 1995, 14; reconfirmed in Deutsche Presse-Agentur (Hamburg), 12 November 1995, on Nexis. The figure for the number seeking asylum in Germany is reported in the last-mentioned source.

12. *Washington Post,* 19 October 1992, on Nexis. For discussion, see also Ivo Banac, "The Dissolution of Yugoslav Historiography," in *Beyond Yugoslavia: Politics, Economics, and Culture in a Shattered Community,* ed. Sabrina P. Ramet and Ljubiša S. Adamovich (Boulder, Colo.: Westview Press, 1995).

13. As recounted later in the *Observer* (London), 4 August 1991, on Nexis.

14. SRNA (Belgrade), 29 June 1995, trans. in FBIS, *Daily Report* (East Europe), 30 June 1995, 25, my emphasis.

15. Matija Bečković, president of the Serbian Writers' Association, in a speech on 4 March 1989, as published in *Kosovo 1389–1989,* special edition of the *Serbian Literary Gazette,* nos. 1–3 (1989): 45.

16. Aryeh Neier, "Kosovo Survives!" in *New York Review of Books,* 3 February 1994, 26.

17. *The Statesman's Yearbook, 1994–1995,* ed. Brian Hunter (New York: St. Martin's Press, 1994), 1619.

18. L. S. Stavrianos, *The Balkans since 1453* (New York: Holt, Rinehart & Winston, 1996), 511; Jens Reuter, *Die Albaner in Jugoslawien* (Munich: R. Oldenbourg Verlag, 1982), 21; and Dušan Janjić, "National Identities, Movements, and Nationalism of Serbs and Albanians," *Balkan Forum* (Skopje) 3, no. 1 (March 1995): 28.

19. This paragraph draws upon Ivo Banac, *The National Question in Yugoslavia: Origins, History, Politics* (Ithaca: Cornell University Press, 1984), 298–300; and Ivan Babić, "U službi Srpske okupacione vojske u Makedoniji i Kosovu," *Hrvatska revija* (Barcelona) 28, no. 3 (September 1978): 476– 77.

20. Alex N. Dragnich and Slavko Todorovich, *The Saga of Kosovo* (Boulder, Colo.: East European Monographs, 1984), 138.

21. Dimitrije Bogdanović, *Knjiga o Kosovu* (Belgrade: Srpska Akademija Nauka i

Umetnosti, 1985), 244–46. See also Savo Drljević, "Uloga i zadaci vojne uprave na Kosovu i Metohiji 1945," *Obeležja* 15, no. 4 (July/August 1985).

22. Miloš Mišović, *Ko je tražio republiku: Kosovo, 1945–1985* (Belgrade: Narodna knjiga, 1987), 53–54.

23. Janjić, "National Identities, Movements," 31.

24. Branko Horvat, *Kosovsko pitanje* (Zagreb: Globus, 1988), 62.

25. Details in Sabrina P. Ramet, *Nationalism and Federalism in Yugoslavia, 1962–1991,* 2d ed. (Bloomington: Indiana University Press, 1992), 188.

26. Janjić, "National Identities, Movements," 32. See also Ilija Vuković, *Autonomaštvo i separatizam na Kosovu* (Belgrade: Nova knjiga, 1985).

27. Thirty-one in 1976, and fifty in 1980.

28. These incidents are detailed and documented in Ramet, *Nationalism and Federalism,* 2d ed., 193–94.

29. *New York Times,* 1 November 1987, 6. For details and documentation concerning these underground organizations, see Sabrina P. Ramet, *Social Currents in Eastern Europe: The Sources and Consequences of the Great Transformation,* 2d ed. (Durham, N.C.: Duke University Press, 1995), chap. 8.

30. This measure, which seemed to imply that rape of a Serbian woman by a Serbian man was "not so bad," was immediately denounced by feminists in Serbia and elsewhere in Yugoslavia.

31. *NIN* (Belgrade), no. 1941 (13 March 1988): 16.

32. Ruža Petrović and Marina Blagojević, *The Migration of Serbs and Montenegrins from Kosovo and Metohija: Results of the Survey Conducted in 1985–1986* (Belgrade: Serbian Academy of Sciences and Arts, 1992), 116.

33. Ibid.

34. *Los Angeles Times,* 15 March 1984.

35. See the discussion in Ivan Kampuš, "Kosovski boj u objavljenim najstarijim izvorima i u novijoj Srpskoj historiografiji," *Historijski Zbornik* (Zagreb) 62, no. 1 (1989): esp. 3, 14.

36. "Srbija kao Job," in *Pravoslavlje,* organ of the Serbian patriarchate, 1 December 1989, 1–2.

37. *Politika* (Belgrade), 17 June 1988, 5.

38. For details, see Darko Hudelist, *Kosovo—Bitka bez iluzija* (Zagreb: Centar za informacije i publicitet, 1989), 155–246.

39. Estimate by the Council on Human Rights in Kosovo, cited in Julie Mertus, *Open Wounds: Human Rights Abuses in Kosovo* (New York: Human Rights Watch/Helsinki, March 1993), 95.

40. Fabian Schmidt, "Strategic Reconciliation in Kosovo," *Transition* (Prague), 25 August 1995, 17.

41. *Economist* (London), 1 April 1989, 40.

42. *Daily Telegraph* (London), 24 March 1989, 9.

43. Regarding the last-mentioned provision, see Radio Ljubljana (24 March 1989), in *BBC Summary of World Broadcasts,* 29 March 1989.

44. *Chicago Tribune,* 26 March 1989, 10, and 28 March 1989, 3; Reuter News

Service, 28 March 1989; UPI, 28 March 1989; UPI, 1 April 1989; and Reuter News Service, 9 May 1989—all on Nexis.

45. Elez Biberaj, *Kosova: The Balkan Powder Keg,* Conflict Studies no. 258 (London: Research Institute for the Study of Conflict and Terrorism, February 1993), 6–7. For confirmation of some of these points, see the *Times* (London), 1 April 1989, 8; and *Vjesnik* (Zagreb), 18 July 1990, 3.

46. Biberaj, *Kosova,* 7.

47. The editorial offices of *Rilindja* were thereupon transferred to Tiranë. The paper is now edited in Tiranë, printed in Switzerland, and smuggled into Kosovo.

48. For a summary of the provisions of this constitution, see *Flaka e Vëllazërimit* (Skopje), 14 September 1990, 4, trans. in FBIS, *Daily Report* (East Europe), 18 September 1990, 50–51; and *Vjesnik,* 14 September 1990, 1. See also Tanjug Domestic Service, 18 September 1990, trans. in FBIS, *Daily Report* (East Europe), 19 September 1990, 66.

49. The prime minister of this last provincial government was arrested only five years later, in May 1995. See *Süddeutsche Zeitung* (Munich), 29–30 September 1990, 7; Serbian radio (Belgrade), 14 May 1995, trans. in *BBC Summary of World Broadcasts,* 16 May 1995; and *Süddeutsche Zeitung,* 16 May 1995, 9. Regarding the previous arrests, see Tanjug Domestic Service, 14 September 1990, in FBIS, *Daily Report* (East Europe), 17 September 1990, 51. Regarding the impact of the 1990 changes, see also Reuter News Service, 8 June 1995, on Nexis.

50. Tanjug Domestic Service, 10 August 1990, trans. in FBIS, *Daily Report* (East Europe), 13 August 1990, 56.

51. *Flaka e Vëllazërimit,* 27 January 1991, 4, trans. in FBIS, *Daily Report* (East Europe), 31 January 1991, 57; confirmed in Tanjug Domestic Service, 26 November 1990, trans. in FBIS, *Daily Report* (East Europe), 27 November 1990, 67; reconfirmed in *Rilindja* (Tiranë), 19 March 1995, trans. in FBIS, *Daily Report* (East Europe), 24 March 1995, 53.

52. *Rilindja* (Tiranë), 22 February 1995, 5, trans. in FBIS, *Daily Report* (East Europe), 24 February 1995, 43. See also TVSH Television Network (Tiranë), 14 April 1994, trans. in FBIS, *Daily Report* (East Europe), 15 April 1994, 46.

53. Radio Tiranë Network (Tiranë), 27 October 1992, trans. in FBIS, *Daily Report* (East Europe), 28 October 1992, 30.

54. ATA (Tiranë), 31 May 1995, in *BBC Summary of World Broadcasts,* 2 June 1995; and ATA, 2 October 1995, in *BBC Monitoring Service,* 5 October 1995. See also TVSH Television Network (Tiranë), 12 January 1994, trans. in FBIS, *Daily Report* (East Europe), 13 January 1994, 30; and *Borba* (Belgrade), 25 January 1994, 3.

55. AFP (Paris), 23 September 1992, in FBIS, *Daily Report* (East Europe), 24 September 1992, 44; confirmed in ATA, 6 October 1992, in FBIS, *Daily Report* (East Europe), 7 October 1992, 28; reconfirmed in Croatian Radio (Zagreb), 28 August 1992, on Nexis.

56. *Neue Zürcher Zeitung,* 21 March 1995, 7; confirmed in Kosova *Daily Report* (Priština), 24 October 1994, in FBIS, *Daily Report* (East Europe), 26 October 1994, 61.

57. AFP, 23 September 1992, in FBIS, *Daily Report* (East Europe), 24 September 1992, 44. Examples in Ramet, *Social Currents,* 2d ed., 423.

58, ATA, 3 October 1995, in *BBC Monitoring Service,* 5 October 1995.

59. Biberaj, *Kosova,* 10.

60. Predrag Tasić, *Kako je ubijena druga Jugoslavija* (Skopje: Self-published by author, 1994), 69.

61. Poll conducted by *Zeri i Rinise,* cited in Belgrade Domestic Service, 10 February 1991, trans. in FBIS, *Daily Report* (East Europe), 12 February 1991, 59.

62. Radio Croatia in Albanian (Zagreb), 7 October 1991, trans. in FBIS, *Daily Report* (East Europe), 9 October 1991, 42.

63. Kosova *Daily Report* (17 May 1994), in FBIS, *Daily Report* (East Europe), 18 May 1994, 44.

64. *Telegraf* (Belgrade), 2 November 1994, 10–11, summarized in FBIS, *Daily Report* (East Europe), 7 November 1994, 59–60. It is worth remembering that in 1990 the Serbs of Croatia, who constituted a mere 11.6 percent of that republic's population, had been offered cultural autonomy but had rejected the offer as "insulting," insisting instead on political and administrative autonomy.

65. For an example of police harassment, see Radio Tiranë Network, 24 May 1992, trans. in FBIS, *Daily Report* (East Europe), 26 May 1992, 58.

66. *Frankfurter Rundschau,* 16 June 1992, 2.

67. Kosova *Daily Report* (30 January 1995), in FBIS, *Daily Report* (East Europe), 1 February 1995, 38.

68. *Politika,* 7 May 1992, 10.

69. *Vreme* (Belgrade), 30 May 1994, 25–27, trans. in FBIS, *Daily Report* (East Europe), 16 June 1994, 52–54.

70. Kosova *Daily Report*, 6 March 1995, in FBIS, *Daily Report* (East Europe), 7 March 1995, 55.

71. *Borba* (Belgrade), 21 October 1994, 12, trans. in FBIS, *Daily Report* (East Europe), 2 November 1994, 40–41.

72. Tanjug Domestic Service, 16 January 1995, trans. in FBIS, *Daily Report* (East Europe), 18 January 1995, 60. See also *Večernji list* (Zagreb), 1 April 1995, 24.

73. Fabian Schmidt, "Kosovo: The Time Bomb That Has Not Gone Off," *RFE/RL Research Report* (Munich), 1 October 1993, 28.

74. TVSH Television Network, 3 February 1995, trans. in FBIS, *Daily Report* (East Europe), 6 February 1995, 56.

75. *Delo* (Ljubljana), 13 January 1995, 16, trans. in FBIS, *Daily Report* (East Europe), 13 February 1995, 43. See also *Il Sole 24 Ore,* 8 June 1995, on Nexis.

76. Raznjatović, as quoted in *Kosova Daily Report* (Priština), 3 May 1994, in FBIS, *Daily Report* (East Europe), 4 May 1994, 45. On 20 May 1995, an unnamed speaker addressed a gathering of 200 Serbs, including several Serbian Orthodox bishops, in the courtyard of Gračanica Monastery and called for the expulsion of "at least" 670,000 Albanians from Kosovo. Reported in *Rilindja,* 23 May 1995, 6, trans. in *BBC Summary of World Broadcasts,* 25 May 1995.

77. *Kosova Daily Report* (Priština), 3 April 1995, in FBIS, *Daily Report* (East Europe), 5 April 1995, 56.

78. Tanjug, 2 June 1994, in FBIS, *Daily Report* (East Europe), 3 June 1994, 41.

79. Deutsche Presse-Agentur, 29 June 1995, on Nexis.

80. This is documented in the following sources: Radio Croatia in Albanian, 14 May 1991, trans. in FBIS, *Daily Report* (East Europe), 15 May 1991, 40; TVSH Television Network, 28 February 1994, trans. in FBIS, *Daily Report* (East Europe), 1 March 1994, 42; TVSH Television Network, 22 June 1994, trans. in FBIS, *Daily Report* (East Europe), 23 June 1994, 30; TVSH Television Network, 16 February 1995, trans. in FBIS, *Daily Report* (East Europe), 17 February l995, 58; ATA, 20 May 1995, trans. in *BBC Summary of World Broadcasts,* 24 May 1995; Mertus, *Open Wounds,* xiv, 2–17, 98–99; and *Kosova Daily Report* (Priština), 4 October 1995, in FBIS, *Daily Report* (East Europe), 12 October 1995, 71.

81. This is documented in Mertus, *Open Wounds,* xiv–xv, 10–13, 31–33. On this point, see also Radio Tiranë Network, 15 December 1993, trans. in FBIS, *Daily Report* (East Europe), 16 December 1993, 45.

82. This is documented in the following sources: TVSH Television Network, 15 October 1994, trans. in FBIS, *Daily Report* (East Europe), 17 October 1994, 75; *Rilindja,* 22 February 1995, 5, trans. in FBIS, *Daily Report* (East Europe), 24 February l995, 43; and Mertus, *Open Wounds,* 33–37.

83. This is documented in the following sources: Radio Tiranë Network, 23 February 1994, trans. in FBIS, *Daily Report* (East Europe), 24 February 1994, 45; TVSH Television Network, 12 March 1994, trans. in FBIS, *Daily Report* (East Europe), 14 March 1994, 59; TVSH Television Network, 2 April 1994, trans. in FBIS, *Daily Report* (East Europe), 4 April 1994, 46; Mertus, *Open Wounds,* 4–9; *Kosova Daily Report,* 1 June 1995, summarized in FBIS, *Daily Report* (East Europe), 2 June 1995, 71; *Kosova Daily Report* (25 July 1995), summarized in FBIS, *Daily Report* (East Europe), 27 July 1995, 43; Albanian TV (Tiranë), 30 September 1995, on *BBC Monitoring Service,* 3 October l995; and *Rilindja* (Tiranë), 19 October 1995, 2, trans. in FBIS, *Daily Report* (East Europe), 26 October 1995, 4.

84. Fabian Schmidt, "Has the Kosovo Crisis Been Internationalized?" *RFE/RL Research Report,* 5 November 1993, 37.

85. For examples, see *Rilindja,* 29 September 1994, 3, trans. in FBIS, *Daily Report* (East Europe), 4 October 1994, 60–61; AFP, 2 December 1994, in FBIS, *Daily Report* (East Europe), 5 December 1994, 55–60; *Rilindja,* 11 March 1995, 3, trans. in FBIS, *Daily Report* (East Europe), 15 March l995, 54; AFP, 29 May 1995, on Nexis; *Kosova Daily Report*, 12 and 13 June 1995, summarized in FBIS, *Daily Report* (East Europe), 21 June 1995, 57; *Kosova Daily Report*, 20 June 1995, summarized in FBIS, *Daily Report* (East Europe), 22 June 1995, 58; and Albanian TV, 1 July 1995, in *BBC Summary of World Broadcasts,* 1 July l995.

86. Oesterreich 1 Radio (Vienna), 24 July 1995, in *BBC Summary of World Broadcasts,* 25 July 1995.

87. Mertus, *Open Wounds,* xiii.

88. See, e.g., *Fjala* (Priština), November 1991, 2, trans. in FBIS, *Daily Report* (East Europe), 19 November 1991, 42; Radio Tiranë Network, 4 August 1994, trans. in

FBIS, *Daily Report* (East Europe), 5 August 1994, 30; TVSH Television Network, 15 October 1994, trans. in FBIS, *Daily Report* (East Europe), 17 October 1994, 75; *Kosova Daily Report*, 26 May 1995, summarized in FBIS, *Daily Report* (East Europe), 30 May 1995, summarized in FBIS, *Daily Report* (East Europe), 30 May 1995, 74; *Kosova Daily Report*, 12–13 June 1995, summarized in FBIS, *Daily Report* (East Europe), 16 June 1995, 43; and TVSH Television Network, 18 July 1995, summarized in FBIS, *Daily Report* (East Europe), 20 July 1995, 42.

89. TVSH Television Network, 3 March 1994, and 8 March 1994, trans. in FBIS, *Daily Report* (East Europe), 9 March 1994, 45.

90. These figures are all derived from *Neue Zürcher Zeitung,* 6 March 1995, 14.

91. Reuters, 20 June 1995, on Nexis; AFP (4 July 1995), on Nexis; *Neue Zürcher Zeitung,* 6 July 1995, 2; and *Süddeutsche Zeitung,* 6 July 1995, on Nexis.

92. *Kosova Daily Report,* 23 August 1995, in FBIS, *Daily Report* (East Europe), 25 August 1995, 58.

93. Mertus, *Open Wounds,* 61–89. For examples, see *Kosova Daily Report* (10 August 1993), in FBIS, *Daily Report* (East Europe), 11 August 1993, 59; TVSH Television Network, 24 February 1994, trans. in FBIS, *Daily Report* (East Europe), 25 February 1994, 59; Tanjug Domestic Service, 15 July 1994), trans. in FBIS, *Daily Report* (East Europe), 18 July 1994, 44; TVSH Television Network, 20 July 1994, trans. in FBIS, *Daily Report* (East Europe), 18 July l994, 43; Tanjug Domestic Service, 17 October 1994, trans. in FBIS, *Daily Report* (East Europe), 19 October 1994, 44; Tanjug Domestic Service, 19 October 1994, trans. in FBIS, *Daily Report* (East Europe), 21 October 1994, 43–44; *Süddeutsche Zeitung,* 3–4 December 1994, 8; Tanjug, 14 December 1994, in FBIS, *Daily Report* (East Europe), 16 December 1994, 30; *Rilindja,* 18 December 1994, 11, trans. in FBIS, *Daily Report* (East Europe), 29 December 1994, 44; *Balkan News and East European Report* (Athens), 5–11 March 1995, 29; *Süddeutsche Zeitung,* 13/14 April 1995, 8; Reuters, 8 June 1995, on Nexis; *Balkan News and East European Report,* 11–17 June 1995, 3; and Yugoslav Telegraph Service (Belgrade), 15 June 1995, trans. in *BBC Summary of World Broadcasts,* 17 June 1995.

94. AFP, 21 September 1995, on Nexis; and Croatian Radio (Zagreb), 21 September 1995, trans. in *BBC Monitoring Service,* 23 September 1995.

95. AFP, 8 September 1995, on Nexis.

96. *Rilindja,* 22 February 1995, 5, trans. in FBIS, *Daily Report* (East Europe), 24 February 1995, 43; confirmed in *Neue Zürcher Zeitung,* 6 March 1995, 14.

97. Tanjug, 28 June 1995, in *BBC Summary of World Broadcasts,* 30 June 1995.

98. Quoted in Tanjug, 23 May 1995, in *BBC Summary of World Broadcasts,* 24 May 1995. See also Serbian charges reported in *Balkan News and East European Report,* 25 June–1 July 1995, 19.

99. Reuters World Service, 20 July 1995, and Deutsche Presse-Agentur, 20 July 1995, both on Nexis.

100. Deutsche Presse-Agentur, 23 August 1995, on Nexis. This figure is confirmed in *Moneyclips,* 25 August 1995, on Nexis.

101. Quoted in *Christian Science Monitor,* 22 August 1995, 6.

102. On the U.S. and Albanian governments' criticism, see *Christian Science Monitor,*

22 August 1995, 6.; on the Albanian government, see also the *Times* (London), 22 August 1995, on Nexis; on the Egyptian government, see Deutsche Presse-Agentur, 28 August 1995, on Nexis; on the unwillingness of the Croatian Serbs to be shipped to Kosovo and the coercion employed by the Serbian authorities, see *Moneyclips, 25 August 1995*, on Nexis.

103. *Vreme International* (Belgrade), 21 August 1995, 16; confirmed by UPI, 22 August 1995, on Nexis.

104. AFP, 9 September 1995, on Nexis.

105. Quoted in *Christian Science Monitor,* 22 August 1995, 6.

106. Albanian TV, 16 September 1995, trans. in *BBC Monitoring Service,* 19 September 1995.

107. Ibid.; also *Kosova Daily Report*, 30 August 1995, in FBIS, *Daily Report* (East Europe), 1 September 1995, 61.

108. *Kosova Daily Report*, 1 September 1995, summarized in FBIS, *Daily Report* (East Europe), 8 September 1995, 43–44.

109. *Kosova Daily Report*, 29 August 1995, in FBIS, *Daily Report* (East Europe), 1 September 1995, 60–61.

110. Ibid.

111. Albanian TV, 18 September 1995, trans. in *BBC Monitoring Service,* 21 September 1995.

112. *Kosova Daily Report*, 7 September 1995, and *Kosova Daily Report*, 8 September 1995, both trans. in FBIS, *Daily Report* (East Europe), 12 September 1995, 43–44.

113. *Neue Zürcher Zeitung,* 24 July 1996, 5.

114. See ATA, 31 May 1995, in *BBC Summary of World Broadcasts,* 3 June 1995.

115. *Rilindja,* 5 March 1995, 3, trans. in FBIS, *Daily Report* (East Europe), 10 March 1995, 41.

116. Ibid. See also reference in *Vreme,* 7 March 1994, 26–29.

117. For a recent rumor, see *International Herald Tribune* (Paris), 6 June 1995, on Nexis.

118. Quoted in *Elsevier* (Amsterdam), 29 October 1994, 86, trans. in FBIS, *Daily Report* (East Europe), 1 November 1994, 44.

119. Albanian TV, 12 September 1995, in *BBC Monitoring Service,* 15 September 1995; and Albanian TV, 30 September 1995, in *BBC Monitoring Service,* 3 October 1995.

120. Reuters World Service, 8 November 1995, on Nexis.

121. *New Europe,* 15–21 October 1995, 3.

122. Tanjug, 11 October 1995, in *BBC Monitoring Service,* 13 October 1995.

123. Quoted in Deutsche Presse-Agentur, 12 December 1995, on Nexis.

124. ATA, 5 May 1996, in *BBC Monitoring Service,* 7 May 1996; and Agence France Presse, 8 May 1996, on Nexis.

125. AFP, 9 September 199), on Nexis; and Tanjug, 7 October 1995, in *BBC Monitoring Service,* 9 October 1995.

126. "Kosovsko pitanje—srpski odgovori," in *Vreme International* (Belgrade), 9 October 1995, 22.

127. *Washington Times,* 5 May 1996, A8.

128. For an argument that democratizing societies may be prone to go to war, see Edward D. Mansfield and Jack Snyder, "Democratization and the Danger of War," *International Security* 20, no. 1 (Summer 1995).

129. Albanian TV (Tiranë), 3 May 1996, trans. in *BBC Monitoring Service,* 6 May 1996.

130. A fifth wounded was Muslim. See Reuters World Service, 24 April 1996, on Nexis.

131. Deutsche Presse-Agentur, 23 April 1996, on Nexis.

132. ATA, 30 April 1996, in *BBC Monitoring Service,* 2 May 1996.

133. *Naša borba* (Belgrade), 25 April 1996, trans. in *BBC Monitoring Service,* 29 April 1996.

134. Agence France Presse, 3 May 1996, on Nexis.

135. ATA, 6 May 1996, in *BBC Monitoring Service,* 9 May 1996.

136. *Illyria* (The Bronx), 27–29 June 1996, 1, 4.

137. See ibid., 8–10 August 1996, 1, 3; 15–17 August 1996, 1; 19–21 August 1996, 2; 10–12 October 1996, 1; and 31 October–2 November 1996, 2. See also Agence France Presse, 15 October 1996, on Nexis; and ATA (Tiranë), 7 November 1996, on *BBC Monitoring Service: Eastern Europe*, 11 November 1996.

138. *Illyria,* 17–19 October 1996, 2.

139. Ibid., 2–4 September 1996, 1, and 5–7 September 1996, 1.

140. Ibid., 5–7 August 1996, 2.

141. For a recent demand for independence for Kosovo on the part of Rugova, see *Süddeutsche Zeitung* (Munich), 13–14 July 1996, 7.

142. Agence France Presse, 6 May 1996, on Nexis.

143. Prepared testimony by Dennison Rusinow, research professor at the University of Pittsburgh, before the House Committee on Foreign Affairs, Subcommittee on Europe and the Middle East, as reported in Federal News Service, 5 October 1994, on Nexis. For a recent confirmation, see Beta news agency (Belgrade), 15 November 1996, trans. in *BBC Summary of World Broadcasts,* 18 November 1996.

144. Reuter News Service, 2 May 1996, on Nexis. Bildt is the European Union's high representative for Bosnia-Herzegovina.

145. For discussion, see L. W. Sumner, *The Moral Foundation of Rights* (Oxford: Clarendon Press, 1987).

146. On positive rights, see Reinhardt Albrecht, *Hegel und die Demokratie* (Bonn: Bouvier Verlag Herbert Grundmann, 1978), 21–22.

Conclusion

1. For a broad view of this and other problems, see Jan Berting et al., *Human Rights in a Pluralist World: Individuals and Collectivities* (Westport, Conn. and London: Meckler, 1990).

2. Pedro Ramet [Sabrina P. Ramet], "The Interplay of Religious Policy and

Nationalities Policy in the Soviet Union and Eastern Europe," in *Religion and Nationalism in Soviet and East European Politics,* ed. Pedro Ramet, rev. ed. (Durham, N.C.: Duke University Press, 1989), 41, emphasis in original.

3. *Neue Zürcher Zeitung,* 23–24 November 1996, 3; and *Wall Street Journal,* 29 November 1996, sec. A, p. 1.

4. *Neue Zürcher Zeitung,* 22 November 1996, 1; see also the interview with Zoran Djindjić in *Vreme* (Belgrade), 16 November 1996, 16–17.

5. Quoted in *Seattle Post-Intelligencer,* 26 November 1996, sec. A, p. 2. See also *Financial Times,* 27 November 1996, 2.

6. Vuk Drašković, speaking in English, on ITN World News (London), 28 November 1996, received in Seattle, 7:36 p.m.

7. See the discussion in Kurt Taylor Gaubatz, "Kant, Democracy, and History," *Journal of Democracy* 7, no. 4 (October 1996): 138, 147–48.

8. But see also Immanuel Kant, *The Metaphysics of Morals,* trans. Mary Gregor (Cambridge: Cambridge University Press, 1991), 23, 77–78, 129.

9. Quoted in Joseph M. Knippenberg, "The Politics of Kant's Philosophy," in *Kant and Political Philosophy: The Contemporary Legacy,* ed. Ronald Beiner and William James Booth (New Haven: Yale University Press, 1993), 165.

10. Knippenberg, "The Politics of Kant's Philosophy," 165.

11. Quoted in ibid., 160.

12. Quoted in ibid., 160.

13. Kazimierz Poznański, "An Interpretation of Communist Decay: The Role of Evolutionary Mechanisms," *Communist and Post-Communist Studies* 26, no. 1 (March 1993): 3.

14. Ibid., 3, 7; and Kazimierz Z. Poznański, "Property Rights Perspective on Evolution of Communist-Type Economies," in *Constructing Capitalism: The Reemergence of Civil Society and Liberal Economy in the Post-Communist World,* ed. Kazimierz Poznański (Boulder, Colo.: Westview Press, 1992), 76–77, 80.

15. Kazimierz Z. Poznański, "Epilogue: Markets and States in the Transformation of Post-Communist Europe," in *Constructing Capitalism,* ed. Poznański, 199, 202.

16. Poznański, "Interpretation of Communist Decay," 4.

17. Ibid., 7.

18. Robert M. Hayden, review article, *Slavic Review* 55, no. 2 (Summer 1996): 444.

19. Ibid.

20. Robert M. Hayden, "Constitutional Nationalism in the Formerly Yugoslav Republics," *Slavic Review* 51, no. 4 (Winter 1992): 673.

21. *New Europe* (Athens), 8–14 October 1995, 17.

22. *Prague Post,* 11 July 1995, 3.

23. Radio Romania (Bucharest), 15 March 1996, trans. in *BBC Monitoring Service: Eastern Europe*, 19 March 1996.

24. George Schöpflin, "Nationalism, Politics and the European Experience," *Survey* 28, no. 4 (Winter 1984): 71.

25. Ibid., 75.

Index

About the Author

Sabrina P. Ramet is a professor of international studies at the University of Washington. She has lived for extended periods of time in England, Germany, Austria, Yugoslavia, Japan, and the United States. She is the author of five previous books, three of which have been published in expanded, revised editions: *Nationalism and Federalism in Yugoslavia, 1962–1991,* 2d ed. (1992); *Social Currents in Eastern Europe: The Sources and Consequences of the Great Transformation,* 2d ed. (1995); and *Balkan Babel: The Disintegration of Yugoslavia from the Death of Tito to Ethnic War,* 2d ed. (1996). She has also edited or coedited eleven other books, and four more are in progress. Her articles have appeared in *Foreign Affairs, World Politics, Slavic Review, Orbis, Problems of Post-Communism,* and other journals.